Reading History: The American Revolution

Lucy Calkins, Janet Steinberg, and Grace Chough

Photography by Peter Cunningham

Illustrations by Jennifer DeSutter

HEINEMANN ◆ PORTSMOUTH, NH

To Anne Goudvis and Stephanie Harvey, with thanks for their collegiality and generosity in sharing with us their amazing resource, The American Revolution and Constitution.

Heinemann
361 Hanover Street
Portsmouth, NH 03801–3912
www.heinemann.com

Offices and agents throughout the world

The authors and publisher wish to thank those who have generously given permission to reprint borrowed material:

Illustrations, by David Wenzel, copyright © 1998 by David Wenzel; and Excerpt(s) from *The Liberty Tree: The Beginning of the American Revolution,* by Lucille Recht Penner, text copyright © 1998 by Lucille Recht Penner. Used by permission of Random House Children's Books, a division of Penguin Random House LLC. All rights reserved. Any third party use of this material, outside of this publication, is prohibited. Interested parties must apply directly to Penguin Random House LLC for permission. (Reprinted under the title *Liberty! How the Revolutionary War Began* in 2002).

"Paul Revere Warns: 'The British Are Coming' 1775." HistoryCentral.com. Used by permission.

From *King George: What Was His Problem? The Whole Hilarious Story of the American Revolution* © 2008 by Steve Sheinken. Illustrations © 2008 by Tim Robinson. Reprinted with permission of Roaring Brook Press. All rights reserved.

The Split History of the American Revolution © 2013 by Capstone. All rights reserved.

The Tiger Rising. Copyright © 2001 by Kate DiCamillo. Reproduced by permission of the publisher, Candlewick Press.

The American Revolutionaries: In Their Own Words. Text copyright © 1987 by Milton Meltzer. Used by permission of HarperCollins Publishers.

The Revolutionary War, by Josh Gregory. Used by permission of Scholastic, Inc.

George Washington Crossing the Delaware by Emanuel Gottlieb Leutz. Art Resource, NY

Cataloging-in-Publication data is on file with the Library of Congress.

ISBN-13: 978-0-325-07717-8

Series editorial team: Anna Gratz Cockerille, Karen Kawaguchi, Tracy Wells, Felicia O'Brien, Debra Doorack, Jean Lawler, Marielle Palombo, and Sue Paro
Production: Elizabeth Valway, David Stirling, and Abigail Heim
Cover and interior designs: Jenny Jensen Greenleaf
Photography: Peter Cunningham
Illustrations: Jennifer DeSutter
Composition: Publishers' Design and Production Services, Inc.
Manufacturing: Steve Bernier

Printed in the United States of America on acid-free paper
23 22 21 20 19   RWP   5 6 7 8 9

Acknowledgments

THIS BOOK was written late in the process, and therefore was able to stand on the shoulders of all the other nonfiction books in the series. It builds upon work that was begun in third grade that involves helping students read expository and narrative nonfiction, noting the text structure and using that structure to organize their thinking. It borrows on earlier work teaching students to read up the ladder of text complexity, using prior reading to provide the background knowledge that can enable work with more complex texts. Work on domain-specific vocabulary and on looking both within and around the tricky word is here as well. Instruction on debate and on how reading argument texts informs the debate is in Bend II. And the Teachers College Reading and Writing Program's (TCRWP) work with writing about reading, too, illuminates this unit.

We thank Annie Taranto for her work with vocabulary and debate; Audra Robb, with her work in interpretation, summary, and writing about reading; Kathleen Tolan and Emily Butler Smith for their work with social studies; and Kelly Boland Hohne for her support with nonfiction learning progressions. This book benefits from the Project's alliance with the Colonial Williamsburg foundation, and we thank them for their support. Anna Gratz Cockerille, co-author of *Bringing History to Life* from Units of Study in Opinion, Information, and Narrative Writing helped us plan this unit so that it supports not only state-of-the-art reading work but also the adjacent unit in writing. And we received writing help not only from people mentioned earlier but also from Amy Tondreau, Ali Marron, and Peter Cipparone. Thanks to all of you.

We would finally like to thank the truly remarkable Tracy Wells, the editor for this book. Tracy brought a deep knowledge of history to her work as the editor of this book. She was able to alternate between editor and coach and historical researcher because of that background. A million thanks.

There is an entire team at Heinemann, supporting our efforts, and we're grateful to them all. Vicki Boyd, Heinemann's new president, leads that organization with warmth and energy. Whenever we've needed her extra dose of support, she's been there. Abby Heim is at the helm of the TCRWP's work with Heinemann, and she steers the effort with finesse. Lisa Bingen is the most enthusiastic, dedicated marketing force that anyone could ever imagine. Meanwhile, behind the scenes there is a whole team of people working under the guidance of Elizabeth Valway, and we thank her for talent, productivity, and sky-high standards. We are grateful also to both Peter Cunningham, who has been the photographer for Units of Study since their inception, and to David Stirling, who works with Peter's photos and the book design to create pages that bring our beautiful children to life.

There is a behind the scenes team at Teachers College, too, and how grateful we are for their power, persistence, and grace under pressure. Thanks especially to Mary Ann Mustac, Sara Johnson, Beth Neville, Dana House, and Kathy Neville. Each of those names represents a whole universe of work, and their leadership makes the world of difference.

This unit is what it is today because of the teachers who piloted versions of the unit. We are grateful to the fourth-grade teachers from PS 36 in Staten Island, as well as to their leaders, Barbara Bellfutto and Stephanie Basset. The teachers at PS 249 also helped guide our work—thanks to them and to their leaders, Elisa Brown, Siolen Kelly Ho, and Ms. Coffee. Two colleagues, Emily Strang-Campbell and Alexandra Roman, also helped us pilot the units. PS 173's fourth-grade teachers were particularly helpful piloting the assessments.

—Lucy, Janet, and Grace

Contents

BEND II Preparing for Debate

BEND III Engaging in a Second Cycle of Research

An Orientation to the Unit

READ THE NEWSPAPER TODAY. Each issue that appears on the front page today has a backstory, and in the United States, that backstory usually involves the issues that were there at America's inception. To whom, and for what, do we pay taxes? Who gets to make the decisions that affect our lives? Are the voices of ordinary people being heard? Liberty for what and for whom? What is worth dying for?

This is a unit about the American Revolution and the beginnings of this country. It's a unit about the Sons of Liberty and the two lanterns that signaled to Paul Revere from the steeple of the Old North Church ("one if by land, two if by sea") and the rides through the countryside that William Dawes and Dr. Samuel Prescott made (not just Paul Revere, after all, and that's part of the story, too). It's a unit about the Minutemen and the Boston Massacre, which wasn't necessarily such a massacre at all, and the Constitutional Convention, complete with the debates over whether to break free from the mother country.

But, actually, if you are teaching this unit in Singapore or Finland or Chile, or if you are teaching from a state that teaches the American Revolution in fifth grade and not in fourth, you could shake loose from this particular content, and the unit would still stand as a unit on researching history. It is also the second of two nonfiction reading units for fourth grade, and as such, it is a unit that moves fourth-graders along on very ambitious trajectory of skill development.

The unit is written to complement *Bringing History to Life*, the unit from Units of Study in Opinion, Information, and Narrative Writing that helps students write information texts on the American Revolution. The expectation is that you will start this unit a few days before you start the writing unit, and although there are almost no references to the other books within these units, the units on writing and in reading will support each other nicely.

This unit builds upon the work of the first fourth-grade nonfiction unit, *Reading the Weather, Reading the World*, and guides students on a journey of learning to read like historians. In the first bend, students embark on a research project about the events leading up to the American Revolution. You'll teach them how to begin building their knowledge about the era by reading accessible texts, and you'll show them how researchers pay attention to text structures in order to organize their notes and their thinking. As students narrow their research focus to a subtopic, you'll teach them how to synthesize the new information into what they already know, paying special attention—as historians do—to the people, geography, and chronology of the event they are studying. You'll introduce your students to primary sources, and teach them strategies for tackling these more difficult texts. By the end of the bend, your students celebrate their new learning by sharing that learning with each other.

Bend II moves the chronology forward to the eve of the American Revolution. Students continue their research in preparation to debate the question of independence from Great Britain. During this bend, you will teach your students that historians learn about multiple points of view in order to gain a more complete picture of events in the past. Your students will prepare to take sides on this great question, with some of them researching the viewpoint of the Patriots and the others researching the Loyalists' perspective. As they gather their evidence and angle it to support their side, your students will hone their skills of supporting a position with reasons and solid evidence. The bend culminates with a reenactment of the Second Continental Congress, with your students debating the heady question of independence for America.

Bend III will take a new turn, as students work in partnerships to begin a new research project, this time on the time period after the Second Continental Congress. After students begin to orient themselves to their new topics by reading accessible texts, you will teach them strategies for tackling the increasingly complex texts that they will encounter. You will teach them to preview and paraphrase, and to study all parts of a text to extract the main ideas. In this bend, vocabulary will have a special emphasis, as you teach students strategies for learning not only the definitions of new domain-specific words, but also how those words are used at a deeper level. As the end of the bend draws near, you will teach students how to draw on their growing body of knowledge to consider new questions and answers about their topic. The unit culminates with a celebration, as students not only reflect on the tremendous learning they have achieved but also think about the big lessons that they can draw from events in the past. Because of the work they have done in this unit, your students will begin to see how the past and the present are connected, and how the past continues to affect us today.

SUPPORTING SKILL PROGRESSIONS

By now, your students should enter this unit with fairly strong skills at organizing research projects, skimming through texts to select those that are relevant to subtopics of interest, reading across those texts on that subtopic, and accumulating information and ideas on that subtopic. As this unit begins, you'll remind your students to use their research skills, allowing them to do that with some independence, while your instruction homes in on particular nonfiction reading skills, especially those that relate to reading history.

You'll continue to support students' abilities to read both expository and narrative nonfiction texts in such a way that they'll be able to summarize what they've read, talking or writing about the main ideas and supporting details. This unit's work with the strand "Main Idea(s) and Supporting Details/Summary" will shift a bit from the previous units. Although you'll remind students that they know the value of previewing a text, noting the text structure and reading the text in such a way that they can take structured notes, your emphasis will be on selecting the most important main ideas and sorting supporting details that relate to those ideas. You'll remind students that they need to select the most important main idea(s) and the most important supporting details, and to write brief notes. It is important for your students to know how to write summaries in which they crystallize what they've learned into a few sentences that capture only the most key idea(s) and perhaps one or two important supporting details.

Your students will be reading about another time and place, and "Envisioning" will be very important to them, just as it will be when they read historical

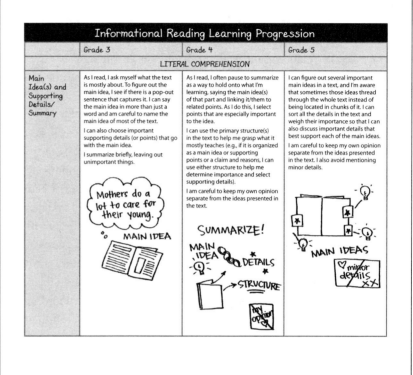

fiction. You'll remind your students that it's not only writers who need to make movies in the mind but also readers. To do that work, readers draw on information not only from earlier in the text but also from their prior knowledge. When reading history, students follow the signals texts give, sometimes reading the history almost as if it is a novel and sometimes reading it as a more technical text, building mental models as they read, fashioning mental timelines, maps, diagrams, and charts. You'll teach students that readers of history pay special note to dates and places, adding both to their mental models.

An especially major strand in this unit relates to the skill of "Inferring Within Text/Cohesion." This strand is not really about the structure(s) of the text. Rather, it is about the *content* of the text and about the important "through lines" that hold texts together. Students need to be able to see the relationships within a text. They need to glean that an event has set off a chain of other events, and that one individual has influenced the outcome of a whole battle. This strand of the learning progression also reminds us that readers need to be able to think about the relationships that exist between abstract ideas and iterations of those ideas. For example, Ben Franklin sitting in on the meeting of the Iroquois confederacy has everything to do with the first Continental Congress. Ben Franklin learned how they ran a government and used that knowledge to help set up our government—that is, one event caused, or influenced, another. This is the *stuff* of the texts and of content, and it is built around relationships. But to discern those relationships, it helps to pay attention to "Inferring Within Text/Cohesion." By fourth grade, students are expected to discuss relationships across the text, noticing how these elements of the text relate to one another. Let's take a look at this part of this part of the progression:

In the shifts between third and fourth grade that were discussed in *Reading the Weather*, we reflected on the importance of "Cross Text(s) Synthesis" strand. Students will need to read across texts on a topic and be able to integrate what they have learned from multiple sources in order to speak and/or write knowledgeably about that topic (work expected of them by the Common Core State Standards [CCSS] strand, Reading: Informational Text [RI], standard RI 4.9). You'll see that in this unit as in the last, students read across subtopics, synthesizing what they learn. It's also important to note that some of your fourth-graders may be doing fifth-grade level work and you'll notice that by studying what they have written in terms of subtopics.

This unit will also support students as they tackle the "Analyzing Perspective" strand, another key way that students in fourth grade are expected to

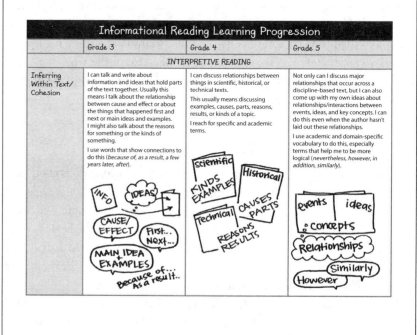

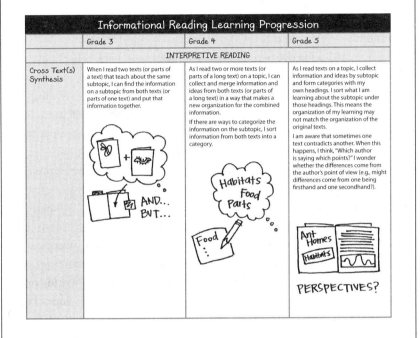

Informational Reading Learning Progression			
	Grade 3	Grade 4	Grade 5
INTERPRETIVE READING			
Cross Text(s) Synthesis	When I read two texts (or parts of a text) that teach about the same subtopic, I can find the information on a subtopic from both texts (or parts of one text) and put that information together.	As I read two or more texts (or parts of a long text) on a topic, I can collect and merge information and ideas from both texts (or parts of a long text) in a way that makes a new organization for the combined information. If there are ways to categorize the information on the subtopic, I sort information from both texts into a category.	As I read texts on a topic, I collect information and ideas by subtopic and form categories with my own headings. I sort what I am learning about the subtopic under those headings. This means the organization of my learning may not match the organization of the original texts. I am aware that sometimes one text contradicts another. When this happens, I think, "Which author is saying which points?" I wonder whether the differences come from the author's point of view (e.g., might differences come from one being firsthand and one secondhand?).

compare and contrast texts. The expectations in this area (which relate to CCSS RI 4.6) are a major shift from third grade. In third grade, students needed to be able to name the point of view, if it's very obvious ("I think this part is told from a penguin's point of view!"), and to know that their own point of view was not the same as that of the author. This means that the students need to read texts and focus on what they think about the topic, as well as what the author is really saying about it. Now, in fourth grade, students need to identify the point of view of a text, which to put it bluntly, is all about the pronouns. Is it an *I* who is writing the text? (Is the author using *I/my/mine*?) Who is the *I*? A general on a battlefield? A soldier on the same field? Is it a bystander who saw the events from a distance? If a text is a first-person account, students need to think about what focus and information that might offer them. For example, a soldier on the battlefield might offer the perspective of experiencing a battle up close and feeling how scary it is to be in a battle. Or, if it is a third-person account, students need to be able to think, "Hmm, this lets me know some background information about the battle, but it doesn't let me feel how it was to be right there."

You'll want to continue to push students to reach for slightly more challenging texts as they read across texts on a topic, and support them in shoring the foundation work in "Word Work" and "Fluency" that is critical in every unit. Then, too, this unit offers key opportunities to help students in "Building Vocabulary." You'll see that the work supports students in building a stronger vocabulary of both domain-specific and academic vocabulary words. Students will study words such as *revolution* across the unit, learning more about these terms and the other terms with which they are connected, and coming to new understandings of the terms.

Also, as students read across texts, analyze texts more deeply, and reach for more difficult texts, it is more important than ever that they be "Growing Ideas" as well. As mentioned in the last unit, students are expected to develop their own ideas more fully. This means that they will have an idea, read a little more, develop the idea further, take the risk to think in new ways about the idea, and perhaps write about it. They are expected to wonder and to question: "Is this always the case? Could this be connected to—?" You'll expect to see them trying out ideas, talking to others about those ideas, reading more, thinking more, writing, and so on. Across this whole year, students will work to both develop and defend ideas, and you'll expect to see them growing stronger at that work. And as students grow ideas, they should also be working within the thread, "Questioning the Text."

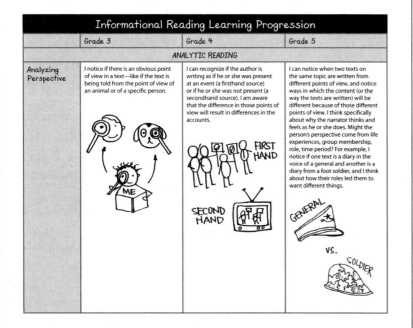

Informational Reading Learning Progression

	Grade 3	Grade 4	Grade 5
ANALYTIC READING			
Analyzing Perspective	I notice if there is an obvious point of view in a text—like if the text is being told from the point of view of an animal or of a specific person.	I can recognize if the author is writing as if he or she was present at an event (a firsthand source) or if he or she was not present (a secondhand source). I am aware that the difference in those points of view will result in differences in the accounts.	I can notice when two texts on the same topic are written from different points of view, and notice ways in which the content (or the way the texts are written) will be different because of those different points of view. I think specifically about why the narrator thinks and feels as he or she does. Might the person's perspective come from life experiences, group membership, role, time period? For example, I notice if one text is a diary in the voice of a general and another is a diary from a foot soldier, and I think about how their roles led them to want different things.

OVERVIEW

This unit has been designed so that it can support students in both reading and writing (*Bringing History to Life*) about the focal topic, the American Revolution. Another historical topic could be inserted into these books in the place of the American Revolution, and this unit could be a free-standing reading unit, without any connection to a parallel writing unit. But to help you imagine the flow of the unit, let me overview how we envision the writing unit unfolding alongside this one.

If you are teaching the two units in synchrony with each other, and if students do not have any prior knowledge of the American Revolution (which is our assumption), you'll want to start a few days earlier with the reading unit so that once kids have read for a few days, they'll be ready to get started with the writing unit, *Bringing History to Life*. While most units that support students' writing about a content area topic postpone writing until after weeks of research, we have found that after even just a few days of researching, it is helpful for students to get their mental arms around what they have learned by flash-drafting an information text, in this case, one called "All about the American Revolution." You'll point out to students that whenever writing an information text, it is important to structure it logically into subtopics that are organized in some principled way. For history, the easiest structure is chronological. Chances are good that your students' flash draft writing on the American Revolution (or on an alternate history topic, if that is your choice) will start with the lead-up to the war.

In *Bringing History to Life*, after students do some writing about the American Revolution, they are each expected to choose a subtopic on which to focus. If you are teaching this book and the writing unit alongside each other, we especially suggest that you channel students to choose topics that are related to the early parts of the war, reserving the final bend of the unit for topics that are related to the later parts of the war. You'll find that most of the texts that students read will have focused on the reasons for the war, the Boston Tea Party, Paul Revere, the minutemen, and so forth, so this won't take much (or any) guidance. In any case, students will spend the bulk of Bend I (in both the reading and the writing units) doing some research on the subtopic they choose. Within a very short time, they'll use their growing information writing skills and their starting knowledge about the subtopic to write another flash draft text, this time on the more focused topic. Over the days that follow, in *Bringing History to Life*, students will write a fictionalized you-were-there narrative that recreates a moment related to their topic and an essay arguing for the topic's importance (or lack thereof). That writing ends Bend I of the writing unit, *Bringing History to Life*.

In the next section of the writing unit, students select another focal topic to research and write about—this time, perhaps exploring a topic that occurs after the Second Continental Congress. But as you will see, this book interjects a brief sequence of days devoted to debate. If you are teaching the two units in sync with each other, you'll probably want to use both writing and reading time to help kids get ready for their debate, because this will require a lot of opinion writing as well as reading.

Bend I: Researching History

The first bend begins with students forming teams to prepare for conducting research on the American Revolution. You will have given a bin of materials to each research team, and each bin will contain books, photographs, articles, and lists of video links. You will remind your students that before diving into a nonfiction text, it is really important to preview it and to read more accessible texts first to glean an overview of the topic. Students begin, then, to orient themselves to the events leading up to the American Revolution.

Although the research process that your students will be involved with will resemble the work they did in the previous nonfiction unit, *Reading the Weather, Reading the World*, the texts that students will be reading won't be easy, and the sheer amount of information can be overwhelming. For that reason, you will provide lots of scaffolds. For example, you'll encourage some of your students to get an overview of their topics by watching videos. You may set some partnerships up to read duplicate copies of articles.

Reading complex nonfiction requires an emphasis on the crucial skills of synthesis, main idea, and summarization—all skills that are especially important on high-stakes tests, including PARCC and SBAC. You'll rely on the Informational Reading Learning Progression, especially the "Cross Text(s) Synthesis" and "Main Idea(s) and Supporting Details/Summary" strands, to support this work. Over the next few days, you will remind your students of what they learned during *Reading the Weather, Reading the World*, before taking them beyond that learning, helping them to look over headings, subheadings, and transitional cues to discern obvious structures, generate expectations, and use those structures to summarize chunks of the text. Students will pause periodically as they read to summarize the big points and to select details that especially support those big points.

The evidence is very strong that readers who take time to preview a text, note the text structure, and summarize a text in ways that reflect that structure will do significantly better on every other dimension of nonfiction reading. It is important to keep in mind, though, that note-taking and prioritizing big points and supportive details can either hurt or help a student's reading. Across these lessons, we aim to lift the level of note-taking in a way that also lifts the level of students' reading. Your students will likely need to practice these skills in multiple ways, so we encourage you to carefully consider the homework embedded across the unit, noticing how it helps students to both develop necessary skills and maintain their volume of reading.

Of course, this unit aims to teach not just nonfiction reading but also the special challenges inherent in the reading of history texts. You'll communicate to your students that when studying history, it is important to pay special attention to time, place, and people (specifically, the relationships and networks linking people together). You'll help students learn that by keeping an eye on an emerging timeline, map, or relationship, they can synthesize what they are learning and thinking about the information.

Across Bend I, you will notice an emphasis on student independence and ownership. For example, one day you will channel students to begin creating their own versions of the class-created tools. The decision to give students time to construct their own tools, rather than handing out pre-made graphic organizers for students to fill in, is a deliberate one. Although this will take a bit more time and the results will look messier, engaging in this process now will equip students to create their own tools and mental models when they encounter complex historical texts in the future.

After the first four sessions, your students will be ready to shift from researching the American Revolution in general to studying a subtopic that is particularly interesting to them. One student may be especially interested in Paul Revere, another in the First Continental Congress, a third in the Boston Massacre. To explore these subtopics, you'll ask students to reread key passages with a new lens, looking for details they may have overlooked the first time, to dramatize moments that bring the characters and the events in history to life, and to investigate primary sources.

You will also support students in synthesizing information across different texts on a subtopic, noticing ways in which texts are similar and different in their content and presentation of a subtopic. As part of this, you will highlight not only what texts teach but also how authors use dramatically different, strategically chosen craft moves to teach that information.

Bend I carries students up to the moment when the British colonists began to seriously consider independence from Great Britain. Students will focus on the position of the Patriots, and you may find that many, if not all, of your students will choose to research the most famous, iconic people and events leading up to the American Revolution, such as Benjamin Franklin, the Sons of Liberty, the Boston Massacre, the Boston Tea Party, or Paul Revere's ride. As students conduct their research, you will help them understand that while they are learning history, this is a reading unit, and they should approach their learning about history through the lens of becoming stronger readers. And at this end of this first bend, students will celebrate their learning by teaching each other about their research and by giving themselves an honest self-assessment of their achievements and progress.

Bend II: Preparing to Debate

In the second bend, you'll teach your students that any account of an event—a current event or one that occurred in the past—was constructed by a person who speaks from his or her own viewpoint. That one perspective is never the whole story. More than this, any one perspective will inevitably reflect the position and ideologies of the person constructing it, making some people's voices and views more dominant than others. Proficient readers are aware of the perspective from which a text is written, and they think, "What views are represented? What voices are heard, and what voices have been silenced? Whose views haven't been revealed?"

Prior to now, your students will mostly have been reading the mainstream story of the American Revolution. The texts will sometimes have presented two sides of a controversy—the students read, after all, that the British wanted to levy a tax to reimburse themselves for the expenses caused by the French and Indian War—but if your students are anything like those in most of our pilot classrooms, they will have identified wholeheartedly with the colonists' story. They won't have taken other perspectives to heart.

In this bend, you will teach your students that responsible historians go in search of as much information on a topic as they can—seeking to gather up all the facts they can before weighing in and taking a stance of their own. In this way, you will send a clear message about the importance of being active, not passive, readers of nonfiction.

Across this bend, students will draw on the skills they've learned—to read and understand point of view, to uncover important details and facts, to angle evidence to fit an argument, and to think about which they believe and why—all in preparation to debate whether or not the colonies should declare independence. Each student will read with a role in mind—Patriot or Loyalist. Though some may be initially reluctant to take on the side of the British, the engaging work of debate, argumentation, and stepping into character will soon overshadow their momentary reluctance. This bend culminates in having your students reenact the Second Continental Congress debate about independence.

Your students will step into history and become delegates to this Congress, debating the question "Should the colonies become independent from Great Britain?" We've designed Session 13 as a mid-unit celebration, where families and administrators are invited in to experience the debate. We recommend that you build on your students' excitement and make that day one that will stand out in their minds at the end of the year and for years to come.

Bend III: A Second Cycle of Research

The third bend begins as third bends often do, with an opportunity for children to restart the process they learned earlier in the unit. At this point, if you are teaching *Bringing History to Life* alongside this unit, students will move into Bend II of that unit. Students will engage in a focused investigation of a new subtopic, ideally this time investigating one that takes place after the Second Continental Congress (although it is more challenging to find source material that children can read for these topics, so you may not be able to support this in the first year or two of this unit). Most of them will probably work with a partner on a topic of choice, and you may need to do some behind-the-scenes manipulation to be sure that students who struggle as readers work with a topic for which you have an abundance of more accessible resources.

Teachers who are teaching both this unit and the sister writing unit, *Bringing History to Life*, will note that although the writing unit allows for some students to continue pursuing a study that is already underway, we are not advising this if you are teaching the two units concurrently. That is, we suspect that if your students are reading about the American Revolution as well as writing about it, devoting at least two periods a day to that work, they may have exhausted most of your accessible resources on their first subtopic, and that you'll therefore want them to pursue a second topic. We also anticipate that you may want their focus to shift towards topics that take place after the Second Continental Congress, just to maintain a chronological feel to the unit. As mentioned earlier, that, of course, entirely depends on your resources, because the most important thing is that students have accessible reading materials and are researching topics of interest to them.

To launch students' upcoming research, you will aim to support them with strategies to handle the challenging texts they'll need to read. They need to know that as they go forward in life, there will be times when the sourcebooks on a topic will be very challenging. When that is the case, you'll teach students that they can find texts that are far more accessible on the topic and read those in preparation for handling the others. That is, prior knowledge on a topic is the one thing that gives readers a leg up on reading texts that would otherwise be too complex. It is important for students to realize that they can take action and create the prior knowledge that they need.

On the other hand, you will also acknowledge that students may need to scaffold their work and sometimes need to review what they have done in the past to help them read more complex texts. You'll teach readers to recognize when a text is too hard and to shift strategies accordingly. If your readers decide to persist with a too-hard text, they essentially need to rewrite the text so that it *is* accessible, translating it down a notch as they read so they can grasp what it is saying. That is, when necessary—which should be rarely—readers can make their way through texts that are too hard by reading chunk by chunk and stopping often to paraphrase.

If you acknowledge that some of the time, kids will be reading texts that are too hard for them, it becomes clear that you'll also need to support students in the critical skill of monitoring for meaning. As fourth-graders, your students should come to an informational text expecting the parts of the text to work together so that they teach main ideas. It's crucial that students learn to monitor for when their understanding breaks down. You'll show students strategies they can turn to in these situations, moving through the text part by part, paraphrasing, and considering how parts of the text fit with the whole topic.

Some of the sessions in this bend closely follow the teaching in *Bringing History to Life*, and their primary purpose is to help your students to make connections between the writing about history they may be doing and the reading they are undertaking in this unit. Fourth-grade readers (and writers!) need to consider not just how facts are strung together on a page but also how an author uses structure and text features to highlight what is most important

about the information. Whether or not you are teaching the companion writing unit, these sessions will stand your students in good stead when they are attempting to determine how authors clue readers in to what matters most.

Bend III also tackles how to help students with academic and domain-specific vocabulary. The research on vocabulary development suggests that developing a richer vocabulary becomes increasingly important as students become older and their texts become more complex. While easier texts often embed the definition of a word into the text, harder texts often require readers to bring knowledge of vocabulary words to their reading. The other big change that happens at about this time is that increasingly, when students encounter tricky words in a text, the hard part is not saying those words, but defining them. A student can pronounce words like *boycott*, *garrison*, and *sovereignty*, but one then has to discern the meaning of the unfamiliar word. This becomes increasingly difficult because often these new, hard words are defined by other hard, technical words.

Your teaching, then, is angled towards the goal of helping students be resourceful word solvers, able to draw on strategies in order to solve words as best they can. You will teach students that in addition to figuring out how to say a word and getting the gist of it, they have to know words well. That means they should be able to give examples of the word, talk about its variations and the ways it is similar to and different from those variations, and give examples of how the word tends to be used.

In the last session of the unit, you invite students to transfer all they know about interpretation to their work with the American Revolution. Interpretation is, of course, a skill that nonfiction as well as fiction readers use. It is especially important when students are reading history, because history is, by definition, interpretive. Most of the texts our students read are interpretations made by different historians. And one of the reasons that history matters is that the stories of long ago can teach us lessons that help us live our lives today.

Stories in history are told over and over again, not just because the facts matter but because they carry themes that matter. The stories of George Washington crossing the Potomac, the Boston Tea Party, the Sons of Liberty, and Thomas Paine's *Common Sense* are told again and again in literature, in film, and at the dinner table. They are told and retold not just as reminders of what happened but as lessons about what's possible, lessons about what's important in our lives as human beings and as Americans. In the same way that a piece of literature offers universal themes that speak to each reader in unique ways, complicated moments from the past and the stories of those times offer ideas about conflict, perseverance, leadership, and character—ideas that are meaningful to people living in any era. By now, you and your students have realized that the American Revolution is chock-full of these stories.

Readers of history need to learn that history is not just about memorizing dates and facts. History is about ideas. Some of these ideas are commonly taught in history courses, while others are developed by the critical and thoughtful reader. Across this unit, you have taught your children not just to memorize facts and events but also to develop and internalize ideas. In just a few weeks, your students will learn to think like a historian.

ASSESSMENT

Your instruction will always be informed by assessments, and those assessments will be ongoing. You'll use running records and other observations of your students, examinations of reading logs, writing about reading, their talk about reading, and performance assessments to track student progress and to align your teaching to what your best knowledge is of what they can do, can almost do, and can't yet do.

You have taken running records many times, surely at least twice, before you start this unit. If students have been reading nonfiction at the same rate as fiction, you will probably have noticed that they read at the same levels in nonfiction as in fiction. If your students seem to be reading more fiction than nonfiction, you may need to move students down a notch in nonfiction at the start of this unit, and then provide enough support so they can move quickly back up. Watch students' reading logs for possible declines in volume of reading.

Assuming you have taught two units prior to this one, students who are entering this unit reading at benchmark will be reading level R or S texts with approximately 96% accuracy, fluency, and comprehension. If your school has access to a system that supports you in conducting running records of nonfiction texts, you might choose to use that system to support you in administering nonfiction running records to students. Even if you don't have such a system, you can use any text that has been leveled, ask students to read a piece of it, and conduct running records. The TCRWP website does not provide leveled nonfiction texts for conducting running records.

Regardless of which approach you choose, this unit supports dramatic growth. Small-group work can reinforce this. The strands of text complexity in nonfiction (see Chapter 5 in *Reading Pathways, Grades 3–5: Performance Assessments and Learning Progressions*) will be enormously helpful to you as you plan your small groups. That chapter shows ways nonfiction texts grow and scaffold from one level to another in relation to main idea, vocabulary, structure, and knowledge demands.

Literal comprehension is necessary, but it's not enough. You will also want to assess your students' higher-level comprehension, looking specifically at all the skills of synthesis, point of view, and the relationships between parts. This unit begins with a performance assessment, available in the online resources, which is designed to highlight and support these comprehension skills. The performance assessment assesses four main skills that are critically important across this unit and on the high-stakes assessments your fourth-graders will be taking. In particular, this unit focuses on these skill areas:

- Main Idea(s) and Supporting Details/Summary
- Cross Text(s) Synthesis
- Analyzing Perspective
- Analyzing Parts of a Text in Relation to the Whole

More details pertaining to the assessment can be found in the Start with Assessment letter, immediately following this introductory section, and in the online resources.

The biggest decision you will want to make right away pertains to the scoring of the performance assessment. In *Reading Pathways, Grades 3–5: Performance Assessments and Learning Progressions*, you will read about ways in which you can hold a norming meeting with other teachers so that all the teachers across your grade level can collaboratively score students' performance assessments, assessing that work in roughly equivalent ways. The learning progression, combined with a big effort to create protocols or agreements among the answers expected on the assessments can enable you and your colleagues to come to a shared view on what makes good, better, best work in particular reading skills.

But what we think is most important is that you try to turn as much of the scoring of the assessment as possible over to the kids. In doing this, students will need to create their own protocols and agreements on what they feel constitutes level four, three, or two work. Pay attention to how the kids score the work and think about the knowledge they have gained to make that judgment call. This is a perfect time to assess if your students have transferred their learning. To support your students with this work, you'll draw on the Informational Reading Learning Progression and on student-facing rubrics, created from the progression.

A word of caution: If your students have not grown up with the Units of Study in Teaching Reading, this entire year will probably be on the challenging side for your students. If that is the case, you may be more comfortable if you score their pre-assessment and then ask your students to work in partners to understand how you scored them and to try revising their work immediately, using your scoring as feedback. Scoring takes a fair amount of your time, however, and if doing so postpones the unit or the unveiling of the learning progressions, it is probably not worth the trade-off.

Once students have studied the Informational Reading Learning Progression and gleaned an understanding of the indicators that might suggest they are doing higher-level work, this fills them with a sense of direction and resolve, and it puts a tincture over the whole unit. As students self-assess their work on analyzing perspective, for example, you have almost painted the future teaching on that topic with a dye that makes that teaching stand out in your students' minds more across the unit. They know it is a skill that will be assessed, so they sit up and look alert! At the point in the unit when you teach about analyzing perspective, they're apt to think, "Oh, this is about perspective. That was on the pre-assessment." By prioritizing this work on the assessment, you've demonstrated that you place a high value on this learning, and students will likely respond accordingly.

GETTING READY
Gather Texts

Because this unit has a substantial research component, you will need to spend some time before hand collecting engaging, appropriate, leveled material on the topic you are studying. You will want to make sure that you have a supply of texts on the most popular subtopics surrounding the American Revolution. In the online resources, we provide a list of suggested materials, as well as a text list of leveled texts on the topic of the American Revolution, to support the work your kids are doing.

You will notice that we refer to mentor texts that we use throughout this unit. We recommend the same mentor texts that are used in the sister writing unit, *Bringing History to Life—The Revolutionary War* by Josh Gregory and *Liberty!: How the Revolutionary War Began* by Lucille Recht Penner, as well as, if possible, *Short Nonfiction for American History: The American Revolution and Constitution* by Anne Goudvis and Stephanie Harvey.

If possible, create bins with approximately half a dozen books in each that are leveled to match readers at a particular band of text difficulty (or ideally, at more specific levels). You will also want to include primary source material, as well as maps and video resources. Include in each bin a toolkit of resources tailored to your students' needs. This will include articles and also videos.

Partnering Students

Throughout the unit, you'll probably want readers to work in same-level partnerships and, if possible, same-level research teams. The unit doesn't emphasize the importance of the research teams within Bend III, but classrooms that piloted the unit felt that social structure was helpful.

Conducting Read–Alouds alongside the Unit

The read-aloud text we recommend for the unit is *Liberty!: How the Revolutionary War Began* by Lucille Recht Penner. Your students will absolutely love this text. Within it, there are mountains of information and pictures that will help students imagine what life was like at the time of the American Revolution. The book also offers lively cartoons that give kids a glimpse into the times of the Revolution and into peoples' thoughts. You will likely admire the book's snippets of text that are perfect for quick strategy and skill instruction.

While you probably won't read this book from cover to cover, it is sure to become a favorite as you share excerpts in read-aloud and in lessons across the unit. During Bends II and III, you'll continue to use sections of *Liberty* as well as some additional texts, such as Josh Gregory's *The Revolutionary War* and Rosalyn Schanzer's *George vs. George*. You will also want to make your own selections of texts to read aloud to your class during the latter parts of the unit. Choose texts that you find engaging, and encourage your students to share texts they think would be helpful for the class, too. You will want to carve out a separate chunk of time each day, outside of reading workshop, for reading aloud sections of these read-aloud texts.

❧ ONLINE DIGITAL RESOURCES

A variety of resources to accompany this and the other Grade 4 Units of Study for Teaching Reading are available in the Online Resources, including charts and examples of student work shown throughout *Reading History*, as well as links to other electronic resources. Offering daily support for your teaching, these materials will help you provide a structured learning environment that fosters independence and self-direction.

To access and download all the digital resources for the Grade 4 Units of Study for Teaching Reading:

1. Go to **www.heinemann.com** and click the link in the upper right to log in. (If you do not have an account yet, you will need to create one.)

2. **Enter the following registration code** in the box to register your product: RUOS_Gr4

3. Under **My Online Resources**, click the link for the **Grade 4 Reading Units of Study**.

4. The digital resources are available under the headings; click a file name to download.

(You may keep copies of these resources on up to six of your own computers or devices. By downloading the files you acknowledge that they are for your individual or classroom use and that neither the resources nor the product code will be distributed or shared.)

◆ START WITH ASSESSMENT ◆

Dear Teachers,

'm remembering the buttons on the duplicating machines that flash: not ready, not ready. My hunch is that is how you feel as you plunge into this unit: not ready, not ready.

Here is my advice. Read the front matter of this book if you haven't done so already—it really orients you. And the good news is that you can postpone day one of the unit for 24 hours anyhow, while you give your students yet another performance assessment designed to assess a few skills critically important within this unit and across the standardized assessments many students take.

There is a mountain of evidence suggesting that your students' learning and your teaching are mobilized and intensified when your classroom becomes more assessment-based in the very best sense of that word. John Hattie, author of *Visible Learning* (2008), reviewed studies of more than 20 million learners to understand factors that maximize achievement. He found that one of the most important ways to maximize achievement is to provide learners with crystal-clear and ambitious goals, as well as frequent feedback that highlights progress toward those goals and provides doable next steps. Today's assessment sets the stage for this powerful work.

If things didn't go perfectly the last time your students did a performance assessment—if you wished they were writing on Post-its instead of sheets of paper, or if you worried that they didn't do their best—by all means think with your colleagues about ways to make things go better this time around. Know that the important thing is that you and your colleagues are in sync with each other—not that you follow our suggestions in detail. Know, too, that as we *learn* from people like you, we will be funneling what we learn into our Online Resources where we will keep you updated. Keep us posted about revisions you are making so that we can let other schools and districts know, as well.

So go forward again today, making the performance assessment work for you and your children.

Thanks,

Lucy, Janet, and Grace

Researchers Orient Themselves to a Text Set

IN THIS SESSION, you'll teach students that researchers often learn about a topic by locating accessible resources through which they can build their own prior background knowledge and overview of the topic. They also skim to pay attention to recurring subtopics.

GETTING READY

✔ Create research teams of four students and write the names of the members on a piece of paper. Place the paper in the meeting area where you would like your teams to sit (see Connection).

✔ Gather a collection of texts on your whole-class topic. Be sure you have duplicate copies of some of the easiest overview articles. The research teams all overview the events leading to the American Revolution for a few days and then shift to focus on a subtopic (see Connection, Teaching, and Link).

✔ Select one research team to begin their research while the class watches, and prepare a bin of materials for them to preview (see Teaching).

✔ Ask students to bring their reading notebooks with their reading logs to the meeting area today and every day throughout the unit.

✔ Set out chart paper to create a "Subtopics on the American Revolution before 1775" chart. (see Teaching).

✔ Prepare a chart titled, "Launching a Research Project." This will become the anchor chart for the bend (see Active Engagement and Link).

✔ Prepare a list of overview videos to share with students. If possible provide students with Internet access to view (see Mid-Workshop Teaching).

✔ Provide students with copies of the "Fluency" strand of the Informational Reading Learning Progression checklist for (see Share).

✔ Print out articles to distribute with tonight's homework (see Homework).

THIS SESSION launches a unit-long inquiry into reading nonfiction. You may choose any topic, of course, but we chose the American Revolution, not only because it is emphasized in national social studies standards, but also because the topic aligns this reading unit with the *Bringing History to Life* writing unit from the *Units of Study in Opinion, Information, and Narrative Writing*. For those who teach the two units alongside each other, this reading unit begins two days prior to the writing unit.

Like *Reading the Weather, Reading the World*, this unit is designed to give students practice reading increasingly complex texts, ascertaining the main idea, synthesizing across texts, learning to tackle domain-specific vocabulary, and the like.

This unit can work as a self-standing reading unit, without any expectation that students will do more writing than note-taking and flash-drafting. Teachers who are not teaching the writing unit may want to devise their own report-writing unit alongside this reading unit, as students will benefit from drawing on this research in to write two books—one related to Bend I, one to Bend III.

Today you'll remind your students of all they already know about ways of launching a research project. You'll remind them to preview their texts, to sequence the reading they plan to do in a thoughtful way, to read more accessible texts first, and to be clear about their purposes for reading. During the upcoming week, your students will give themselves a quick orientation to the events leading up to the American Revolution.

We make no bones about it: this work is challenging. The texts that students will be reading aren't easy, and the sheer amount of information can be overwhelming. For that reason, you will see lots of scaffolds. For example, you will see that students are often encouraged to learn from watching videos. You'll also note that in Bend I, students will work in research teams consisting of two matched-level partnerships.

Your work for the next few days will benefit from you knowing the overall design of the unit. It will help for you to read the front matter of this book, but in a nutshell, the plan is that during the later portion of this bend, students' research will focus on one of the subtopics in the list that is generated today. Then in the second bend of the unit, students will study the Loyalists' side of the story (which will have been somewhat missing from the first bend) and will engage in a mock version of the Second Continental Congress. Finally, in the third bend, they will study a subtopic of their choice related to the actual war, the ending of the war, or the development of a government.

Today, students are reminded of how a person begins to plan and to launch a research project, and then the two members of a partnership begin reading duplicate copies of an accessible text that overviews the American Revolution.

Researchers Orient Themselves to a Text Set

CONNECTION

Announce that kids will work in research teams on a whole-class research project, to learn not only about the topic, but also about the kinds of reading that researchers do.

I asked students to come to the meeting area and to sit near a paper on which I'd written their names, with each piece of paper naming the four members of a research team consisting of two ability-matched partnerships. "Researchers. I'm going to call you that—*researchers*—because for the next month, you're going to be doing the particular kind of reading that a person does when following the trail of a research project. You'll work in research teams. The names on the seating chart papers show your teammates. The umbrella topic for this first bend will be the events leading up to the American Revolution in 1775. But here's the thing: you won't *just* be learning about the American Revolution. Instead, you'll be learning about how people conduct research on *any* topic."

Channel kids to recall what they already know about launching a research project, using this to drumroll the first teaching point.

"Today we start the research. Will you think back over all the research projects you've pursued over the last few years and list, with your partner, what you know about launching a research project?"

The room erupted into talk, and I listened, using what the kids said as a preassessment. Soon I stepped in. "So, do you just grab an armload of texts and plow through them, diving into the first source and reading it from cover to cover, then diving into the next in your pile?"

The kids chimed in and I joined them: "No!"

Nodding, I said, "You are right, experienced readers are more strategic than that."

❖ **Name the teaching point.**

"Today I want to remind you that readers take time to plan before plunging into a research project. Readers locate easy sources and plan to read those first. It also helps to scan for subtopics that come up again and again in the resources. If you list those subtopics, you give yourself a way to plan your reading."

◆ COACHING

It is important to note that you can easily substitute another topic instead of this one. We've chosen this so that fourth-graders are given some help reading in history as well as in science, and because we know many classrooms using these reading units of study will also lean on Units of Study in Opinion, Information and Argument Writing (and specifically, Bringing History to Life). This unit parallels and supports that book, although it is also entirely workable as a freestanding unit.

You'll notice that when a teaching point is a reminder, as this one is, it tends to consolidate work that, in prior units, was stretched out over a series of lessons.

TEACHING

Bring a small group to the front of the classroom to demonstrate how to get started as researchers, while channeling the rest of the class to take notes on the process.

"It is one thing to *say* that researchers do those things, and another thing to actually pull all that work off. So let's watch a few researchers begin to do this complicated work as a way to clarify what this entails. Jose, Emanuel, Rose, and Jen have agreed to launch their research into the American Revolution, and I'll join them. It's going to be critical for the rest of you to research us, recording the steps you see us taking. You can whisper to each other what you notice us doing and the steps you see us taking. So while the group gets themselves settled up here, will the rest of you get ready to take notes on the work you see them doing?"

Jose, Emanuel, Rose, Jen, and I settled around a basket of books and articles on the American Revolution. I said to the kids, "How do we start?" One student piped in that we should find some easy texts to look at first. Another added, "To find the topics they write about all the time."

Coach a research team to identify subtopics that repeat across books. Create a chart of subtopics with the students.

We quickly located some easier texts, and I said, "So now that we have located some easier overview texts, do we first look them over to see subtopics that come up again and again?" The rest of the research group nodded and dug in, while I glanced significantly at the rest of the class, and pantomimed to remind them to take notes.

Leafing through the pages in the books, members of the group began saying things like, "This one starts with before the war and then goes to the war," and "Mine has pictures of people doing crazy things like emptying boxes from a boat into the ocean."

I jumped in. "Do any of you know what's happening in Jose's book?" and I asked him to show the group the pictures of what I knew was the Boston Tea Party. Some of them scanned the page and read enough of the text to announce, skeptically, that there was a tea party going on. I nodded, and said, "I'm not sure you realize it, but the things you have said so far are all events leading up to the war. That 'tea party' is famous as one of the events that led to the outbreak of war. There will probably be others, too."

I asked the research team, "Are you ready to list the subtopics that seem to come up over and over in the texts you're looking at?" They contributed ideas, and soon we made this list:

You might consider giving a few of the observing students white boards to record notes and having another group take notes on chart paper. This could add complications, however, so it may not be worth the trouble.

The easy books function almost like the picture on the box of the jigsaw puzzle does, giving a big picture of the whole topic before studying more about any particular subtopic.

This entire demonstration should take all of three minutes. The rest of the class can grasp the gist of what you are conveying without you going on and on. Always keep in mind that an entire minilesson is ten minutes long—though the first minilesson in a unit will often be a bit longer. But keep your pace efficient.

Subtopics on the American Revolution before 1775

- End of the French and Indian War
- Problems between Britain and the colonists
- Sons of Liberty
- Paul Revere
- Speeches: Patrick Henry, Sam Adams
- Boston Massacre
- Boston Tea Party

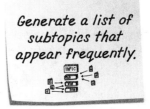

Generate a list of subtopics that appear frequently.

Then I paused and said to the observing class, "Make sure you have jotted down what we have done so far as researchers, while Jose, Sophia, the rest of the group, and I look at some other subtopics that come up a lot further along in their books." While the class wrote silently, recording what we'd done, the small group and I looked further into texts, and soon had added to the list:

Subtopics on the American Revolution before 1775

- End of the French and Indian War
- Problems between Britain and the colonists
- Sons of Liberty
- Paul Revere
- Speeches: Patrick Henry, Sam Adams
- Boston Massacre
- Boston Tea Party
- **Intolerable Acts**
- **First Continental Congress**

ACTIVE ENGAGEMENT

Channel the class to talk about what they saw you and the small group of student-researchers do to launch an inquiry. Listen as they talk, and then list the steps they saw you taking.

"So let's flip things around. The research team you were just watching and I will observe *you* and your partner. Only this time, we'll observe you talking as researchers about what you saw us doing to launch our research into the causes of the American Revolution. Will you researchers talk in partnerships or small groups about what you noticed us doing? The five of us will listen."

The other members of "my" small group and I listened, and within a few minutes, I'd listed the steps the class saw us take to launch a research project. I knew this would grow into an anchor chart for this bend.

These subtopics will thread through the first two bends of this book. They are dominant in the resources your kids are apt to read, so chances are good these will be subtopics your research team identifies as well—but you might suggest topics that your kids don't stumble upon to make your list resemble this one for convenience sake. This is only a suggestions and is, of course, your choice.

In an instance like this, the list that you grow from overheard conversations will become an important scaffold for the work the class will do. Don't hesitate to add steps the class didn't notice or word the steps in ways you think will be helpful to the class. For now, your chart will probably match ours for convenience.

LINK

Distribute resources to each team. Channel kids to skim the materials, revise the existing list of subtopics, and to start reading easy overview texts.

I gave a bin of resources to each team, and said, "Researchers, will you start your reading by doing some work right here? Sort through these materials, and decide on a few to skim first. Will you revise our class list if you encounter new subtopics you expect to learn about? And, be sure to choose an easy, overview text you can read first. That should take about five minutes." I added my tip to our anchor chart, and then knelt down to coach in as research teams started working.

ANCHOR CHART

Launching a Research Project

- Gather sources on the topic to preview.
- Generate a list of subtopics that frequently appear.
- **Choose an accessible book to read for an overview.**

Choose an accessible book to read for an overview.

Set partnerships up to make choices for how they will work together.

After a few minutes, I called for the students' attention. "Now you'll have time to read. Will you and a partner read together today? You'll see there are a few articles in your bin that have duplicate copies. Start with one of those so you can read the same text for now. Look over the text and make a plan for whether you want to take turns reading aloud to each other, or to read silently for a chunk of text, then stop to talk. There is a ton of new information to digest. Get started!"

As students work, you may need to voice over, saying, "Researchers, are the topics we found during the minilesson also present inside your books? Adjust that list if you need to, and add to it."

Coaching Students to Draw on All They've Learned Previously

You'll be busy today! You will want to get the new work of the unit underway by moving quickly among your students, naming and celebrating what they are doing that matches your hopes and channeling them to try some things that are central to the unit. Today's work won't be substantially different from that which they did during the research project on weather earlier this year. But the texts they are reading now will be more challenging.

Support transference from prior units, especially around text orientation.

Be vigilant from the very start whether kids take a moment to orient themselves to whatever text they are reading, getting the lay of the land. The window of time in which you can support students' previewing will be a small one, as they'll soon shift into reading their texts. If readers need help, you might suggest that several of them listen in as you coach one partnership to preview their text. You might gather your readers around the focal partnership and say, "Will you show us all how you look over your text, letting text features and topic sentences lead you to your expectations?" Set the other readers up to notice what the previewing pair does. Continue to coach the partnership as they preview, saying, "So what do you think the main parts will be in this text?" There will be instances when the titles and subtitles do not explicitly highlight upcoming content, so be ready to direct readers to topic sentences of paragraphs or to the paragraphs themselves. Help them see that transitions can clue them into the structure of the text they'll be reading.

Support partners working together with a shared text.

Make sure that when children orient themselves to the text, partners agree on stop-and-talk places at the ends of chunks of the text. They'll only reap the advantages of reading collaboratively if they talk about their reading. The length of those chunks will vary, depending on the density of the texts and the skills of the readers, but certainly fourth-graders should be able to read at least a page before pausing to digest, and usually several pages. When kids retell, think of this as a sort of oral note-taking. Their reconstruction of what they have read should reflect their prior work on gleaning main ideas and supportive points.

Although generally you won't imagine fourth-graders spending workshop time reading aloud to each other, if they do this for today, there are definite advantages. This will keep their involvement high, help them become more fluent readers of *expository* texts, and help you to double-check the level of text difficulty each child can handle.

MID-WORKSHOP TEACHING
Knowing When the Text Is Too Hard

"Readers, I love the way you and your partner are pausing at the ends of chunks of the text to recall what you have learned together. I've even seen some of you recalling what you read by using the palm of your hand for main ideas and your fingers for supporting details.

"If you find that after you read a passage you're having a hard time remembering what you read and can't therefore figure out the main ideas and the supporting details, you may be reading something that is too hard for you. The text could look easy at a glance, but there can be so much information in it, coming at you so quickly, that it is actually harder than you think. If you feel like it is not easy to retell the text, instead of inching through it, rereading it over and over, try to find an easier text on the same topic and read that first. Or watch a video. I'm putting a list of good overview videos beside our computers, so if you or you and your research team want to watch one of these, go ahead."

Rereading Passages for Fluency

Channel partners to select a passage, and to read it aloud well to each other.

"Readers, I know you are wanting to get back to your partner and to share some of what you have learned. Before you do that, will you and your partner mark a passage—just a paragraph, at most—that you have read today that you think is worth sharing?" I gave them a minute to do this.

"Right now, with your partner, take the time to reread the passage you and your partner shared, reading it aloud. But here is the thing: Try to read the passage in a way that makes it easy for listeners to understand what you are saying and to feel why it is important. You'll see that to read a passage really well, you have to know what matters—what will you pop out? What is just a small, tucked detail? Is there a list inside the passage? See if you can read any list that is within your text in a way that accentuates the list."

As children read aloud to each other once, I distributed the "Fluency" strand of the Informational Reading Learning Progression suggesting students note where they were on that progression, and try reading aloud again, taking their work up a notch.

After a bit, I said, "Now will one person from your partnership read to your research team? After the passage is read, talk a bit about it. If there is time, switch off so you hear from the other partnership."

PREVIEWING THE AMERICAN REVOLUTION

Researchers, tonight you'll begin a crash course on the American Revolution. You can start by watching three or four videos. You can find good videos on the list in the online resources. You can also read some of the articles I gave you. If you don't have access to a computer, focus on reading the articles.

Please also think about the reading that you will do at home during this unit. You and I will have a conversation soon about your reading plans.

Readers Use Text Structures to Organize Incoming Information and Notes

IN THIS SESSION, you'll teach students that when researchers preview a text, they try to identify the text structure, to help them understand the important parts and organize their reading and note taking.

GETTING READY

✔ Ask students to bring the nonfiction texts they have been reading to the meeting area and to sit with their research teams (see Connection).

✔ Display the "Common Nonfiction Text Structures" chart from Connection, Teaching, and Active Engagement.

✔ Cue a video clip of Patrick Henry's "Give me liberty, or give me death!" speech at 5:07 for playback (https://www.youtube.com/watch?v=HHo-3LEcgQE; search terms: give liberty John Litel video) (see Connection).

✔ Cue a video clip of a Samuel Adams speech from *Liberty's Kids* Episode #1 (youtube, search term Liberty's Kids #01 1/2) at 5:57–6:54, and display a transcript (see Teaching).

✔ Update the "Launching a Research Project" anchor chart (see Teaching).

✔ Select an excerpt for students to read through the lens of text structure. We use a passage from *Liberty! How the Revolutionary War Began* but you may choose any work-structure (see Active Engagement).

✔ Distribute Post-it® flags for students to mark where the structure of their texts changes (see Link and Conferring and Small-Group Work).

✔ Print copies of "Main Idea(s) and Supporting Details/Summary" and "Cross Text(s) Synthesis" strands of the Informational Reading Learning Progression (see Conferring and Small-Group Work).

✔ Update the "Subtopics on the American Revolution before 1775" chart based on the new knowledge students acquire (see Share).

TODAY you will teach students the crucial skills of synthesis, main idea and summarization—all skills that are especially important on high stakes tests, and on the Informational Reading Learning Progression. Specifically, you will help your students rely on text structures as supports for comprehension. You will remind them of what they learned in the previous session and during *Reading the Weather, Reading the World*, then you'll take them beyond that learning, helping them to look over headings, subheadings, and transitional cues to discern obvious structures, to generate expectations, and to use those structures to summarize chunks of the text. Students will pause periodically as they read to summarize the big points and to select details that especially support those big points.

In this session, as in the last, partners will read duplicate copies of expository texts in sync with each other, pausing after chunks of text to summarize. Pay attention to ways you can provide close-in support for the work your students are doing, as described in the Conferring and Small-Group Work section. Keep on hand the Informational Reading Learning Progression on hand, and especially the "Main Idea(s) and Supporting Details/Summary" and "Cross Text(s) Synthesis" strands, because these can guide your conferring and small-group work. The evidence is very strong that readers who take time to preview a text, note the text structure, and summarize a text in ways that reflect that structure will do significantly better on every other dimension of nonfiction reading.

Although this is, in a sense, a basic skills session, you will also aim to rally your kids' interest in the topic of the American Revolution by showing them clips of two videos and by channeling them to do a bit a persuasive speaking themselves. Helping students to learn from multimedia nonfiction texts is a valued twenty-first-century literacy skill. Of course, if you can't rely on media, you can simply read the transcript instead, but we do urge you to move heaven and earth to be able to show the video, as just two minutes of watching can help students to imagine the times and feel its fervor.

For now, however, Patrick Henry's speech is the appetizer to a session that focuses on helping students use the text structures that are embedded in the texts they read to help them learn from their reading.

Readers Use Text Structures to Organize Incoming Information and Notes

CONNECTION

Channel kids to talk persuasively to each other, advocating for the importance of their research topic.

"Before we go any farther, I'd like you to think about *why* the American Revolution is such a big deal. Why, out of all the possible topics we could be investigating, are we studying this one?" I gave students less than a minute to prepare. "Now, talk to your partner. Give each other little persuasive speeches on why it is important to study the American Revolution. Start with a claim. 'Studying the American Revolution is important because. . . .'"

Play a clip from a dramatized historical speech capturing a similarly persuasive argument.

I listened as the groups gave each other little persuasive speeches, and then said, "You are pretty eloquent! Before the Revolution started, there were a lot of colonists who did just what you did now—they argued for the importance of the Revolution. I'm going to show you a video clip in which the speaker, Patrick Henry, stands up for independence. Listen carefully to see if you can hear how he organizes his ideas. Before we get started, I want to remind you of some typical ways that information texts tend to be organized." I gestured toward our "Common Nonfiction Text Structures" chart. "When people speak, as when they write, they often use text structures to organize their ideas—structures like main idea and supporting details, cause and effect, or problem/solution.

Common Nonfiction Text Structures

Structure	Transition words
Chronological	first, then, next, after that, finally, before, after
Problem/solution	a problem is, a solution is, if . . . then . . . , so that
Cause and effect	because, since, reasons, then, therefore, so, in order
Compare/contrast	different, same, alike, similar, although, but, yet, or

You probably worry that the kids won't know enough about the American Revolution to do this little activity. I encourage you to do it anyway. Kids will learn more if you hoist them into positions that require them to use what they have learned, and the truth is that they can do something with even just the preliminary learning they've gleaned so far. Just keep the time for talking brief, and think to yourself, 'What's the worst thing that can happen?'

FIG. 2–1

"I'm just going to play a minute or two of this very famous speech. It's 1775, and the colonists in Virginia are trying to decide whether to go to war to break free from Great Britain. Listen to Patrick Henry's speech, and see if you can figure out which text structure he uses to organize his powerful thoughts." I played a video clip of the last minute of Patrick Henry's "Give me liberty or give me death" speech, from the 1936 short film, *Give Me Liberty*.

After the video, students noticed Henry's recurring theme of "We must fight" and the reasons he supplied for going to war, and that he used a clear boxes-and-bullet structure. Some students pointed out that he also used a problem-solution structure, talking about the problems some people have with the idea of war, and his response to that problem.

❖ **Name the teaching point.**

"Today I want to remind you that when you look over a nonfiction text thinking, 'How is this structured?' it helps to have a handful of optional text structures in mind. Often history texts are structured either chronologically, in a cause and effect structure, or in a problem-solution structure."

TEACHING

Begin by giving students a rationale for considering text structures. Remind them of structures they should already be familiar with, referring back to the earlier nonfiction reading unit.

"Readers, sometimes when I read nonfiction, there are so many facts coming at me, at such a fast clip, that I feel overwhelmed. I think, 'I can't memorize everything' and 'I'll *never* learn everything that this text is teaching me.' I sometimes give up trying to grasp the content of the text. But then I remind myself of something that I want to remind you of as well—and this is it. It can *really* help to think, 'Underneath all the fast-flying facts, how is this structured?' Because if I can find that text structure, I can figure out what to pay attention to and what to ignore for now.

"Do you remember earlier this year when we watched that video about the oryx at the Phoenix Zoo? When I started watching the video, I was frantic to write down all the facts: that oryx is white. He's fat . . . But then I realized: hold it! This is a film about an animal that is endangered, and the zoo is helping to solve that problem—this is a problem-solution text. This helped me take organized notes on just the important parts of the text."

Set students up to join you in watching a different clip of a speech persuading the colonists to go to war, doing so through the lens of text structure. Reference the chart from prior units.

"Today let's watch another video, this time one in which the historical figure Samuel Adams gives a speech to make the colonists realize how badly the British were treating them.

"Let's watch together and think: how is this structured? What key words from the 'Common Nonfiction Text Structures' chart am I hearing that might help me decide what structure this is in?" I played about a minute of the video.

This speech is worthy of discussion, but it is important you become accustomed to keeping your minilessons brief. The topic of today is not the speech—it is simply meant as an appetizer to set up your teaching point and to immerse students in the drum roll leading to the war. If you have devoted social studies time as well as reading time to this study, you may be able to view and discuss the Patrick Henry's speech more deeply during social studies, and then today, to simply return to that speech, thinking this time about its structure.

If you want to cut corners and save time in this minilesson, students could simply talk about the text structures in Patrick Henry's speech, bypassing the second video. Another option to save time is to simply rely on the transcript.

FIG. 2–2 You may want to display a chart with nonfiction text structures and key words as students watch the video clip.

Invite students to think along with you as demonstrate identifying the structure of the text by noticing transition words.

After stopping the video, I put a transcript of Adams's speech on the document camera:

> *Gentlemen of Boston, the hour has arrived.*
>
> *Please, please. Gentlemen, you know me as Sam Adams. Neighbor and friend. Hear me now. Parliament continues to treat us with ill will.*
>
> *First, the Sugar Act raised our taxes. Did we have a say? The answer is, 'Nay.' Then, the horrid Stamp Act nearly drove us to ruin. And who can forget our brothers who lost their lives in the Boston massacre. And now, Governor Hutchinson insists on collecting Parliament's Tea Tax, but did we have a vote?*
>
> *NO!*

"Well, let's think. Which text structure seems to apply here? Hmm. Do you notice the word *first* early on?" I highlighted it. "That would signal that this could be chronological. Let's see, are there other clues that this is set up in order of time?"

I paused to allow the students to read forward with me. As we did this, they called out—and I highlighted *then*, and *and now* on the transcript.

"Wow. Now that we're reading for text structure, the structure of this is pretty evident! Knowing this is organized chronologically (or you could call it *sequentially*) helps us understand, because the structure draws our attention to the most important parts." I added to our anchor chart.

The entire clip of Adam's speech has been transcribed. It is tiny, so you know you can bypass the video if the mechanics of showing videos in minilessons puts too much stress on your system.

The text is structured in much clearer ways than most, and you may decide to substitute a more challenging text. Our goal, for now, was to remind students to search for a text structure and to use it to help them organize their learning and their notes.

ANCHOR CHART

Launching a Research Project

- Gather sources on the topic to preview.
- Generate a list of subtopics that frequently appear.
- Choose an accessible book to read for an overview.
- **Identify the text structure to help determine what's important.**

ACTIVE ENGAGEMENT

Prompt students to try the same work of identifying the structure of a new text.

"Let's take a look at another text, about a different subtopic related to the events that led up to the American Revolution. This one is about the colonists and their reasons for coming to America in the first place. Again, will you read with the lens of text structure? Listen for words that clue you in as to whether this is also chronological, and if not—how *is* it structured?" I put an excerpt from *Liberty!* on the document camera:

> *Why had they left home?*
>
> *Some left in search of religious freedom. The king and most Englishmen belonged to the Church of England. People who tried to worship differently were thrown in prison or even hanged.*
>
> *Others left because they were poor and hungry. They hoped to find jobs and food in America.*
>
> *And some hoped to grow rich. In England, a poor farmer couldn't become a respected landowner. If your parents were poor, you too would probably be poor all your life. But in America, if you worked hard, you might become one of the richest people in the land.*
>
> *It wasn't easy. But it was possible. America was the land of liberty.*

Pointing to the "Common Nonfiction Text Structures" chart, I asked, "Which keywords are you noticing, and what text structure do they point to? Talk to your partner and decide. Of course, there may be more than one text structure at work here!"

I moved quickly from partnership to partnership, listening in. Aliyah and Rose were saying, "Well, I see the word *because* in the middle there. And the whole thing is explaining *why* the colonists had left. So maybe it's cause and effect, but not of the war, just of them coming? Like, all the reasons they left are the causes."

Debrief, noting that there are several possible names for how the text is structured.

I brought the students back together and shared out the conversation I had just witnessed. "I heard you say you could think of this as structured in a cause and effect, even though really we could call it 'effect and cause' since the effect is mentioned first. Some of you saw it as problem and solution (all the problems that caused them to leave, and the solution of leaving) and that works too. There is often more than one possible way to name the text structure."

Notice that this minilesson now has three different texts—the two videos and this print text. In the interest of time, you may decide to forego this example. If you use it, keep a brisk tempo.

As you coach into what your students are doing, remember that you are teaching synthesis. Keep the learning progression for this skill in mind, remembering that you want your fourth-graders to organize information into big points, categories, or ideas, and to fit what they read under those headings. As they read, you want them weigh the importance of each new bit, and to fit the significant details into their emerging outline, setting that new information alongside what they have already learned. Your kids have had lots of practice doing this over the years, and your coaching today can remind them of that.

LINK

Send readers off, with the charge to think about how nonfiction texts are structured and to flag places where the structure changes.

"Readers, like yesterday, will you and your partner read a text that you have in duplicates so you can read in sync with each other? When you start a second text—I know you could be finishing yesterday's—remember to preview it together.

"When the organization of a text seems clear, flag natural stopping spots. In car races, they use flags to let the drivers know to slow down and get ready for a change ahead—because the track is wet or because there's something on the track. In your reading, you'll be placing these flags—Post-its, really—where you notice that the structure of the approaching section seems to be changing. When you read, the flag can remind you to get your mind ready to read the upcoming part as a new structure. The flag can also signal for you to take a second and talk or think to digest what you just read.

"Remember, whenever you're reading informational texts, taking a second to figure out how the text is organized can help you figure out how to organize and prioritize the information coming at you. I'll be looking for your flags as I come around. Off you go!"

You'll want to keep an eye on the frequency of these flags. Your goal should be for readers to read for at least ten minutes without pausing, so if there are flags dotting a page, that is a big problem! Aim for there to be a flag every few pages.

Informational   4th

✓ Main Idea **(MI)**

✓ Details Support Main Idea **(D-MI)**

✓ Summary **(S)**

✓ Text Features **(TF)**

✓ Text Structures

  - Compare & Contrast **(CC)**
  - Cause & Effect **(CE)**
  - Sequence **(SS)**
  - Problem / Solution **(P/S)**
  - Anecdote **(A)**

FIG. 2–3 Bookmark for road mapping.

Supporting Students in the Important Work of Previewing

AT THE START OF TODAY, you will want to make sure that your students preview their texts and use the Post-it flags you've given them to mark the places where the structure of their text changes. You'll only have a small window of time at the start of reading time to support this important work of previewing.

One of the advantages of those flags is that by signaling students that these are good places to stop, think, and take notes, the flags make it less likely that students will inch through texts with pen in hand, copying down every passing fact. If students are flagging micro-structures, putting several flags onto a page, you'll need to coach them to only pause and retell at certain flags. As they grow more skilled, your students need to be able to read information texts at a faster clip and to digest larger swatches of text.

In general, if the text addresses one idea, providing supports for that idea, and then shifts to another main idea, you hope readers will note the switch. Similarly, if a text shifts between an expository section and a micro-persuasive essay, you hope students see that switch, using a flag to alert themselves to alter their ways of approaching the new portion of the text. Keep the "Main Idea(s) and Supporting Details/Summary" and the "Cross Text(s) Synthesis" strands of the Informational Reading Learning Progression close at hand as your work with students, and refer to those progressions often so that students know what the goals are for this work.

For now, you are mostly focusing on helping them to see the structural shifts in texts and to pause periodically to glean the big points that a text makes and the important details that go with each big point.

Support students as they practice identifying text structures.

This work will be challenging for your students and for you. Remember that it is not critically important that the organizational structures that students find embedded in a text are the structures that you would identify. The important thing is that fourth graders know it can help to overview a text and to think, "What do I know about this text structure?" or "What do I know about this genre?" Especially when a reader knows little about a topic, the reader's prior knowledge of genre/text structure can help the reader know what is apt to be important. For example, if the final chapter in a book seems to be a persuasive essay, then the student can look for a claim and for the supportive reasons. He can wonder whether two sides of the argument will be laid out. Similarly, if a reader sees that part of a text is a story of a person, that reader might think, "What is this person known for especially?" and then read, aware that the details that matter will be those that relate to whatever has made that person famous.

Your goal is for students to move beyond looking at trivial facts to notice main ideas, and to go beyond reading with blinders on, thinking only about a specific line,

---

MID-WORKSHOP TEACHING **Studying Text Structures**

"Readers, I noticed that some of you have been flagging parts as you read. This is great! Take a minute to share what you have flagged with your partner. Show each other one flag that you used today, and see if you agree about the way the text is structured.

The room erupted in conversation. During a minute of listening to one partnership after another, I coached in briefly: "Be sure to show your partner the words that helped you see the text structure" "You are right that sometimes there are a few possible ways to name the structure of a text—it could be called main idea and supports, and also pros and cons, for example."

After just a minute, I channeled the class back to reading, reminding them that in a little while, they'd have a chance to teach what they've learned to the other partnership in their research team.

to think about which particulars seem especially important and to think about how the particulars fit together into the whole text.

Provide guided reading support for students who are reading below benchmark level.

Some of your students will have a lot of difficulty doing this work, especially those who read in a sentence-by-sentence way. Make sure these students are continuing to read a great volume of texts on their level. They can't afford to slip backward because you don't have access to texts about the American Revolution that are at levels they can read. If you *do* have accessible texts on other wars, you might set those youngsters up to watch a video about the American Revolution and then to read books on other wars and compare ways the American Revolution was like and unlike those wars. If you have accessible biographies on people from those times, set them up to read those biographies.

If you can support a guided reading group for these students, that would help them. Supply them with copies of a text. In a text introduction, help them preview the text, noting the main subtopics. Help them identify the kind of text they'll be reading and understand how the knowledge of text can set them up to read appropriately. Usually the texts students will be reading about the American Revolution will be studded with concept vocabulary terms. Support them with a few of those words, but also leave some for them to wrestle with on their own as they read, so there will be challenges for them to encounter. The challenging vocabulary may be phrases, not just words; in fourth grade, most high-stakes assessments emphasize the importance of students understanding unfamiliar phrases. Think of "Don't fire until you see *the whites of their eyes*" as an example.

As students read silently while sitting together, move from one member of the group to the next, asking each to read just a bit of text aloud to you. Listen for whether the reader is reading with enough accuracy and fluency that the pace and intonation resembles talk. If the text seems too hard, now is not the time or place to teach the reader all he or she needs to know. Instead, say, "Let me read a bit to you," and quickly read for the student, making a note in your mind that after this guided reading group, you'll channel that reader toward easier texts.

As students read within a guided reading structure, you will want to have in mind some goals other than the goal of helping them handle a slightly hard text. For example, you may have decided that the readers in one guided reading group need help reading the maps, charts, and diagrams and thinking about how they fit with (or don't fit with) the passages themselves. If that is part of your hope, mention this at the start of reading. As you watch readers, coach into their work so as to support this.

You'll probably want to return to a guided reading group across a sequence of days. If one day you helped the students preview a text by identifying words that cued them into guessing the way that part of the text will be structured, the next day you'll simply want to coach them to do this work on their own. You might say, "Let your eyes sweep across the lines of the text, and when you come to a transition word, such as *because*, *but*, *if*, or *so*, it should be like a radar wave going 'bing!' when it detects a signal. You brain goes "bing! Aha! This might signal the presence of a particular text structure." After you detect a transition word, ask yourself, "Does this say anything about the text's structure? If so, what?" You can then watch and coach into this work, but the work will be more independent than it was on the first day of the guided reading group.

Seeing Relationships between New Material and Previous Research

Prompt students to make connections between new and old understandings. Ask them to show these connections as a way to assess their understandings of subtopics and their ability to sort information.

"Readers, for today, let's come back together. Bring the books that you were reading today with you." I waited while the fourth-graders quickly made their way back to the meeting area.

"I'm pretty sure that you are ready to pause and to ask yourself, 'What have I learned?' Because you are reading a second text on the topic of the causes of the American Revolution, you can also ask, 'How does what I've learned from this second source fit with what I already know?' I added more subtopics to our chart.

After children had a moment to recollect what they'd learned, sorting it by subtopic, I channeled them to convene with their research teams and to share and cumulate information.

Subtopics on the American
Revolution

• End of the French and Indian War
• Problems between Britian and
   the Colonists
• Sons of Liberty
• Paul Revere
• Speeches: Patrick Henry, Sam Adams
• Boston Tea Party
• Intolerable Acts
• First Continental Congress

FIG. 2–4

ANALYZING TEXT STRUCTURE

Readers, tonight, you'll want to get a lot of reading done—forty minutes or more. Read from the materials in your resource bin. Use Post-its to note when you sense that the text shifts from one organizational structure to another. For tonight and for the next few days, will you also jot on your flag a code that signals what you notice about the text structure?

If a line or paragraph captures the main idea, add a Post-it there and write MI (for "main idea") on your Post-it. You don't need to flag all the supporting details, because there will be a lot of them. But do try to flag the strongest supporting detail. It could be strong because of the language the author uses. (Perhaps the author says, 'Most importantly . . .' or 'Above all . . .') Or it could be strong because of the emphasis that detail is given in the text.

These are ways you could label flags that indicate the text structure is changing:

CC for compare and contrast

CE for cause and effect

S for sequential (or chronological)

PS for problem-solution

You may find that some of what you read seems to be opinion writing. You may see that the author makes a claim and gives reasons to support the claim. If you find opinion writing, you can flag it like this:

Cl for claim

R1, R2, R3 for reasons

Readers, you can use your bookmarks to help you. Be ready to share your Post-its with your partner in our next session. This is not something you do for life, but a few days of this can improve your reading.

◆ A DAY FOR ASSESSMENT ◆

Dear Teachers,

Think about times in your life when someone has seen you do work that you care about and given you crystal-clear feedback on the next steps you can take. It is a great gift to receive that sort of feedback.

Today can provide that gift to your children. Don't hesitate to look your kids in the eyes and talk about what the great coaches in life do. Great coaches believe so much in the learner and in the work that they ask a lot of the learner. They are willing to say, "That's good—but you can do better." Help your students aim for the stars!

Today set aside time to engage students as active agents of their own reading development. By studying the rubrics and learning progressions next to your assessments of their work, students can see what is expected of them, clarifying next steps so they can work with expediency to move forward. They can approach a new chapter and think, "Wait, what work should I be doing as I read today?" Then, they can work with resolve to achieve those goals.

Performance assessments cannot only guide instruction, they can energize it as well. The greatest contribution these tools make is that they help both you and your students self-assess, collaborate with other learners, learn from feedback, and work collectively toward challenging, clear goals. And in the end, if there is a secret to success, it is this process of continuous improvement.

As you prepare for today's work, remember that the Online Resources will be a resource to you. You'll find a more detailed description of how today's important work might go, as well as relevant rubrics, learning progressions, and exemplars.

To feedback! Thanks, Lucy, Janet, and Grace

Session 3

Special Challenges of Researching History

THIS UNIT aims to teach not just nonfiction reading, but also the special challenges inherent in the reading of history texts. This is one of several sessions to highlight these special challenges. Today, you'll communicate to your students that when studying history, it is important to pay special attention to time, place, and people (and specifically, the relationships and networks linking people together). You'll help students learn that by keeping an eye on an emerging timeline, map, and relationship chart, they can synthesize what they are learning and thinking about the information.

When trying to understand the Stamp Act, the Intolerable Acts, the Boston Massacre, and other milestones leading up to the American Revolution, for example, it is helpful for students to be able to synthesize all of this onto a single timeline and to think about the events that came before and that followed each other. How much time lapsed between these events? By creating a timeline of events, students are able to see the way all the disparate events fit into a cohesive whole and to ask questions about the cause-and-effect relationships.

Similarly, thinking about the relationships between events and geography will always play a big part in any understanding of history. How did the sheer distance between Great Britain and the colonies influence the events? How did the distance between Boston, Philadelphia, and Virginia influence the events? The good news is that as students think about these things, they are experiencing what it means to develop their own theories, based on information. The texts will produce lots of undigested information related to networks of people, place, and time, and this session enables you to give students a way to distill the information. When you encourage students to keep track of people, place, and time, and to use a relationship chart, map, and timeline as tools for thinking about the texts they are reading, the really important message you are sending is that reading is thinking. The reader's job is not just to record the facts. It is to think: to surmise, to speculate, to theorize, to investigate.

IN THIS SESSION, you'll teach students that researchers pay particular attention to people, geography, and chronology when they read history. By paying attention to *who, where,* and *when,* researchers begin to organize their new knowledge.

GETTING READY

✔ If you are using *Bringing History to Life* in your writing workshop, begin teaching Session 1 from that unit today, and teach one reading and one writing session a day. The two sessions won't always dovetail, but will support each other.

✔ Ask students to bring their homework from the previous session to share with one another (see Connection).

✔ Display the chart titled "Lenses to Carry When Reading History" (see Teaching and Active Engagement).

✔ Gather three small whiteboards and dry-erase markers for groups to organize the information they have learned (see Teaching and Active Engagement).

✔ Chart paper and markers to create enlarged set of tools: relationship chart, timeline, and map (see Teaching and Active Engagement)

✔ Select a passage to read aloud from *Liberty! How the Revolutionary War Began,* pages 3–4 (see Teaching and Active Engagement).

✔ Display the "Subtopics on the American Revolution before 1775" chart (see Link).

✔ Prepare to show the "No More King!" video (www.schooltube, search terms: kings schoolhouse) (see Conferring and Small-Group Work).

✔ Print out small versions of the "Subtopics on the American Revolution before 1775" chart for each student (see Homework).

Special Challenges of Researching History

CONNECTION

Let students know that reading researchers have earmarked fourth grade as a time when students especially read-to-learn.

"Readers, yesterday you assessed your work to set goals, and I expect you will work on those goals throughout this unit. You'll have the chance to work on many of your goals today; in particular, those on the 'Inferring Within Text/Cohesion' and 'Analyzing Parts of a Text in Relation to the Whole' strands of the learning progression.

Readers, I'm sure you know that there are adult scientists who research the solar system, the layers of rock under our feet, and the creatures that live in rotting logs. But are you aware that there are also research scientists who go into fourth grades, clipboards in hand, and study the particular work that fourth-grade readers do?" I let the children think about that for a minute, adding, "It's true. And some of those research scientists say that fourth grade is a turning point year in a person's whole life as a reader. They say that *before* fourth grade, kids are mostly learning-to-read, and that starting in fourth grade, the job changes, and now a big part of getting better as a reader is reading-to-learn."

Recruit the students' commitment to flagging observations about text structure and ask them to report to each other on how this work went for them when they did it at home.

"You are reading-to-learn in this unit, and as part of that, you are getting better at looking over a text and thinking, 'What's the job this part of the text is trying to do—and what do I need to do as a reader of this part?' I'm hoping that flagging the text structures like you did last night helped you to be more conscious of the way the text is written. Did you see that the structure of the text assigns you to do certain work? Like, if a part of the book is an essay, you as a reader know, 'I better read for the most important claim the author is making and the reasons supporting that claim.' Will you talk with each other about what it was like to flag the text structures as you read last night?" I asked, "Show each other what you did."

I pulled in to listen as Cynthia said, "When I was reading last night, I flagged the part in the beginning of the Magic Tree House book on the Revolution that told all about the causes of the war. It told why the colonists were upset."

Michael responded, "I called that chronological and stuck on a flag whenever a new problem happened. Things got worse and worse."

The "Inferring Within Text/Cohesion" strand of the Informational Reading Learning Progression, at the fourth-grade level, asks that students can use text structures to identify important information and to relate important pieces of information to one another (idea/example, problems/solution, and cause/effect). On high-stakes assessments, students are often asked to talk about how one part of the text contributes to the rest of the text. The strand "Analyzing Parts of a Text in Relation to the Whole" helps with this task. Students need to know that a paragraph may be there to explain the cause of something that occurred earlier, or to compare one thing to another, or to raise a question and answer it.

I said to the group, "I'm hearing that the assignment to flag places where the text structure seemed to change got you thinking things like, 'That's the second reason he gives to support that claim,'" or 'I'm noticing that he says the main idea in a couple of places,' or 'This is really a whole chapter that just lists one cause after another after another.'"

Provide a transition toward the new work of the day.

"You are doing work. Last night, when I lay in bed thinking about the work you have been doing, I thought, 'Maybe I should get a research scientist to come study my fourth-graders.' But then I realized that I don't want those reading researchers to come and observe your reading-to-learn until you know one more big tip about reading-to-learn. You ready for it?"

❖ **Name the teaching point.**

"Today I want to teach you that people read differently based on the discipline in which they are reading. Readers of science texts read differently than readers of history texts, because different sorts of things are important in science than in history. Researchers of history pay attention to *who*, *where*, and *when*."

TEACHING AND ACTIVE ENGAGEMENT

Stress the value of reading a text again to gain a deeper understanding of the text. Explain that readers of history reread to pay attention to the 3 Ws: *who*, *where*, and *when*.

"Have you ever watched a movie a second time and noticed something that you didn't see the first time? Maybe the first time you were just following the story to find out what happened, but when you watched the movie again, you already knew the storyline, so you paid extra attention to other things. You saw someone buckling their seat belt, and you thought, 'That's important. It's going to come back later,' or you thought 'So that's when the bad guy first appears. Now I am seeing he's sort of scary from the start.' Well, just as movie watchers see more in a movie the second time they watch it, as a reader of history, you'd be wise to reread—and eventually, to read—paying attention to a few elements of the story that are particularly important to historians. And those elements can be summed up in the 3 Ws," I said, as I revealed our new chart.

Some may argue that thinking about geography doesn't pay off as much as thinking about people and the timeline, but there is no question that the relationship between geography and events is important—geography shapes historical events. Always remember your real goal is to teach students skills they can use again and again on countless topics.

Lenses to Carry When Reading History
- Who: key people/relationships
- •
- •
- •
- Where: geography
- •
- •
- •
- When: the timeline
- •
- •
- •

FIG. 3–1   A student's timeline.

"After you have read a history text, grasping the main things that happen, you will want to reread, thinking about who? Where? When?"

Set kids up to help each other develop basic graphic organizers on white boards, drawing from what they already have learned.

"To think of these things, it helps to hold tools near you as you read. I'm going to ask you to quickly, develop some of these tools," I said, as I distributed a small whiteboard and dry erase markers to each group as I identified them. Pointing to the "Who" bullet on the chart, I said, "Those of you sitting on the right side of the meeting area, will you make a tool for thinking about 'Who?' You might draw a relationship chart—a kind of diagram—listing names of important people or groups and drawing lines of connections between them. Think about all the people you've read about in your research so far. Your relationship chart will probably include specific names, as well as groups of people, like colonists, loyalists, or British soldiers. Make sure your diagrams show their relationships. You can do this by drawing arrows or, like with a family tree, by showing how the branches connect."

Pointing to the "Where" bullet, I said, "Will those sitting on this far side make a quick and simple map of the places and the geography connected to our topic? It might help you to think about the major events you've been learning about and where they happened. For example, the Boston Tea Party was in the took place along the shore of Boston Harbor."

Pointing to the "When" bullet, I said, "Will those of you sitting in the center of the meeting area think about *when*? Make a super-quick, informal timeline connected to the American Revolution—look up dates quickly if you need to do so."

I addressed the whole class, "You have only three minutes to make your tools. Help each other and get going—fast!"

As children worked, I recruited three youngsters to work on enlarged versions of each of these on chart paper at the front of the room. Soon clusters of kids were all sitting in the vicinity of a simple relationship chart, timeline, or map.

Read aloud from the shared text, asking kids to attend to (and record) details relevant to their graphic organizer.

"What I am going to do now is to read aloud from where we left off the other day in our book, *Liberty! How the Revolutionary War Began*. As I read, if you learn any new information that relates to your tool, record it."

> It wasn't easy. But it was possible. America was the land of liberty.
>
> **By the mid-1700's,** a huge elm tree **in Boston** had become the symbol of the new land. It was called the Liberty Tree. **The townspeople** gathered under its branches for important meetings.
>
> **Other towns and villages along the Atlantic coast** named trees in honor of the Liberty Tree of Boston. If they didn't have a big enough tree, they put up a tall pole and called it the Liberty Pole.

"I'm going to skip ahead—skipping the part that you probably know about the English settlers, the Pilgrims, making peace with the Indians . . . and about other colonists treating them rudely."

Lenses to Carry When Reading History

Who: people, relationships

- Who are the players?
- What are their relationships?
- Who holds power? Who doesn't?

Where: geography

- How does the geography affect big events?
- How does the geography affect people's lives?

When: timeline

- What is the sequence of big events?
- Are there cause and effect links?

We've bolded parts of the read-aloud you might want to particularly emphasize to support children in adding information to their tools.

*They had a powerful ally—**England**. They called England the "mother Country." The **American colonists were England's children**. Now that her children were in danger, the Mother Country sent soldiers to help the **settler's own troops** defend the colonies against their enemies.*

*This fight, called the French and Indian War, **began in 1754** and continued for almost **ten years** . . . . In **1763**, a peace treaty—the Treaty of Paris—was signed. . . .*

*The **colonial soldiers** hung up their muskets over their fireplaces and went back to their **farms**. They hoped they will never fight again.*

Channel students to write-to-think about the information they just gathered, asking and answering analytic questions about the people, the geography, and the timeline.

"Researchers, it's important not just to record information related to people (and relationships among them), place, and time, because as readers of history, you are always thinking about these elements and how they influence each other. Will you for a few minutes, use writing to think about the information you just collected?

"Those of you thinking about the groups of people: what are you noticing in what we just read, and in all that you know? What sides did people take, and how did this change? When you think about relationships among the people you've read about, what ideas does that give you? Who had power over whom? Who was loyal to whom?

"Those of you thinking about places: your question is 'How does the geography influence what happened?' You have the facts—your job is to think about them, to grow ideas. How did the great distance between Great Britain and the colonies affect their relationship? How did Boston's location on the coast affect the role it played before and during the revolution? How did geography affect the way colonists communicated with Britain—and with each other? Grow ideas by thinking, 'Hmm . . . could it be that. . . ?'

"Those of you thinking about dates, synthesize what you just learned with everything you already know. Think about causes and effects—about what led up to big events, and what resulted from those big events. Think about turning points—those big events that changed things forever afterward. When you really study your timeline, it can give you a lot of ideas about the events back then."

I revealed new content on the "Lenses to Carry When Reading History" chart, updated with the big questions that readers of history ask in relation to the people, place, and time (the *who*, *where*, and *when*).

I stopped reading aloud, and asked children to talk within their groups about their notes. The room filled with conversation. I didn't try to harvest what they'd learned, leaving that to them.

The decision to give students time to construct their own tools, rather than handing out premade graphic organizers for students to fill in, is a deliberate one. You are equipping students to create their own tools and mental models in the future when they encounter complex, historical texts. Although this will take a bit more time and the results will look messier, we strongly encourage you to do the same.

LINK

Remind readers that fourth grade is a time for reading to learn, and that research on discipline-based reading has shown that reading history has its own special challenges.

"Researchers, earlier I pointed out that adults who study young readers think fourth grade is a special year for becoming people who learn from reading, and those adults think that there are special challenges to reading history. Let's think about all that reading history texts involves. Just reading these texts, smoothly and in ways that support comprehension, is no easy thing! Now you are aware that you also have to be attentive to all of the 3 Ws, thinking about how what you are reading fits together on a relationship map, map, or timeline. That is not a small order!

Channel students to begin creating their own versions of the class-created tools. Let them know they will add to these tools as they continue researching.

"It will help you if you are holding the three tools I've recommended today—you have one already made in your groups, but you'll each want your own set of the three tools. So will you at least get started making any tool you don't yet have made? You can copy from the graphic organizers we have up here on chart paper," I said. "I also have bare-bones versions of some graphic organizers that other students made another year if you want to work off those for inspiration."

FIG. 3–2   A student's relationship chart.

Once students had had a minute or two to get started equipping themselves with a more complete set of tools, I said, "I know you aren't finished making yourself a set of tools, but as you read today, will you jot notes onto whatever you have, and will you continue, over the next day or so, to develop a set of tools for yourself?

"Before you and your partner continue reading about the subtopics you've chosen to focus on, will the two of you skim back over what you read yesterday, seeing if perhaps you weren't as attentive as you could have been to the *who*, *where*, and *when*? Then you can get started.

"Take another look at our subtopics chart, and think back over all that you have learned about the American Revolution. Is there more about the *who*, *where*, and *when* that you need to pay attention to?

"Remember that at the end of today's workshop, you and your partner will teach the rest of your research team about the subtopics you have been studying up on. You needn't read the same texts today, if you and your partner want to divide and conquer."

Subtopics on the American Revolution Before 1775

- End of the French and Indian War
- Problems between Britain and the Colonists
- Sons of Liberty
- Paul Revere
- Speeches: Patrick Henry, Sam Adams
- Boston Massacre
- Boston Tea Party
- Intolerable Acts
- First Continental Congress
- Colonial Boycott of British Goods

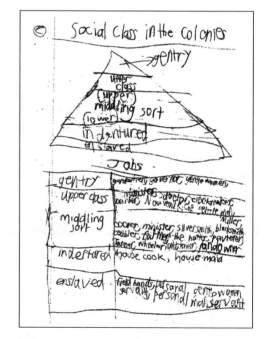

FIG. 3–3

Supporting Students to Use New Tools to Do New Sorts of Thinking

FOR MOST OF TODAY, you will be conferring into individuals' reading and their note taking. It will help if you have in mind a few key things you anticipate you will probably teach during your conferring. For example, you will certainly want to remind students of the instruction you gave prior to today, in which you asked them to read, using flags to mark places where they notice that the structure of the approaching section seems to be changing. Remind them to use those markers to get their minds ready to read in that structure.

You will also want ensure that students' reading today reflects the minilesson and that students are using tools such as relationship chart, timelines, and maps as lenses for thinking about texts. For some students, it might help to first use those tools while watching a video, then later use them with written texts. You might therefore want to convene a small group and set them up to watch the Schoolhouse rock video "No More King!" The video supports notetaking about people and places (though less about dates) and is a good summary of the Patriots' reasons to rebel against the British. After watching that video with a map in hand, Cynthia commented, "I noticed that they started out on the ocean, but they landed at Plymouth Rock. They built a town that started out small and grew bigger and bigger." She looked at her notes, then continued, "Then they grew from just Massachusetts to all thirteen colonies." I whispered in to her partner, Emmanuel, who then asked, "Were there any other important places?" Cynthia replied, "Oh, yeah, they sort of went back and forth between the colonies and England. They kind of showed that the two places were right across the ocean from each other." I reminded them to make sure both partners shared, and moved on to another group.

Jose had watched the same video through the lens of people, and he said, "Well, I was looking through the lens of people this time, and I noticed that they made King George look *really* mean. He was counting his money and ordering people around, all while he was sitting on his throne."

Whether you help students to use these latest tools with video or with texts, the important thing will be that you support them as they talk and perhaps write to grow ideas from what they note about people, places, and times. Encourage them to use phrases such as "This must have meant . . ." or "This gives me the idea that . . ." or "This makes me wonder whether. . . ."

(Continues)

MID-WORKSHOP TEACHING Constructing a Shared Timeline

"Readers, I know many of you have been thinking about the timeline of events leading up to the American Revolution, but you haven't necessarily gotten much of that down on paper. Will you work with your research team to build a timeline on paper? I'm distributing some blank index cards, chart paper, and tape to each team. Working with your team, put one event on each card—write the year, then the event. Once you have done this, your research team can lay the cards out on the chart paper and tape them down to build a timeline for the events leading up to the American Revolution. When you're done, take a look at your own personal copy of the timeline, and make sure you have all the events from your team timeline on your copy, too."

After children worked for a few minutes, I said, "You need to get back to reading, so finish up, at least for now. Once you have constructed your team's timeline, find a place to hang it. And keep reading, noticing if you learn about more events that needs to be placed on the timeline.

"As you are working on your timelines, you may have some lightbulb moments where you say, 'Oh! So this tax didn't happen until five years after the . . ." Or, "Wow! This event happened at the same place as. . . .'"

It will also help if you channel kids to think, "How does this connect with other things I know?" and "What are the surprising parts about this?" Either way, those questions nudge students to think about how the information they have just read fits with or contradicts their existing knowledge from previous readings. The helpful thing about this is that by nudging students to think about the relationship between new and old information, you are helping them to build links, to organize information—in short, to learn.

There are two important things to keep in mind as you support this work. The first is that the tools you have been giving students today and recently are meant to provide them with lenses that they can bring to their nonfiction reading. The work of thinking about text structures or about time, people, and geography will be important work for many of your students, but you will have some students who have not yet learned to ascertain the main idea of a passage and to see the supporting details. Those students might be better served if you encourage them to jot headings and subheadings alongside passages they read, or star sentences that seem to pop out the main idea of a text.

Then too, your hope for all your students is that the tools you have given them become concrete representations of a lens that you hope they bring to their reading. But their focus still needs to be through the lens to the main content. Above all, you want students to read a great volume of text, pausing only after long intervals of reading to take stock of what they have learned. It is a good thing if they can note, as a date flies by them, where this is relative to other events, but if recording a date becomes a major endeavor and everything else screeches to a halt while the student does this in a belabored fashion, that surely would not be a good thing. Balance is critical, and you don't want reading time to become nothing more than a time for colored pencils, flags, and codes. Then, too, keep in mind that the tools you have given students recently are all meant to be temporary scaffolds that students use for a time and then outgrow the need to use.

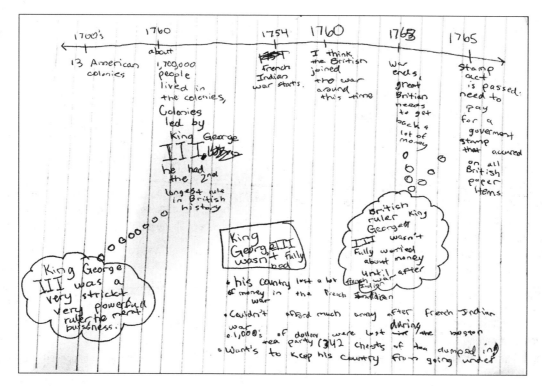

FIG. 3–4   Another student's timeline.

Keeping Students' Energy High

Channel students to share what they have learned about their subtopics.

"In the session prior to this, I set you and your partner up to read, in preparation for teaching the rest of your team what you learned about your subtopic. Right now, within your research teams, will one partnership teach the other partnership some of what you have learned? It may help you to use some of the tools you've been working on—your relationship chart, timeline, or map. Take a few minutes to teach the other partnership what you've learned, then switch places, so the other partnership can do the teaching. You ready? Now, teach!"

Explain that when working in groups, one person's zeal (or apathy) will be contagious, affecting others. Channel students to discuss ways that group members can keep energy high.

After a few minutes, I reconvened the students. "Readers, before we get much farther into this unit, will you think a bit about how your research team is working? The truth is that when you work in a group with others, the others in the group influence you—and you also influence them. Research has shown that if you don't invest yourself, if you decide to be a curmudgeon, you'll turn your whole group into curmudgeons.

"I'm serious about that. I think your teacher from third grade told you about a National Public Radio show in which a man named Will Felps gave a talk called, 'The Bad Apple.' Am I right? How many of you recall hearing about that research?"

Some, but not all, students indicated they remembered hearing this research, so I plunged on. "To study how groups of people operate, Felps had an undercover actor join different small groups. In some of the groups the man acted like he was so exhausted he could barely do anything. They made videos of the exhausted man interacting with the groups he joined, and in every group, before long, every group member's head would be sagging, and they were all stumbling through their work.

"Then the man went undercover as a different bad apple. He became the sort of person who complains about everything, who whines and moans—can you picture the scene? They put him into all these different small groups where people were working really energetically together . . . And you guessed it! Right there on the video, you'd see the other people in his group become as negative as that man had been! The point of all this research was this: Bad apples are contagious—they spoil the bunch.

"So right now, before you go any further, will you and your colleagues talk a little bit about ways you can make sure none of you act as the bad apple in your group? Talk about ways you can keep energy for this work as high as possible."

Invite children to make a plan how their group and the individuals in it will keep energy and investment high.

I listened while children talked in their groups, then spoke to the whole group. "You are saying some smart ideas. When I point my imaginary baton at you, will you share your suggestions?"

As I pointed my pretend baton at one students and another, they shared suggestions ranging from, "We thought we could say things to each other like, 'That's really cool!' so that we pump each other up," to "We thought people could do extra, like websites on the topic," to "We gotta not slouch and talk into our collars so no one can hear."

I sent them off with, "Remember, throughout this unit, and whenever you're working in a small group, your group members are counting on you. Your actions, your attitude, affects those around you."

SESSION 3 HOMEWORK

 CHECKING FOR GAPS IN YOUR KNOWLEDGE

Readers, earlier you laid out some important subtopics on the American Revolution. I'm enclosing that list ("Subtopics on the American Revolution before 1775"). Will you check your knowledge base by asking yourself how much you know about each of the subtopics? Find the gaps in your knowledge and see if you can read to fill in those gaps. Remember as you read, to keep an eye out for dates that you can add to your timeline. Notice the people, too, and the networks of people. Add to the tools you made in class today.

Finally, you should be doing some additional reading (outside the unit). This may be working with a biography, with a historical fiction book, or with added fiction books. Please log this and all your reading.

> **Subtopics on the American Revolution**
>
> • End of the French and Indian War
> • Problems between Britian and the Colonists
> • Sons of Liberty
> • Paul Revere
> • Speeches: Patrick Henry, Sam Adams
> • Boston Tea Party
> • Intolerable Acts
> • First Continental Congress

FIG. 3–5

Session 4

Prioritizing
Notetaking on What's Really Important

T HIS IS A CRITICALLY IMPORTANT SESSION on note-taking and prioritizing big points and supportive details. It continues the work you have been doing
to support students' skills in synthesis, summarization, and determining the main
idea—all skills that are outlined on the Informational Reading Learning Progression.

You'll want to approach the session fully aware that note-taking can either hurt or help
a student's reading. When you lift the level of note-taking, you lift the level of students'
reading. However, there are three ineffective approaches to note-taking. Some students
don't take notes at all. Others inch through a text, recording every passing fact in notes with
no organizational structure, so the readers doesn't pause, reflect, and prioritize to make
something of the information. That kind of note-taking consumes too much reading time,
and doesn't support the higher-level comprehension work that is essential to proficient
reading. Finally, some readers record notes that aren't information based, but are instead
a gush of emotion, loose ideas, generalizations. That sort of writing also chases away time
for reading and doesn't support comprehension or text-based thinking.

Today, you'll emphasize that effective note-takers pause after a big chunk of reading.
Students who are at grade-level proficiency should probably be able to engage in quiet
reading for fifteen minutes by now before pausing to digest. If your students develop a
routine of reading for a large chunk of time and then pausing to review what they have
read to determine significance, to organize, and to think about the incoming information,
this routine will give them very important practice in many of the most important reading
skills. Each time they take notes, the act of doing so will nudge them to work on determining main idea, synthesizing information, and selecting the supportive details that are most
important. This makes it a very big deal that you teach kids to take notes in effective ways.

This will not be easy work for your students to do well. The texts tend to be complex
and dense with information. There will often be a lot going on in these texts—many contain headings and subheadings, text boxes and illustrations, and passages that compare,
contrast, list, and describe. It will be all too easy for your students to get distracted by
flashy but less significant details, to overlook important points, and to not stop to synthesize

IN THIS SESSION, you'll remind students that when researchers
take notes, they read a chunk of the text straight through and pause to talk it
over in their mind before they record important parts.

GETTING READY

✔ Have chart paper and markers to make a list on "Note-Taking from Nonfiction
Books" (see Connection) 👆

✔ Choose a mentor text that contains information on class subtopics. Enlarge
it for students to see. We have chosen the section "Sneaky Taxes" from
Liberty! How the Revolution Began by Lucille Recht Penner, page 6 (see Active
Engagement).

✔ "Taking Notes to Record Important Information and Explain it" one-day chart
(see Active Engagement) 👆

✔ Update the "Launching a Research Project" anchor chart (see Active
Engagement). 👆

✔ Display the "A Detail Is Important Enough to Record When . . ." chart (see
Mid-Workshop Teaching). 👆

✔ Print out copies of the "Note-Taking to Support Nonfiction Reading" checklist
for each student (see Homework). 👆

new learning with what the reader previously understood. You will want to coach your students to check their thinking continually and become accustomed to deciding, "Is this bit of information necessary to understanding this topic, or the part of the topic I'm studying, or is it okay to let this go?" That is, your teaching today will especially emphasize the importance of prioritizing information. You'll encourage students to ask, "Is this important?" and to use that question as the first step in becoming a discerning note-taker, recording important information in such a way that the reader can recall it later on.

"The physical act of notetaking is actually a way to practice the mental habit of note-taking."

Note that the Mid-Workshop Teaching and especially the Share ask students to continue to work on deciding what is important in a text and why. This is arguably one of the most important skills in nonfiction reading and on standard-aligned tests.

Although your session today nudges kids to become more active note-takers, it is important for you to remember that the physical act of note-taking is actually a way to practice the mental habit of taking note. That is, the question, "Is this important?" when used habitually, prompts readers to be analytic whenever they are reading (or listening, or watching!), whether or not they will be taking notes—and this in turn supports a deeper understanding of the text and connection to the topic.

Prioritizing
Note-Taking on What's Really Important

CONNECTION

Remind your students of the work they did yesterday connecting new information to the subtopics. Let them know they will soon be writing to tell all they know across all the subtopics.

"Readers, yesterday you assessed your work and set goals. I expect you will work on those goals throughout this unit. You will have a chance to work on many of your goals today, in particular, those related to cross text(s) synthesis, or main idea(s)/details/summary. Researchers, let's start by remembering some of the subtopics leading up to the American Revolution that seem important.

"Yesterday, you combined your knowledge on these subtopics. But right now, can you think about what you personally could say about any one of these sections if you were asked to write or give a report on it?"

I gave students a moment to think and then said, "Think about what you would write if I asked you to flash-draft an overview chapter called 'All about the American Revolution.' What would you write if I asked you to write a section about this?" as I pointed to an arbitrarily selected subtopic off the list. "How about a section about this?" and I pointed to a second subtopic off the list.

Share excitement over the upcoming challenge of teaching others.

"Do you feel your heart racing just a bit at the idea of writing about these subtopics? If so, that's good. That's how learning goes. At first, you just luxuriate in the topic, soaking up all the new information. But as the time approaches when you have to teach others about what you are learning, all of a sudden your heart begins to pound, you think, 'Do I know enough to teach it to someone else?' and you sit up and look alert.

"I'm telling you this, because some of you need to think about whether you have been reading your texts in a 'Waiting for the Dentist' way, which might not be sufficient for you to teach others what you are learning. At the end of this bend, you'll need to teach people from throughout the class about one subtopic from the list—so choose one which you will focus on for the rest of this bend (and then later in the unit, you can choose another.) To be prepared to teach others about that subtopic, you need to read today in a 'Make this material my own' sort of a way.

Note that last night for homework, you asked students to do something similar to what you are doing here. You may want to alter this so instead of doing this work in class, students merely tell each other about what they did and discovered the night before.

The reference to children writing a text, "All about the American Revolution" refers to one of the early sessions in Bringing History to Life, *a unit of study on writing research reports from* Units of Study in Opinion, Information, and Narrative Writing. *You may not be teaching that writing unit (or any writing unit) parallel to this one, and that is okay. The two units needn't be taught in sync with each other. You can tweak the few places in this book where the writing unit is directly referenced.*

But meanwhile, whether or not you are leaning on that resource, you probably want the kids to understand that they should be learning about their topic in a way that would make it possible for them to write an all-about text on what they have been learning.

Channel partners to identify a subtopic they'll study together.

"At the end of this bend, you'll need to teach people from throughout the class about one subtopic from the list. So, right now, will you and your partner read through our list of subtopics and choose one which you will focus on for the rest of this bend (and then later in the unit, you can choose another)? It will likely help to choose a subtopic you know something about, one you have some resources on so you can learn more."

Ask kids to articulate what they already know about note-taking.

"Let's assess. Thumbs up if it will be easy for you, two days from now, to teach us all about one of these subtopics?" Several kids did so, but many seemed insecure in their new knowledge.

Nodding, I said, "Here is my conclusion. You may need to amp up the way you are reading and taking notes. Let's think for now about your note-taking. What do you know about how to do this well?"

Kids called out observations, and I recorded some of them:

Note-taking from Nonfiction Books
- Readers stop at the ends of chunks to take notes.
- Readers usually structure their notes so their notes match the text.
- Notes are brief, containing the essentials.

❖ **Name the teaching point.**

"Today I want to remind you that researchers take notes about the big points. They also recall the details and think, 'Does this detail go with one of the main points? Is this important?' As you read, think, 'How does what I'm learning fit with what I already learned? Is this a new big point? Does it fit under an existing point?'"

TEACHING

Demonstrate by reading a chunk of text, pausing to consider what's important, then thinking aloud to explain the information. Recruit the kids to do this work alongside you.

"Writing is one of the most powerful tools a person has for coming to new understandings. Let's try to use writing as a way to learn from our read-aloud.

"The goal will be to use writing as a way to think about whatever seems important. Let's read on in our book, and as we do, let's pause at the ends of chunks to ask, 'What's important here and why?' 'What is this making us think?' Because we want to be quick within our minilessons, we'll just read tiny chunks of text before stopping." I began to read aloud the next chapter in *Liberty*.

In the previous fourth-grade nonfiction reading unit, Reading the Weather, Reading the World, *we explain that "Waiting for the Dentist" reading is a kind of bored, nonchalant reading, idly flipping through magazine pages without taking anything in. We contrasted "Waiting for the Dentist" reading with "Reading-to-Become-Smarter" reading, a deeper kind of reading with engagement and commitment.*

Often in your minilessons, you will revisit a bit of text that the students already know, looking at that text through a particular lens. This, on the other hand, is a time when it's appropriate to introduce new text within the minilesson, as the work you are demonstrating is all about taking in new information and processing it through writing. The passage shown here combs through the next session as well, so it is important to use it.

Sneaky Taxes

The bloody French and Indian War was finally over.

But what if the Indians attacked again? What if Spain tried to invade?

The British were still afraid of losing their colonies. So they decided to keep an army in America. Ten thousand British soldiers—called "redcoats" because of their red jackets—were sent across the ocean.

Ten thousand men ate a lot food! And they wore out hundreds of pairs of shoes and suits of clothing. Who would pay for their keep?

The British said the colonists should pay. The British Parliament, which made laws for Britain and its colonies, passed the Quartering Act. It said that the colonists had to provide quarters—places to live—for all the redcoats stationed in America.

Then the British thought of another way to raise money from the colonies. They would enforce the Navigation Acts, which had been passed in the 1600s but never implemented. The Navigation Acts said that the colonists had to buy almost everything they needed from Britain—even when a product could be bought more cheaply from some other country.

"Hmm. What seems important here? What are you thinking?" I left a bit of silence so students had time to think alongside me. "One thing I bet we are all thinking is that the fact that the British wanted to keep an army here seems really important. And also, that the army cost the British a lot of money—money that they ended up getting from the colonists."

Set students up to write alongside you as you demonstrate how to record and explain important information.

"I'm going to do a little writing in my notebook to remember this and explain it in my own words. I'll write what I've learned and what's important about it. Will you write as well? Sometimes it helps to use these sentence starters." I pointed to a small piece of chart paper.

As the children settled into writing, I put a clean piece of paper on the document camera, paused with my pen in the air for a moment, then started to write:

> I learned that *the British didn't want the colonies to be separate, so they decided to keep an army there.* An important detail to support that is *that 10,000 redcoats were sent across the seas.* This seems important because *the decision to put redcoats here meant the army needed places to stay and clothes and food which cost money. It explain why the British taxed the colonists. The*

Taking Notes to Record Important Information and Explain it:

I learned that _____.

An important detail to support that is _____.

This seems important because _____.

This makes me think _____.

---

colonists had to decide not just if they were loyal to England but if they wanted to pay for that support. <u>This makes me think that</u> maybe the whole war got started out of this fear that the British had of the colonists being separate. If they had just relaxed maybe they could have actually kept the colonies.

Debrief in a way that highlights that writing about information can be a way to come to new thoughts about that information.

"Wow, I just came to a new thought as I was writing this! Did you guys come to new thoughts too? I don't think I would have thought it in that way if I hadn't pushed myself to write about it. That's the power of writing."

ACTIVE ENGAGEMENT

Read on a little more and let the kids know this time they'll be writing on their own. Recruit one child to take notes in a way that others can see.

"Let's read on," I said. "I'm going to again read a chunk of text and only then, pause. This time I want to watch your writing, so will one of you take notes up here?" I passed the marker pen to Curtis and said, "You ready to listen?" I then read on:

> *And not only that, they also had to sell almost everything they produced to Britain—even if they could get better prices elsewhere. It didn't seem fair!*
>
> *So people paid smugglers to bring in illegal foreign goods and to sell the colonies' own goods to other countries. They did business with their butcher, their baker—and their smuggler!*
>
> *When the British saw what was going on, they sent warships to patrol the American coast. Smugglers who were caught were fined and imprisoned. This made the colonists angry.*

"I know we're pausing *way* more often than you will, but let's ask those questions: What's most important here and why? What is it making you think? You can again use the template if it helps," I said, and pointed to our chart, "Taking Notes to Record Important Information and Explain It."

As the children took notes in their notebooks, Curtis did so under the document camera:

> <u>I learned that</u> the colonists started to boycott the butchers and the bakers and to buy from the smugglers—going around the British so they wouldn't have to pay taxes. <u>This seems important because</u> the colonists were getting brave. <u>This makes me think that</u> the colonists were mad, so the British will be even more afraid. This may be how the war started.

I pointed out, "Notes like these will help you a lot as you continue to research. They will be reminders of important information, and also give you the chance to write to explain what's important." I added to our anchor chart.

You could take the time to point out that you have decided the number of soldiers—10,000—is an important detail because it had consequences, while the fact that the soldiers wore redcoats is not important—it had no consequence nor does it support the general point. It is helpful for students to rank details, to determine which detail is more important and why.

The amount of text you read before pausing is briefer than is ideal. You certainly don't want this minilesson to channel your students to stop at every tenth line to record notes!

Launching a Research Project

- Gather sources on the topic to preview.
- Generate a list of subtopics that frequently appear.
- Choose an accessible book to read for an overview.
- Identify the text structure to help determine what's important.
- **Pause at the ends of chunks to recall the text in a structured way.**
- **Record only the important things.**

Pause at the ends of chunks & recall the text in a structured way.

Record only the important things.

LINK

Send kids off to read and to take notes, reminding them of all they should be keeping in mind.

"Readers, today you'll continue to research and learn more information about the subtopic you're researching related to the American Revolution. You can decide if you want to read a shared text with your partner or if the two of you are reading different texts about the subtopic you both are investigating. Either way, you are learning not just for yourself but also for the class you'll be teaching later.

"Do remember to use all you know about nonfiction reading. For example, preview the texts before you read them and flag the places, at ends of chunks of texts, where you plan to stop and jot. Make those chunks be large ones so you are pausing after ten or fifteen minutes—and before that, no note-taking. And be sure not only to write down what is important, but also *explain* what's important in your own words. That's a lot to do—get started!"

Coach your students to make informed choices. Do partnerships read the same text? If so, why? If not, why would they choose to read different text?

Reading and Writing as Tools for Learning

TODAY'S FOCUS IS IMPORTANT enough that you may decide to devote your conferring and small-group time to the topic of today's minilesson. You'll benefit from a few minutes to take stock, categorizing the note-taking work that students are doing, and then working with small groups.

You may want to create more social supports for note taking. You could ask partners to talk about what they have learned rather than to generate notes. This would help them to understand that the point of notes is to serve as memory aids and to help learners reconstruct what they have learned.

MID-WORKSHOP TEACHING   Prioritize When Taking Notes

"Fourth-graders, let me stop you for a minute. I want to tell you a way to make your notes as useful as possible. Make sure that you write down *important* information, not just any fact or detail that you happen to read. Sometimes facts that are cool can distract you. You want to be laser focused on only the details and ideas that matter to the big points you think the author is making.

"Will you use the 'A Detail Is Important Enough to Record When . . .' checklist to review the notes you've taken so far, crossing out some if you think actually you shouldn't have taken them? Share ideas with your partner.

"Readers, I know you may not be done reviewing your notes and your partner's, but it is time to get back to reading. As you read, use this checklist to make sure your notes are going to help you remember important information or readers you can use your progression."

Now that you have had a chance to think about the details that are important, this is a good time for you to think about the goals you have set and to use the "Main Idea(s) and Supporting Details/Summary" strand from the Informational Reading Learning Progression to help you look at your own details. See where you are in the progression and decide on your next steps.

> **A Detail is Important Enough to Record When...**
>
> It connects to something bigger – to a main idea, an issue, a key subtopic. [ISSUE IDEA SUBTOPIC] ← [★ ▬▬]
>
> It sparks thinking – and the jotting adds to my thinking. (☁) ← [★ ▬▬]
>
> It is important to the topic and I haven't recorded it before. [TOPIC] ← [★ ▬▬] ≋NEW≋

There will be other students who are skilled at note-taking that recapitulates the text. You might encourage these students to take notes of their thinking, questions, and ideas about what they read. Provide such students with prompts that they can ask themselves as they think about what they just read. The prompts might include "What are the surprising parts? How does what you learned fit with what you already knew? What does the new information make you think?"

Students will often feel insecure about writing what they think! They'll say, "I'm not sure," or "I don't know." Help them to use phrases such as "This might be important because . . . ," "Could it be that . . . ," "Probably they . . . ," and "It must have been that . . ." to capture their tentative, growing ideas.

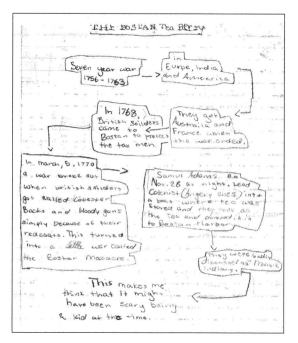

FIG. 4–1   Later today, your students' writing might look like this.

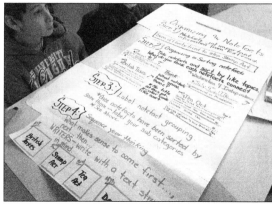

FIG. 4–2   Another way students took notes

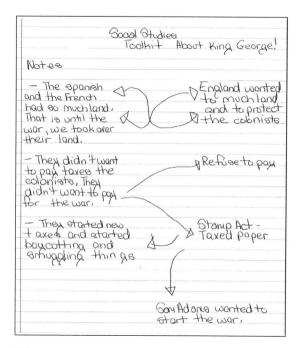

FIG. 4–3

Ranking and Sharing Main Ideas and Supporting Information

Channel researchers to rank the main ideas taught in a text, determining the most important idea. Encourage students to state the main idea in different ways.

"Researchers, will you gather in the meeting area? I need your full attention," I said. "Today I want to point out that it is important that you master not only the skill of taking notes, but also the skill of using your notes to do important work. You'll want to become skilled at reviewing your notes as a way to reflect on questions such as, 'Which themes are especially important in this text?' 'Which details especially support those big ideas?'

"The text you have been reading probably puts forth a few big ideas. Perhaps the first part of the text makes one main idea, then the next part of the text makes another main idea. You need to be able to look over the whole text, almost as if you are in an airplane, flying over it so as to see all those parts and think about how they go together.

"When you can see all the parts of a text, as when you lay your notes out and look over them, you should be able to determine the most important big idea in the text. It's often hard to see that idea when you are reading the text, but when you review your notes, you have a way to lay all the parts out in front of you. Then you can ask that all-important question, 'Of all the many ideas put forward in this text, which ranks as the *most* important idea?'

"Readers, right now will you review your notes on one topic, or from one text, and try to do that thinking? Do that work alone."

As students worked, I moved among them, helping them to step back from their notes on the whole text enough to be able to tell the story of how that whole text goes. Then I helped them think, "What is the main point the text is making?" Sometimes students wanted to find that main point in their notes, and often I encouraged them to do it without their notes, to write it from the knowledge they'd gained from their research so far.

"Students, two more challenges. Once you can say the main point of a text, try to do this: Say that main point in a word. Come up with about ten possible words that might hold the main point, and then narrow in on the one that works best. Try also to say that main point in a few sentences. You should be flexible enough you can say it in a long way or an abbreviated way."

FIG. 4–4   Main Idea and Supporting Details work

NOTE-TAKING TO SUPPORT NONFICTION READING

Readers, read for about forty-five minutes tonight, but save time for not only notetaking, but also for reviewing your notes. The "Note-taking to Support Nonfiction Reading" checklist might help you make sure your notes help you read your nonfiction.

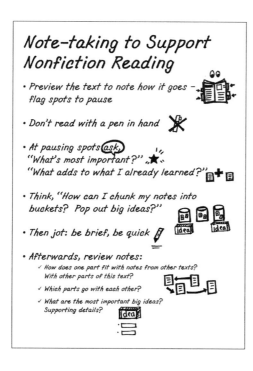

Synthesizing across Texts

IN THIS SESSION, you'll remind students that researchers synthesize information about a key subtopic by reading an overview text, then reading across several sources about that one subtopic, and thinking about how the new information fits with what they've already read.

GETTING READY

✔ Prepare to display your notes on the class read-aloud from Session 4 (see Teaching).

✔ Choose two other texts containing a similar subsection on taxes. Enlarge them for students to see. We have chosen "Tax the Colonists" from *King George: What Was His Problem?* p. 3, and *The Split History of the American Revolution*, p. 4 (see Teaching and Active Engagement).

✔ Prepare three versions of class notes about a subtopic to show how you synthesize information from different sources. We begin with our notes from Session 4 on "Sneaky Taxes," then we add notes from "Tax The Colonists" for our second version, and end with a version combining those two with notes from *Split History* (see Teaching and Active Engagement).

✔ Update the "Launching a Research Project" anchor chart (see Link).

✔ Make small copies of the "Phrases that Help Synthesize Related Information" chart for each student (see Share).

TODAY'S SESSION continues to support students, this time from multiple sources. By now, your students will be ready to shift from researching the American Revolution in general to studying a subtopic that is particularly interesting to them. One student may be especially interested in Paul Revere, another in the First Continental Congress, a third in the Boston Massacre. Whatever the subtopic that captures a student's interest, that researcher will need to synthesize information from a variety of sources.

You'll again want to rely on the learning progression to support your students' development of this important skill. As you teach, you'll want to have in mind the skill of cross text(s) synthesis and you will be apt to look like at the second-, third-, fourth-, and fifth-grade levels, bearing in mind that students will come into our classrooms at a wide range of places along the spectrum, and your job is to move them from wherever they are, as far as you can move them. A knowledge of pathways in skill development is important not only for you, as a teacher of reading, but also for your students so that they can progress toward clear goals.

Our learning progression suggests that third graders should be able to explain how a new piece of information adds to what the reader has already learned. Third graders should be able to read from two texts or parts of two texts, and put that information together to help them find information on any subtopic. Fourth graders should then be able to merge relevant information from multiple sources to discover and collect new information and organize this in a way that is new and invigorating.

The instruction you give today is not new—you taught a similar lesson during the earlier fourth-grade nonfiction unit, *Reading the Weather, Reading the World*, and several simpler versions of this lesson in third grade. It is likely that kids struggled with this work in third grade, and hopefully by now, it is becoming easier for them. The minilesson in this session is simpler than the mid-workshop and the share—be sure to get to them!

Synthesizing across Texts

CONNECTION

Help kids understand synthesis by comparing the work of integrating text information to something that they connect to and enjoy.

"Let's talk about making cupcakes. If I want to give you guys cupcakes to eat, I first need to make them. We know what cupcakes look like, so I could just start making something that looks like that—right?

"Wrong! Because to make a cupcake, I have to put ingredients together that aren't cupcake-ish at all! The directions start like this":

> *Combine flour, sugar, baking powder, and salt in a large mixing bowl. Add shortening, milk, and vanilla. Beat for 1 minute on medium speed. Scrape side of bowl with a spatula. Add eggs to the mixture.*

"The recipe continues, but you get my point. Or do you? Because this minilesson really is not about cupcakes at all. It is about reading. And what I want to tell you is that by now, you are probably finding that certain aspects of the American Revolution are especially interesting to you. To learn about any one of those subtopics (and especially to be able to teach others about that subtopic), you need to combine information from many sources and from your own mind. To learn from reading, and especially to write something for others based on your reading, you need to synthesize information from many sources, just like you pull together all of those different ingredients to make cupcakes.

"You know that already. Earlier this year, you gleaned information from lots of topics to learn about droughts, tornadoes, and earthquakes. And anyhow, you know how to make cupcakes, and making knowledge is not all that different. The individual ingredients aren't much. A teaspoon of baking powder. A cup of flour. They need to be combined together to make the cupcake. In the same way, your information and your sources need to be combined together to make learning.

"You can't just read one article or book after another as if each is separate from the others. You need the information from one source to get smushed in with the information from another source. That flour needs to get stirred in with the eggs and the butter!"

It is important to vary your methods of instruction so that you recruit kids' interest. This connection aims to do that. Notice that your example—making cupcakes—is a totally accessible one. You don't want to compare nonfiction reading to something that is equally complex or the comparison won't have a lot of teaching power.

You see we will go to all lengths to try for engagement! Many people who speak to adults start with an anecdote that illustrates the teaching point.

Name the teaching point.

"Today I want to remind you that learning is all about making connections. When you read more than one text on a topic, it is important to pause in the midst of reading the second text (or the third) and think, 'How does this connect to what I already learned? Does this add on to what I learned earlier? Change what I learned earlier?'"

TEACHING

Demonstrate how you locate a new text that elaborates on what you read before. Read the new passage aloud, asking students to think, "How does this connect to what I already read?'

"So researchers, yesterday we read the 'Sneaky Taxes' section from *Liberty!*, and took some notes." I displayed my notes.

> <u>I learned that</u> the British didn't want the colonies to be separate, so they decided to keep an army there. <u>An important detail to support that is</u> that 10,000 redcoats were sent across the seas. <u>This seems important because</u> the decision to put redcoats here meant the army needed places to stay and clothes and food which cost money. It explains why the British taxed the colonists. The colonists had to decide not just if they were loyal to England but if they wanted to pay for that support. <u>This makes me think that</u> maybe the whole war got started out of this fear that the British had of the colonists being separate. If they had just relaxed maybe they could have actually kept the colonies.

If we want a complete understanding of this topic—The Taxes—we'll have to look at other sources, other books. I held up another book, *King George: What Was His Problem?* and said, "First we need to find a subsection that talks about the same topic. Doing that can be tricky, because there probably won't be a section titled the same way. We need to look for a subsection in this book that's about the causes of the Revolution, and in particular, about the taxes."

Musing over the table of contents, I read a few chapter titles aloud. "'First Shots Fired'?" I glanced up at the kids, and many of them shook their heads, no. I tried again, "'Showdown at Saratoga'? 'Losing and retreating'?" No. No. But then I came upon a section called "Tax the Colonists." The kids agreed this was a possibility, and soon I was preparing to read that section aloud. I said, "Remember, keep in mind what we already learned from 'Sneaky Taxes,' and think, 'Does this add to what we know? Change it?' Listen up and get ready to think about that. As soon as you hear a bit of

Notice that this teaching point says, "I want to remind you . . ." This is not a new teaching point.

If you feel that your students may not remember the important parts from the reading from the previous session, you may decide you need to quickly reread the passage from the preceding day or at least the class notes on the passage.

information that elaborates on something we read in the first text or changes it, give me a thumbs up." I projected the section from *King George* as I read it aloud:

Tax the Colonists

Here's the bad news: war is really expensive. The British were left with a mountain of debt. And now they had to keep 10,000 soldiers in North America to protect all their new land. That's not cheap. The British prime minister George Grenville started thinking of ways to raise some quick cash. You can guess the idea he came up with can't you?

That's right: he decided to tax the British colonists. Grenville really felt that the thirteen colonies owed Britain the money. As he put it: "The nation had run itself into an immense debt to give them protection; and now they are called upon to contribute to a small share toward the public expense." Grenville's plan was called the Stamp Act. When colonists signed any legal document, or brought paper goods like newspapers, books, or even playing cards, they would have to buy stamps too (the stamp showed that you paid the tax). A few members of the parliament warned that the Stamp Act might spark protests in the colonies. But young King George III (he was twenty-two) liked the idea. He didn't expect any problems [from the colonists].

Insert the new information into your notes to help students visualize the process of synthesis. Read aloud the synthesized information to confirm that the new notes fit with the original notes.

I called on Jose, who pointed out, "It says that a guy named Greenville felt that the colonists owed England the money so he taxed them. It then said that Parliament knew it would spark protests, but the king liked the idea of taxing the colonists."

"Yes! That's new information. Now we can insert this new bit of information into yesterday's notes from *Liberty*." I did so. "Will you listen while I read the revised notes, and give me a thumbs-up if you agree that these two parts, synthesized in this way, go together."

Class Notes from "Sneaky Taxes" and "Tax Those Colonists" combined

I learned that the British didn't want the colonies to be separate, so they decided to keep an army there. An important detail to support that is that 10,000 redcoats were sent across the seas. This seems important because the decision to put redcoats here meant the army needed places to stay and clothes and food which cost money. It explains why the British taxed the Colonists. The colonists had to decide not just if they were loyal to England but if they wanted to pay for that support. <u>This makes me think that</u> maybe the whole war got started out of this fear that the British had of the colonists being separate. If they had just relaxed maybe they could have actually kept the colonies.

In this demonstration, the "synthesizing" merely involves adding in new information to extend earlier notes. If you feel your students are ready for more sophisticated work, you might decide to alter this demonstration to show children that new information can sometimes change or challenge earlier notes.

The British PM Greenville came up with the idea to tax the colonists. Parliament and King George agreed with him although there were lots of people in Parliament who knew this would spark protests.

Debrief in ways that accentuate the replicable work you have done.

"Readers, did you see what I just did? I looked through another source to find more information on my topic. To do this, we had to skim to locate a similar subsection from another text. Then I pondered, 'Does this new thing I'm reading about taxes add to or change my earlier notes?' And I added all the new information to my notes, making them better.

ACTIVE ENGAGEMENT

Set children up to continue this synthesizing work in their research teams.

"Okay, it's your turn to try this synthesizing work. I'm going to read you another relevant section from yet a third text, *The Split History of the American Revolution* by Michael Burgan. Listen for more information you can synthesize into causes of the American Revolution, in particular the taxes." I projected the section from the book *The Split History of the American Revolution* as I read it aloud.

> But the relationship between the colonies and Great Britain grew tense after 1763. That year the British won the French and Indian War, in which Great Britain battled France for control of North America. Britain's victory gave it control of Canada and the eastern half of what became the United States. The war had been costly, and British officials demanded that colonists help pay for the future defense of the colonies.
>
> In 1764 Parliament passed the American Revenue Act, known as the Sugar Act, which taxed goods including sugar, wine, coffee, and some types of cloth. The Sugar Act was the first law to raise new money in the colonies. Many merchants believed the new taxes would hurt their businesses.

"Talk with your partner—what can you add or change and where could you add or change it? Please take what we wrote from *Liberty!* and *King George: What Was His Problem?* and then add to it using *The Split History of the American Revolution*." As students worked, I circulated, calling out coaching tips.

"Think about whether the information actually elaborates on the first text. If it just repeats the same information in different words, skip it." Soon partners had constructed a new synthesized text.

LINK

Review the steps you've asked students to take as they synthesize notes from several sources.

"Readers, let's quickly review the steps. First, you read an overview to get a basic understanding of your subtopic. Then, you found related subsections from another book, pausing after you read a chunk to think about whether the information you just learned about adds onto or changes information you'd gleaned from the overview text. As you read, you slotted the new information alongside your earlier notes on the topic. Let's add that to our anchor chart."

"Before your research team disperses to read, will you think about what subtopics you'll each research today? I recommend that two of you focus on one subtopic—such as the Sons of Liberty, the Boston Tea Party, or Paul Revere—and two focus on another subtopic. That way you can later teach each other what you have learned.

"Yesterday, you and your partner decided on a subtopic you were interested in exploring together. Likely you chose a different subtopic than the other members of your research team. That way, you can later teach each other what you have learned.

"When you have decided the subtopic you will research today, remember to read an overview text first, and after that, remember to read subsections from several different books that relate to that subtopic. Take notes that allow you to synthesize information."

If you are using the writing unit Bringing History to Life, *students will have been asked to choose a subtopic such as those you listed. In Bend II of the writing unit, students are asked to research either this subtopic or another one. If you are teaching both reading and writing units in sync, you'll probably postpone Bend II of the writing unit until after Bend II of reading, and at that point, you'll channel students to a new subtopic. The important thing is that starting today, channel your struggling students to work with a partner on a subtopic for which you have easier books and more videos.*

Support Readers Who Struggle to Extract Information from Nonfiction Texts

TODAY, you will probably find yourself taking on two main jobs during conferring. The first is to support students in synthesizing across multiple texts. The second is to remind them, as always, to draw from all the skills, strategies, and behaviors that they have in their repertoire as they read and research today.

Since independent time will start with the meeting of research teams, you will likely want to start out by coaching into these meetings. You might advise team members to flip through books to find the sections related to their chosen subtopic, perhaps tagging those with color-coded Post-its. You have suggested that each team research two subtopics, with two students researching one and the other two students researching another. There will be a lot of books being passed around, so encourage the groups to work together on this and to share the books with each other.

Next, you might look across the room, looking at the kinds of notes students are taking. You might continue to see some students taking notes that are nothing more than a long line of facts. They are probably also reading with pen in hand, jotting down any random factoid as it passes by them. These will also be readers who progress at a snail's pace. You will want to learn why they have continued to resist the instruction you've given them. Certainly, the "Main Idea(s) and Supporting Details/Summary" strand of the Learning Progression will help with this.

Some readers may be chunking texts and writing notes after reading a chunk of text, as you've instructed, yet their notes may suggest they aren't thinking about what the main ideas are, and the most important supporting details. Teach those kids to think in boxes and bullets, main ideas and supports, and to be more discerning in what they choose to record. They might Post-it what they believe could be the main point of a part of the text, and then continue reading and rereading, looking back to weigh whether that is, in fact, the most important point. Help them to consider where the point was supported across most of the text. Remind them that sometimes the author will not come straight out and say the main point, leaving it up to readers to do that.

MID-WORKSHOP TEACHING
Supporting Elaboration with Internalized Conversations

"Researchers, eyes up here for just a second. In a little while, you are going to get together with other members of your research team to teach each other the topic that you have been studying. When you teach your classmates about your topic—say, the reasons the colonists were angry at the British—will you leave time for others in your research team to add onto or to reflect about your information. So after you teach, leave time for the listeners to look over their notes, to think about questions and ideas they have, and to engage in conversation.

"Once the talk off the first person's comment begins, I hope that if you have found something that adds to the conversation, you'll try to use a transition such as, 'An example of that is . . .' and then give the example. 'I agree because . . .' or 'To add on . . .'

"Here's the thing. You should each be able to have this kind of conversation *with yourself* about whatever you are reading . . . and do so right now. So stop reading right now, and think about the topic you are studying. In your mind, say a sentence about what you have been studying—just restate something you have learned. Do that now."

I waited, giving everyone time to have a thought. "Now say, 'For example . . .' or 'To add on . . .' and then say more. Keep going, using other transitional phrases as well to hold your own in-the-mind-conversation about your topic."

I left more silence for kids to do that. "Let me stop you. That's the sort of work you'll be doing with each other later, so for now, get back to your reading."

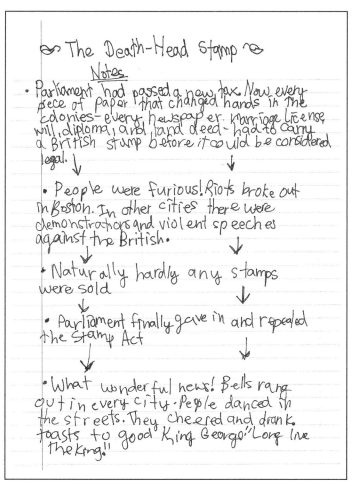

FIG. 5–1   A student's notes reflect information synthesized from two texts.

Finally, for those kids who have taken notes in a structured fashion—boxes and bullets, two-column entries, or diagrams and maps with annotations—you may offer some help synthesizing notes from a second text into the notes from the first text. The concrete logistics of this will be important. Make sure the notes are on one side of a page so that a researcher can literally scissor them apart. You can also help researchers to make notes off their notes—to draw arrows between bits that connect, to star important things, and to write marginal thoughts. That is critically important work.

Meanwhile, when children struggle to take reasonable notes, your job will be to determine whether the issue is a note-taking issue, a determining importance issue, a synthesizing issue or a reading issue. Chances are very good that the real issue is that the child is attempting to learn from a text that he or she cannot read with at least 96% accuracy, fluency, and comprehension. Such a child will need encouragement and support in locating an easier text—and perhaps, after reading that easier text on the topic, the child will have enough background knowledge to be able to return to the original text, this time reading it with more success.

As students read across texts to teach each other information, you might want to refer back to their goals. Use the progression to watch their growth in the strand "Cross Text(s) Synthesis." How are they connecting across the texts and to their prior knowledge? As you do that, remember to notice where they are in the progression and think about what's next. You could also look at the strand "Inferring Within Text/Cohesion" and think about the new relationships students are discovering between the text and the connections they are making. Use the progression to help students think about next steps.

Conversation Leads to Better Understanding of Text

Remind students of phrases they have used to synthesize information through conversation. Set up research teams to talk using these phrases.

"Researchers, remember earlier when we talked about making cupcakes? We talked about how you put together stuff that isn't cupcake-ish: baking powder, butter, flour, eggs . . . Then the trick is you need a mixer that combines those ingredients. Well—the greatest mixer in the world for ideas is conversation. So you're going to get a chance to have the sorts of conversations that help you to synthesize.

"You already know that there are phrases people use to combine information and ideas. You studied these in third grade, but they become all the more important as you get older. So get started talking about your subtopic, and I'm going to give each one of you a miniature copy of this chart. Actually read from it as you talk. Try to see how these transitional phrases get you combining one person's ingredient with another. Get started!"

After a few minutes, I called for students' attention. "Researchers, this is my question. Have you made a conversational 'cupcake'? Has something lovely and interesting emerged from your talk? Talk about what the conversation has been like."

Phrases that Help Synthesize Related Information:

What it does:	Transition to Use:
In order to _tell more_	The author also says... In addition to... Also... To add on, X says...
To _connect_ one text to another	This author says something similar. S/he says. . . So and So believes that. . .
Describing something	This looks like. . . Picture. . .
Explains/Clarifies	Let me show you what I mean. . . The way this happens is. . .
Gives an _example_	An example of this could be. . . For instance, one time. . .
Builds on something	Because this is true. . . This means that. . .

SYNTHESIZING AS YOU READ

Readers, tonight continue reading about a subtopic you studied today in school. Remember to use your relationship chart, timeline, and geographical map. They will help you understand the connections between people, events, and places. Keep these tools on hand to help you put together all that you are learning.

You will also want to continue synthesizing your notes. Remember to pause after reading a chunk of text. Think back over what you read. Find the most important idea, and think about whether that adds to the ideas in your notes. If it does, add that idea to your notes.

Remember that your job during this unit is twofold. You are learning about the American Revolution. You are also learning about reading nonfiction. Using tools such as relationship maps, timelines, and maps can help you get stronger as a nonfiction reader. Learning to synthesize information is another way to be a stronger reader. Tonight, push yourself to do some important intellectual work as you read.

Remember, too, that you and I have made a plan for the additional reading you will do. Follow your plan and log the amount of reading you do.

The Role of Emblematic Detail in Nonfiction

IN THIS SESSION, you'll teach students that researchers not only construct a big picture of their topic through reading and synthesizing, they also pay careful attention to the details that reveal tone and point of view.

GETTING READY

✔ Prepare two excerpts from a secondary source to read aloud, so that students can listen for the main ideas. We used "The Famous Ride of Paul Revere" and Henry Wadsworth Longfellow's poem "Paul Revere's Ride." Assign "The Famous Ride of Paul Revere" to a research team ahead of time, so that they can read for the main ideas The excerpt (from Anne Goudvis and Stephanie Harvey's not-to-be-missed resource, *The American Revolution and Constitution* [Heinemann: 2015]) and a link to "Paul Revere's Ride" are available in the online resources (see Teaching and Active Engagement). ✋

✔ Prepare boxes-and-bullets notes of "Paul Revere Warns" (see Teaching).

✔ Print out copies of the "Cross Text(s) Synthesis" strand of the Informational Reading Learning Progression for grades 3, 4, and 5 for each student (see Share and Homework). ✋

T EACHING IS A BALANCING ACT. You teach one thing, advocate for it, and then the kids overdo it, and you have to teach something quite different. In the Teachers College Reading and Writing Project community, we have talked about this as "running from one side of the boat to the other." This is one of those sessions that serves as a correction. Prior to now, in this unit and in the nonfiction unit that preceded it, there have been lots of sessions in which you taught kids to glean main ideas from texts. Repeatedly you have taught kids to look for clues that will help them to determine importance, letting some of the extraneous detail fall away. And surely that is important, because all too often kids approach a text, intent on copying down and memorizing every single little fact. They inch through the text, reading a few paragraphs in a day, and their minds are so full of trivia that nothing sticks.

But if your teaching is too focused on main idea, kids can let go of the detail entirely—and detail is as important to history as it is to fiction. Nonfiction reading requires dramatic storytelling, reflection, and exposition. When writers approach emblematic movements, they often get to what they think is the good part of the story, which is expressing their point of view in engaging and reflective ways. They create a tone using detail: imagery; action; and setting and conflict detail, giving emotional weight to the moment. Think, for example, of the details in any novel you know well, like *The Tiger Rising*. Think about Sistine rubbing her hand up and down Rob's rash-covered legs and then again, up and down her own legs, praying that Rob's rash would be contagious and she, too, could be excused from school and able to spend long hours with Rob's carved animals. Think about her tromps through the woods, her sermons from Willie Mae. Those detail are absolutely essential to the story of *The Tiger Rising*.

In the same way, detail is essential to any understanding of history. That is why Jean Fritz, one of the most famous writers of history books for children, says, "I dote on small details. In researching Ben Franklin, I read in one book after another that Franklin learned ten swimming tricks. What were they?" Fritz couldn't rest until she knew what all ten of those tricks were. Fritz' book, *George Washington's Breakfast* tells the story of a little boy who went on a similar quest: this time, to learn what George Washington ate for breakfast. The details matter.

This session, then, gives you a chance to teach kids that once they have synthesized texts, once they have determined the main contours of a topic, they can reread to fill in the details, to bring out the color of the times, places, and events. You invite kids to use what they know about reading with a lens to this time, reread key passages, looking for detail that they overlooked the first time they read these texts.

"Once students have synthesized texts, once they have determined the main contours of a topic, they can reread in order to fill in the details, to bring out the color of the times, places, and events."

If you are using *Bringing History to Life* for your writing workshop, you'll find that this session exactly supports Session 5 of that unit, and this reading session is probably best taught before that one. In that session, you remind students to research in ways that allow them to see and record details and then to bring some of those details into their own report writing. So peek ahead to the upcoming session, and if you can find ways to preview it here, do so.

The Role of Emblematic Detail in Nonfiction

CONNECTION

Reinforce students' abilities to synthesize by asking them to participate in a brief whole-class conversation in which they use transitional phrases to glue information and ideas together.

"Researchers, think of a time when you went to a show or a concert. If the performance was really good, afterward the audience probably applauded furiously, and then the performers came out for an encore. They played just a little more of the music, sang just one more song. I'm talking about this because the work you did during yesterday's share was really, really good—and I think there needs to be an encore. I'm going to start us off on a conversation about the events leading to the American Revolution. It will be about the colonists' relationship with Britain. Will you all look at your notes, look at the chart of 'Phrases that Help Synthesize Related Information,' and try to join into this conversation?"

I began, "I think that before the Revolution, many of the colonists felt happily connected to Britain."

George said, "An example of that could be that they called Britain the mother country."

Talin said, "To add on, they were glad that Britain helped with the French and Indian War."

I interjected: "But then the colonist's feelings began to change. Some had problems with Britain."

Patricia elaborated, "For instance, when Britain tried to get the colonists to pay for its army by taxing tea, they decided to no longer drink tea."

Atif added, "Picture this. One night, lots of people climbed onto a British ship and threw the tea into the harbor."

Closing the conversation out, I said, "You've gotten really good at drawing on, or synthesizing, a lot of sources to begin to construct a general understanding of our shared topic."

This connection relates to the previous session and not to today's session. It is here just to extend the work that was begun during that session. Usually connections act as an entrance ramp, bringing people toward the day's new work. Today's connection is an exception. It is more a review of the previous day's work.

If your students are ready for a more advanced spin on this, you could give them a few phrases that can lead them toward citing one of the texts they have been reading, and then ask them to actually quote from that text. The phrases that set up this work might be, "In . . ., so-and-so writes . . ., then the cited passage . . ."' or "So-and-so explains this in . . . She points out . . . , the cited passage . . ."

Name the teaching point.

"Today I want to teach you that once researchers construct a big picture of the topic by synthesizing the facts, they also record the drama of history. Often specific details will dramatize the point of view of real people in history."

TEACHING

Set readers up to read a passage several times: first, to extract main ideas, and then to note and draw forth revealing detail and get a sense for the tone and texture.

"Researchers do synthesize the basic facts of history—the big events of what happened in sequence. But what really brings history to life is specific detail. Right now, I'm going to show you some bulleted notes taken from a passage about Paul Revere." I displayed the following:

- Colonists storing arms in Concord
- British decided to capture the weapons.
- Paul Revere warned the Colonists.

"The thing is these barebones facts don't in any way capture the drama of that night. If this is all any of us knew of Paul Revere, he would long since have been forgotten. Let me read out the actual passage to you (the one from which these bulleted notes were taken). As I read, could you jot down any specific detail and any direct quotation that might seem important?"

I read the following passage aloud:

> The British were going to march, our spies told us. Soon, they would cross the Charles River. From there they could capture Samuel Adams and John Hancock, who were in Lexington planning the fight against the British. Then they could march on to capture our patriot weapons, stored in Concord. Adams and Hancock had to be warned. The townspeople had to be warned, too, so that they could defend our weapons. The Regulars—the British soldiers—were coming, and people needed to know!

> I had a plan already. First, I hurried to Christ Church, to give a warning to those waiting across the river. We had agreed on a code: one lantern would be lit in the church steeple window if the British were to leave Boston by land, two lanterns would be lit if they were to leave by the river. Light two lanterns, I told my friend who waited in the steeple.

Passage from Jane Sutcliffe, "Famous Ride of Paul Revere," Appleseeds, October 2001. © Carus Publishing Company. Reproduced with permission.

After reading, I again asked children to turn and talk. Then I convened the group. "So what detail would you want to capture in your notes? Let's start with Ryan."

Ryan went right to the most famous detail of all. "I'd put down that Paul Revere had a signal, that they were to light lanterns to say which way the British soldiers were coming and make it 'one if by land and two if by sea.'"

I nodded. "Those words have been remembered for hundreds of years—they help us feel the drama of that night, don't they? I noticed you didn't mention the name of the church, and somehow, that detail, too, has gone down in history. The lanterns were hung from *the belfry of the Christ Church*." I asked for other details that kids noticed.

Izzy thought it was important that Paul Revere was part of a small group of people who had been tracking the British movements. "I think that means he was one of the Sons of Liberty," she said.

I nodded. "Remember that earlier, I suggested that as a reader of history, you need to keep track not only of the people, but also of the relationships. You are right to think that Paul Revere seems to have been one of the Sons of Liberty. Good call." I added, "I also want to point out that the author of this passage has called Paul Revere's ride 'the most famous ride in history.' If I were in Ryan's group studying Paul Revere and someone said his ride was the most famous ride in history, I would definitely put that quotation in my report."

Debrief in ways that accentuate the replicable and transferable nature of what you and the kids have been doing.

"So researchers, my bigger point is that oftentimes when you read nonfiction, you read it first for the main ideas. But once you have established those ideas, it is also helpful to reread, paying attention to the details. After all, detail is what makes for power in any story—-so if you leave the detail out of your notes, out of your learning, you leave out the power."

ACTIVE ENGAGEMENT

Give students a more independent experience reading for the detail that brings a subject to life. Read a second text, asking them to signal when they hear a detail that they might record.

"Readers, I want you to try to add more detail to help you understand the tone and point of view of Paul Revere's ride. This time, I'm going to suggest you listen to a poem—and as I read, when you hear detail that you might want to capture if you were Ryan's group, give a thumbs-up." And I began to recite Longfellow's classic poem, "Paul Revere's Ride."

Written nearly a century after Revere's ride, Longfellow's poem was a call for courage as the United States stood on the brink of the Civil War. His vivid depiction of Revere's ride is moving and powerful—but it was not intended to be a completely accurate and objective work of history. Longfellow took liberties with his depictions of events—most notably, giving Revere sole credit for the ride, when in fact William Dawes and Samuel Prescott undertook the journey with him, and Prescott was the only one made it to Concord in time to warn the militia. Longfellow's poem can help students feel the excitement of those events so long ago, but caution is advised when looking at poetry as a historical source.

Listen my children and you will hear

Of the midnight ride of Paul Revere . . .

As I recited a few stanzas of the poem, children noted bits they would record, if this were the subject of their research and thought of the tone and point of view of Paul Revere.

LINK

Send readers off with a sense of mission and urgency.

"Today you have forty precious minutes to devote to researching these amazing topics, culling main ideas and then noting specifics. Please make sure that for some of that time, you are not reading—but rereading. It's easiest to discern the detail that will be important when you first have a sense for the big contours of a topic. Then notice the details that help you understand the tone of the text and the point of view of the people involved in the moment. Meet with your research team, make a plan, and then get started researching! I'm going to be coming around to admire this important work."

Supporting Productive Conversations that Identify and Explore Connections

TODAY YOUR CONFERRING will presumably start when the students are meeting with their research teams or their partners, and then continue once students are reading. As you listen to the initial conversations that students have before they get started on this work, you may find yourself tempted to jump in and "fix" their talk, but it's important to resist that temptation. It is no small thing for kids to learn to work collaboratively in small groups, and you do want to help them do that well, not just today but always. That means that you'll profit from simply watching for a few minutes. Ask yourself, "How does this group start a conversation? Do they struggle to figure out what needs to be done and to build an agenda for getting that job done as efficiently as possible?"

If students have difficulty in launching the work of their group today, you can help by first watching for predictable problems. While your students are discussing their plans, they aren't talking about texts, but you'll see that issues that come up when they *do* talk about texts surface now as well. For example, perhaps the pattern in their conversation is that one student speaks, then another says something totally unrelated. Later, when they are talking about a text, they'll follow that same pattern. One person says an idea about a text, and the next pops right away from that idea, neither elaborating on it nor asking for evidence of the idea. If you had no knowledge of these students' conversational pattern, you might think the issue revolved around students'

MID-WORKSHOP TEACHING   Synthesizing Point of View

"Readers, Jose asked me an important question, and I think it will help all of you to hear it. He said, 'How do I put together two points of view and think about the time, place, and the consequences of their decisions?' Jose and I worked together to take the important details of the article he was reading that laid out two points of view, and I thought it would help you to hear what Jose did. As he reads it to you, think to yourself, 'How is the way he wrote and took notes the same as the way we did earlier as a class? How is it different?'"

Jose read aloud, "In this article, 'Tea Troubles: The Boston Tea Party'* the author explains the Sons of Liberty's stance and describes reasons for and against their argument. The reasons *against* them throwing the tea overboard is that if they do, they will be destroying property. The ramifications for this could be severe. The reasons *for* doing this is to let Britain hear their voice and see that we will not take all the injustice they are throwing at them."

"Okay, everyone quickly talk to a partner. How is the way Jose wrote notes similar to or different from the way we did earlier?"

After a few minutes, I said, "I heard you talking about how Jose laid out the two most important main ideas in the beginning of his writing. Then, he gave some key details. These details added to one of the main ideas, but more importantly, by holding onto the important details in the texts, he was able to notice how the author lays out different perspectives on the Boston Tea Party. That was different from what we just did."

What a perfect time as well to take out the Informational Reading Learning Progression and look at the strand marked "Analyzing Perspective." Look to see if your students are able to synthesize what they are reading to understand various points of view. After a few minutes, I said, "Everyone, remember that you need to write details for a text you are reading today. And every time you read, you should be thinking about how to hold onto what is most important. Okay, back to reading!"

* from A. Goudvis and S. Harvey, *The American Revolution and Constitution* (Heinemann: 2015)

---

use of texts. But if you see that even when talking about plans for the day, students do not listen to, respond to, or elaborate on each other's ideas, then the issue probably revolves around listening. In that case, you may want to provide some coaching to these students about how to listen and respond to each other in a way that leads to greater understanding. This may be a class where very few people really listen to and respond to what others say.

When you confer with students as they read, it may help if you have a few lenses that you bring to those conferences. We suggest you might help students think about how the events that they are reading about are connected to each other. To do this, you might see if the student is continuing to jot dates onto his or her timeline. Whether the student is recording dates or not is not crucial, but it is important for students to think between one event and another. Ask questions such as "What might this be a result of?" "What might this have led to?" "What do you think caused . . . ?" We suggest this for several reasons. First, far too many students read with blinders on, taking in only that part of the text which is immediately in front of them. Thinking about how one part of the text connects with another part is critical work, and this is nowhere more true than when reading narrative nonfiction. History is all about causes and effects, problems and solutions, events and consequences. This is a perfect time to help students become accustomed to these ways of thinking. Then, too, most of the high-stakes, world-class-aligned tests put a great premium on students being able to talk about how one part of a text connects to another. Your questions will help students be more ready for these questions.

Taking Stock

Set children up to evaluate their synthesis work using the "Synthesis" strand of the checklist. Channel them to notice what they are doing well and what they could improve.

"Researchers, it is time for you to take stock of the work you are doing as nonfiction readers. I know that a couple of days ago, you looked at the learning progressions for a few skills. I'm going to suggest that we bring out the 'Cross Text(s) Synthesis' Progression once again, and that you think about the notes you have been taking, the thinking you have been doing, and be the harshest possible critic of your abilities to synthesize within a text and across texts.

"To do this, I'm going to ask you to look over your notes and find a place where you think you have done your strongest synthesizing work. Get out the notes, and find at least one of the texts that you were reading, too, if you can."

I gave children some time to gather their materials. "Now I have some questions for you to ask of yourself and your synthesizing work."

"Take a look at this progression to assess the part of your work that you think is the strongest. Where do you think this work falls—under the 3, 4, or 5 column? How do you know? Talk with your partner about your self-assessment and be sure to hold your work up against the checklist.

"Readers, you did a good job using the progression to think about your strongest work and identify the areas in which you are doing well. We know how important it is to pat ourselves on the back when we're doing great work. We also know that it is just as, if not more, important to set goals for ourselves, to look at our work through another lens and ask, 'What can I do to make my work even stronger? What have I not done already that I can push myself to do now?' Go ahead and take another look at the checklist and your work. Talk with your partner. Is there an area that you want to work on? Is there a part of the checklist you feel you did not meet? Make this area into a goal for your future reading and note-taking. You can start working on this goal right now!"

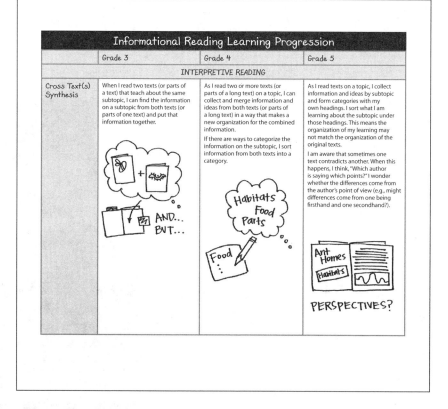

SYNTHESIZING TEXTS

Readers, tonight, as you read a nonfiction text or two on your subtopic, keep working on the synthesis goals you set. I've included a copy of the "Cross Text(s) Synthesis" strand of the progression so you can refer to it as you make your work stronger. To do this, you'll want to read and make sense of main ideas, but also, will you pay attention to the details? It's the details that bring the historical information you're learning to life.

Be sure to spend some time working on the plan you and I made for your additional reading. Be sure to log the reading you do tonight.

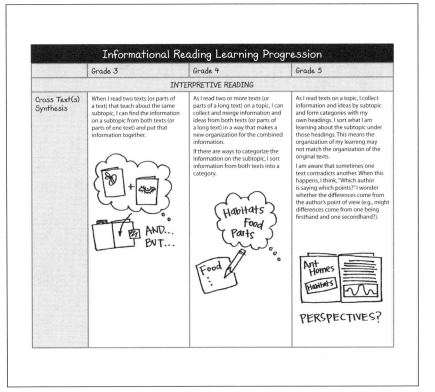

Informational Reading Learning Progression

	Grade 3	Grade 4	Grade 5
	INTERPRETIVE READING		
Cross Text(s) Synthesis	When I read two texts (or parts of a text) that teach about the same subtopic, I can find the information on a subtopic from both texts (or parts of one text) and put that information together.	As I read two or more texts (or parts of a long text) on a topic, I can collect and merge information and ideas from both texts (or parts of a long text) in a way that makes a new organization for the combined information. If there are ways to categorize the information on the subtopic, I sort information from both texts into a category.	As I read texts on a topic, I collect information and ideas by subtopic and form categories with my own headings. I sort what I am learning about the subtopic under those headings. This means the organization of my learning may not match the organization of the original texts. I am aware that sometimes one text contradicts another. When this happens, I think, "Which author is saying which points?" I wonder whether the differences come from the author's point of view (e.g., might differences come from one being firsthand and one secondhand?).

Readers Develop Strategies for Reading Primary Sources

IN THIS SESSION, you'll teach students that readers of history draw on particular strategies to read primary source documents.

GETTING READY

✔ Have chart paper and markers ready to record questions students would ask about a primary source (see Teaching).

✔ Display the "Questions to Ask about a Primary Source" chart (see Teaching).

✔ Prepare copies of "The Wigmaker's Boy and the Boston Massacre" and "Tea Troubles: The Boston Tea Party" for students to familiarize themselves with these events ahead of time, as needed. (see Teaching).

✔ Select primary source visuals to display for students to analyze. Visuals are available in the online resources (see Teaching, Active Engagement, and Mid-Workshop Teaching).

✔ Add a primary source document relevant to each partnership's subtopic to the relevant research team bins (see Link).

✔ Print copies of the "Critical Reading" strand of the Informational Reading Learning Progression for each student (see Homework).

✔ See online resources for primary documents.

I N THIS SESSION, you'll teach students to use close reading skills to make sense of primary sources. In *Lens of History*, the fifth-grade writing unit from *Units of Study in Opinion, Information, and Narrative Writing*, Emily Butler Smith and I write about the importance of primary research by pointing out that accomplished chefs—like Julia Child, James Beard, Alice Waters—always recommend beginning with the best ingredients you can find. For Alice Waters this has meant working closely with local farmers to ensure that the food served in her world-renowned restaurant, Chez Panisse, is the best it can be for her patrons. She knows that by beginning with the best raw ingredients, she guarantees that the food will taste the best, have the purest, most natural flavors. Any chef knows that cooking with farm fresh local foods is vastly different from opening a can of soup or warming up a frozen dinner.

Cooking and learning about history are not so very different. Yes, when you teach your students to study history it is much easier, simpler, neater to provide them with processed sources—secondary sources. But even the best secondary source is filtered through the viewpoint of its author, which can color the interpretation of events. Instead, the best thing for your students' minds and for their understanding of history is to do just as the best chefs do and to use unprocessed ingredients. In history, that means relying on primary source documents.

As the Library of Congress argues, "Examining primary sources gives students a powerful sense of history and the complexity of the past. Helping students to analyze primary sources can also guide them toward higher-order thinking and better critical thinking and analysis skills." Today's session focuses on teaching students the importance of using the best ingredients, primary sources, to study history.

This won't be easy. Your students will need a variety of tools and strategies to make use of the primary sources they study. You will need to teach them to look and read closely, to question, to categorize, and to compare and to contrast, as they study these documents.

Readers Develop Strategies for Reading Primary Sources

CONNECTION

Use a reference to the game of telephone to point out the importance of reading primary documents.

"Readers, you know the game of telephone, don't you? I whisper something to one of you, like 'Power to the people,' and that person whispers it to the next person, and that person whispers it . . . and the chain goes on like that. Finally the last person gets the message, and instead of 'Power to the people' it will be 'Popcorn Pimple,' or something equally far-fetched.

"The game of telephone is a silly little game, but it illustrates a gigantic truth. If you want to get as close to what the original source actually said (in this case, that was me saying 'Power to the people') you either need to go back to the original source, or to someone as close as possible to that original source.

Coach students to look at how a story can change from the original source over time, and if it changes you need to confirm the accuracy of the changes that were made.

"To study history, it is important for you to spend some time going back to documents that originated in the era you are studying. It isn't usually easy to read those—they are called primary sources—because the ones from the past are often written in what feels like old-fashioned English, for starts, but there are many ways in which studying primary source documents is really the *only* way to grasp the flavor of the times, the points of view of the people who were actually there."

❖ **Name the teaching point.**

"Today I want to teach you that readers of history value primary sources, and they know that just as there are strategies to draw upon when reading narrative texts or persuasive texts, there are also strategies that pay off when reading primary source documents."

TEACHING

To give students a quick grasp of the special challenges inherent in reading primary sources, pretend you just stumbled on a primary source and ask them to help you make sense of it.

"Readers, if I said, 'I want you to read a bit of presidential history' and showed you a text that was written in old-fashioned printing on yellowed paper with burnt edges and the text said, 'Behead him,' will you think about what questions you would need to ask to make sense of this text?"

The kids quickly generated questions, and I jotted them on chart paper:

- Who wrote it? When? Why?
- Who is the person it references? That is, what is it really saying?
- What were the conditions under which this was written?
- How authentic is this?

"You can see that until those questions are answered, the document wouldn't mean much, right? I mean, it could be a note that a president wrote when he was five or six years old, and he could have been speaking about an insect, or a toy soldier!"

Point out that the questions the kids generated aren't very different from the questions that historians ask of primary sources, and share those questions.

"The interesting thing is that the questions you generated are pretty much the same as the questions that the Colonial Williamsburg Foundation—a big fancy organization that teaches teachers how to teach history—has come up with as well. These are the questions they teach young historians to ask of primary sources. As you look over them, notice how similar they are to the questions you came up with."

"One of the interesting things about reading primary sources is that sometimes you need to be a bit of a detective to figure out the answers to all those questions. I mean—imagine that if you passed a note to a friend, and I intercepted it, then someone found it 200 years later and studied it. They wouldn't necessarily see on the note the conditions under which you wrote it, or even who you are, who the recipient of the notes is. They may not even know who or what the note was about."

Channel students to look at a visual primary source about the Boston Massacre and ask themselves the questions you have taught them to ask.

I displayed Paul Revere's engraving of the Boston Massacre, then said, "Let's look at a primary source from the time of the American Revolution. This is actually an image, not a print text, but an image can be a primary source, too."

If you want to playact this, you could do so. In that case, you might simply say, "Kids, I just found this on my desk," and unfold some little wad of paper that might have some note that is sure to cause a stir such as, "The school will be closed for three days next week." Again, you could recruit kids into generating the questions that need to be asked to make heads or tails out of that mysterious document. They'd ask the right questions: Who wrote it? When is it dated?

We know that many students won't have prior historical knowledge to bring to this discussion. If so, you can help provide them with context for analyzing the primary sources by having them read a short secondary source about these events ahead of time. We recommend "The Wigmaker's Boy and the Boston Massacre" and "Tea Troubles: The Boston Tea Party," which are available in the online resources.

"Readers, you often come up with questions as you read. You learn a bit of information, you pause and wonder, keep reading, and either your questions are answered or sometimes revised and carried forward as you continue to read, but usually these questions are specific to the topic or text you are reading about. If you're reading about the French and Indian War, you come up with questions about the French and Indian War, or if you are reading about the Stamp Act, you come up with questions about the Stamp Act.

"Well, today as we work together to tackle the reading of primary sources, let's use these questions that readers use when they are reading any primary source," I said as I gestured toward the "Questions to Ask about a Primary Source" chart.

Demonstrate the process you use to analyze the image, showing that you draw on this analysis and your prior knowledge to understand the image.

"So, I'll start by taking a good look at the image and working my way through the questions on the chart. The first question is 'What do you notice?' Well, that one is pretty obvious—I see a line of soldiers in red coats shooting and killing a group of unarmed people. There's a title: 'The Bloody Massacre perpetrated in King Street, Boston.' So, now I'm thinking that this is a picture about the Boston Massacre.

"Oh, but wait, there's more to see than that. If I look more closely, I see that this shooting takes place in a city—I see lots of buildings and signs that say 'Butcher's Hall' and 'Custom House.' I know the Custom House is important, because that's where the Boston Massacre took place. But what about Butcher's Hall? Hmm . . . if I keep looking, I see that the soldiers almost seem to have *smiles* on their faces. I wonder if the creator of this image intended to say that the soldiers were butchers?

"So, then, who created this image? You can't always tell by looking, but let me see if I can figure that out." I looked for a moment, then pointed and said, "Here at the bottom of the image, it says 'Engrav'd, printed and sold by Paul Revere, Boston.' I know that later, Paul Revere was the guy who rode to warn the colonists that the British soldiers were coming. I think he was one of the Sons of Liberty.

"And I see that it was made in Boston in 1770. That was soon after the Boston Massacre happened, so that makes me think that Revere's memory of the event must have been fresh."

I continued working through the questions, until I finally came to the last one. "The last question I have to ask about this picture is 'Why was it created?'

"That's an interesting question. I'd think that a silversmith would probably make pictures of something happier. I know Paul Revere was angry at the British, so I wonder if he made this to help other people understand why he was angry."

Questions to Ask About a Primary Source:

- What do you notice?
- What type of document is it? primary / secondary
- Who created it?
- When and where was it made? 1776 / BOSTON
- Why was it created?

History teachers across the United States often ask students to consider multiple perspectives on the Boston Massacre by comparing Revere's engraving of the Boston Massacre with other depictions of the event, to teach that history is influenced by the perspective from which it is told. We deliberately do not so in this session, because we are saving that work for Bend II, where we make very big deal out of the importance of hearing all sides of a story.

ACTIVE ENGAGEMENT

Set students up to analyze another primary source image, drawing on the information they can glean from the image and all that they already know about the event it depicts.

I displayed an image of the Boston Tea Party on the document camera. "Now it's your turn to give this a go. Here is another primary source for you to analyze. At a glance, can you tell what it's about?" I heard a resounding chorus of "Boston Tea Party!"

"That's right. Now, take a moment with your partner, and carefully look at the image. Then work together to answer the questions on the chart. As you think about the questions, remember to draw on the details of the image *and* what you already know about the Boston Tea Party."

I listened in on partners' conversations. Patrick said, "Well, I notice a boat full of Indians rowing toward a ship with knives and tomahawks in the air." Atif replied, "I think these are the people, the colonists, dressed up as Indians. I think they want to blame the Indians."

Meanwhile, others pointed to people on the wharf, with their arms in the air, waving hats. "It's like a party," they said.

Debrief in ways that accentuate the replicable and transferable nature of what you and the kids have been doing.

"Remember, researchers, when you are reading and analyzing a primary source, you have a series of questions to ask about that source. Historical documents were created by people—people who lived in a particular place at a particular time, people who had their own points of view about events. So when you are looking at a primary source document, ask yourself all the questions from our 'Questions to Ask about a Primary Source' chart so that you understand not only what the document is saying, but why it was made and whose viewpoint it reflects."

LINK

Provide students with additional documents to read and discuss in partnerships.

"Readers, I know you want to get back to your research. You only have another two days before you'll be teaching others about the subtopic you have been studying, so I know you are urgent to get a lot of reading done. You'll notice that I put a primary source (or a reference to one) that I believe might be relevant to your topic in your bin of materials. Today, continue doing whatever research you are on about, but will you make sure that you spend at least a bit of time reading over a primary source that can help you learn about your topic.

"Off you go!"

Coach students to first think of the lens they will look through with the primary source with and then the questions they will ask.

Supporting Students in Analyzing Primary Sources

PRIMARY SOURCES are the foundation stones of history, and students need the skills to analyze primary source documents and place them into their proper historical context if they are to know how to read like a historian. Of course, secondary sources are useful for gaining an understanding about an event or a time period, but there is nothing like a primary source to allow the voices of the past to be heard, in their own words and with their own viewpoints. Primary sources are what make history come alive.

Studying primary source documents is challenging. You can anticipate, therefore, that your students will run into a variety of predictable problems as they try this work. Even at the very start of this work, you can immediately spot problems if you notice some students flip through primary source documents quickly, without stopping to ask questions or develop theories. Encourage them to study each document as if they were examining a beetle under a microscope. Meanwhile, you'll probably want to make a public fuss over students who do spend time reading documents closely. You may call

---

MID-WORKSHOP TEACHING   **Readers Synthesize Information from Primary Sources into Their Notes**

"Readers, when you read a primary source, remember that the information you learn needs to be synthesized with all that you learned earlier. The important detail goes into your notes. You will already have notes on some big points about the American Revolution, and when you study the primary source, you are not just reading that one new document, you are also thinking between that document and all that you already know. You have to ask, 'How does this new piece of information fit with the big points I've been learning?'

"Right now, tell your partner the big points your authors have brought forward."

I listened as children did that, then said, "Researchers, eyes up here. Atif has been studying the Boston Tea Party. He just named one of his big points by saying, 'The Boston Tea Party was one important way that the colonists protested the taxes by the British.' Let's say Atif wants to add in something from the primary source you all studied in the minilesson. What could he say?"

Kids pointed out that he could add that the colonists dressed up as Native Americans. "Hmm. Okay . . . and how would that support the point that this was an important way to protest?"

The room was silent. "Think again about the primary source document," I said and showed it. "What do you notice about this depiction of the Boston Tea Party that *does* support Atif's point that the colonists thought the Boston Tea Party was an important protest?"

Atif chimed in. "Maybe I could say that the colonists all came down to the dock to watch people throw the tea into the sea." Others chimed in, "And you could say they cheered and waved their hats."

I nodded. "So all of you, remember that primary source documents will help you bring in the detail that will color your knowledge of the event. You give the tone and flavor of the event with those details. The only thing I want to add is this. Be sure you say, 'According to Paul Revere's engraving . . .' or 'In his journal, so-and so wrote . . .'" Be sure you tell where this wonderful primary source information comes from."

---

out, "Wow, I saw Atif look at one small person in the corner of an image for a whole minute," or you may say, "Class, I have got to interrupt. I just saw something really impressive. Zoe almost seems to be tracing a map with her finger, trying to figure out the distance between Boston and Lexington. What detailed study."

You can also anticipate that some students will jump into studying primary sources without orienting themselves to the features of the text. These students will bypass the title, the author, and the accompanying pictures. Be ready to talk up the special need for previewing texts when working with primary sources.

Then, too, you may see students who are so enthralled by the primary sources in front of them that they are sketching these maps, cartoons, and images in their notebooks. It will be important to remind students that researchers look at images analytically. One way to help these students is to give them copies of primary sources that they can paste in their notebooks, and encourage them to highlight and underline pieces of the text or image, and jot their own comments in the margins of the texts.

Text complexity is an important issue to consider when using primary sources. You will want to look for students who seem stuck on a particular text, not able to glean anything from its words. One way to help students make sense of complex texts is to set them up in temporary heterogeneous partnerships, where a stronger reader reads the document to a more struggling reader, or at least helps them through it. In this way, struggling readers can still do the important work of close reading even when facing texts above their independent level.

You may find that text complexity makes it especially difficult for your struggling readers to find an entry point into a primary source. You may want to guide these students toward visual primary sources, such as historical illustrations, maps, or political cartoons. Lifting the burden of eighteenth-century language will give students an opportunity to practice their skills in analyzing what they see and synthesizing that information with all that they know about the subject from their research. If your class research topic deals with more recent history, however, the language of primary sources may not be such a barrier, and you may find that text-based primary sources from more modern history are more accessible to your students.

Seeking Out Primary Sources, Not Skipping Over Them

Ask students to note the similarities and differences of primary and secondary sources. Explain that secondary sources often contain primary sources, and highlight differences between them.

"Readers, let's get together for a few minutes. Bring whatever you have been reading lately." Once the children had assembled in the meeting area, I said to them, "Most of you have been reading a primary source today, as well as a secondary source. Would you put an example of each in front of you and talk to your partner about how they are similar and how they are different?"

As the children started talking, I listened in. "Class," I said, interrupting. "Joselyn has been reading *What Was the Boston Tea Party?*, and she was just telling her partner that in the middle of this book, she came upon a whole series of pictures and they are different from the other ones in the book. They're on a different kind of paper and they look old. She realized that even though the book she is reading is a secondary source, it contains primary sources in it. Would the rest of you see if that is true for you as well?"

As students talked about this, I noted some confusion so I asked students for their attention and said, in a voiceover, "Some of you are asking how you can tell the difference between primary and secondary sources. That is a good question. Primary sources are original documents, artifacts, records, papers, or other resources created by individuals who participated in or witnessed past events, or who were at least contemporaries of those who did.

"The style of image or the drawing can provide clues. Check out the captions, because if the document is a primary source, the caption will often tell who made the document and may provide a little background about that source.

"And you are right that often times secondary sources will have primary sources embedded in them. Don't skip over the primary source when you're reading. That primary source has the real words of the real people who lived back then, and you don't want to miss out on that! Your job as a reader, then, is to read the secondary source, read the primary source, and to ask, 'How do these fit together? And how do they fit with what I already know?'"

In third grade, students were encouraged to use technology to find primary sources. Their knowledge of primary sources, then, may harken back to that work a bit.

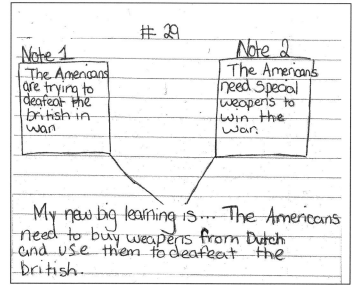

FIG. 7–1   A student comes up with new learning from two sources of information.

DEVELOPING YOUR OWN IDEAS

Readers, tonight, continue reading about the American Revolution. In just a few days, you will teach others what you have learned about a part of the revolution. Before you do that, be sure that you have spent time collecting information and ideas from books. I also want to make sure you have developed some of your own ideas.

You can develop your ideas like you did during our earlier nonfiction units. Reread your notes and think, "What do these ideas show me about the topic?" If you have studied two causes of the American Revolution, you can think, "What are some similarities between these two? The differences?" You can also ask yourself, "How do these two causes relate to each other?" Spend a few minutes studying the section of the learning progression on "Critical Reading: Growing Ideas," noting where your work currently falls and pushing yourself to immediately make your work growing ideas stronger.

This will help you grow your own theories. When you do that, you are reading like a historian. Your own ideas and insights about the causes of the American Revolution are valuable.

Meanwhile, make sure that you also continue the other reading you are doing, in addition to your research. Be sure to log all of your reading on your log.

Informational Reading Learning Progression

	Grade 4	Grade 5
	ANALYTIC READING	
Critical Reading *Growing Ideas*	I develop my own ideas about what I have read. Those ideas might be about values, the world, or the book. My ideas are grounded in text-based information and ideas, and I draw on several parts of the text(s). I raise questions and larger theories about the topic or the world. I read and reread with those questions in mind, and this leads to new insights. My reading helps me to develop my ideas. I think and sometimes write things like "Is this always the case?" or "Could it be . . . ?" I am not afraid to think in new ways.	I can synthesize several texts in ways that support an idea of my own. I select the points that do the best job of supporting my idea(s). For example, "How will this author add to or challenge my argument?" I think and sometimes write things like "Is this always the case?" or "Could it be . . . ?" I can apply what I have learned and my own ideas to solve a problem, make an argument, or design an application.
Questioning the Text	I think about what implications my theories and what I have learned might have for real-world situations. I can apply what I have learned. I'm aware that texts can be written to get readers to think and feel something about an issue or topic, and I can say, "I see what you want me to think/feel, but I disagree."	I consider what a text is saying about an issue, idea, or argument and whether I agree or disagree. I weigh and evaluate a text for how convincing and reliable it is. I consider who wrote the text and what the author might gain from the text. I can talk back to texts.

Session 8

Readers Bring Their Topics to Life

WHAT IS HISTORY, really, but one grand sweeping narrative? History is all about characters—many very colorful—who have desires, meet with obstacles, and draw on resources within themselves and others to respond to those obstacles. Reading history asks readers to apply many of the same skills that they are asked to use when reading fiction. Just as the smell of a woodstove or the particular sound of a screen door slamming may conjure up for you the places of your childhood summers, it is important that when reading history you let particular images—the lanterns hanging from the belfry of the old North Church, and Paul Revere, rowing across the Charles River with cloth wrapped around the oars to muffle the sound—conjure up pictures of another time, another place.

It is important, too, for readers of history to walk in the shoes of the people in the stories, to imagine themselves awakening in the dead of night to hear a pounding on the door and a voice saying, "The Redcoats are coming, the Redcoats are coming!" How life must have been turned upside down in that moment, when ordinary farmers, silversmith, printers, left behind their homes, their families and head off to join a war with the people they once thought of as "the Mother Country."

This session invites your students to transfer some of what they know about reading literature to their work with nonfiction. You will encourage them to envision, to make movies in their minds as they empathize and imagine their way into vicariously experiencing the story. You'll teach them to transfer reading skills that they think of as belonging to fiction reading into their work with history texts. (This session builds upon the last two, and for those of you who are teaching *Bringing History to Life* in your writing workshop, it aligns to Session 6, especially.)

IN THIS SESSION, you'll teach students that researchers can bring their topics to life when they draw on all they know about reading fiction to make a scene come alive.

GETTING READY

✔ Prepare a passage from a narrative nonfiction text and a narrative fiction text to read aloud, for students to compare and contrast how they think about them. We chose an excerpt from Milton Meltzer's *The American Revolutionaries*, page 110, and *The Tiger Rising* by Kate DiCamillo pages 5–6 (see Connection).

✔ Select a quotation about the envisioning and empathy essential to fiction reading that also applies to nonfiction reading. We suggest a quote from John Gardner's *The Art of Fiction* (see Teaching and Active Engagement).

✔ Select a primary source quote with enough vivid detail that students could reenact it. We chose Washington's speech from *The American Revolutionaries*, page 110 (see Teaching and Active Engagement).

✔ Ensure each student has a copy of the "Fluency" strand of the Informational Reading Learning Progression (see Conferring and Small-Group Work).

✔ Compile examples of longer sentences to support students in fluency (see Conferring and Small-Group Work).

✔ Today, students will need to sign up for a topic they are willing to teach others in the next class session (see Share).

Readers Bring Their Topics to Life

CONNECTION

Ask students to jot thoughts in response to a narrative nonfiction passage depicting an episode from Revolutionary War times, and then to share their thinking with a partner.

"Researchers, before we do anything else today, I'm going to read an excerpt from one of our texts. The scene is a cold gray hillside in December 1777, when General Washington's tired and hungry men pitched their tents and began to cut down trees to make shelters. A twenty-seven-year-old Connecticut surgeon noted conditions in his diary. As I read aloud what the surgeon wrote, I'll ask you to quickly jot down some of your thinking."

As you read aloud, picture the scene. It is extraordinary how important it is that you are doing the mental work that you hope students are doing as well. Read with an awareness that this is written from the point of view of a soldier. These are entries from his diary.

December 21.

Preparations made for hutts. Provisions Scarce. . . . Sent a Letter to my Wife. Heartily wish myself at home, my Skin & eyes are almost spoil'd with continual smoke. A general cry thro' the Camp this Evening among the Soldiers, "No Meat! No Meat!"—the Distant vales echo'd back the melancholy sound, "No Meat! No Meat!" . . .

What have you for your Dinners Boys? "Nothing but Fire Cake & Water, Sir." At night, "Gentlemen the Supper is ready." What is your Supper Lads? "Fire Cake & Water, Sir" . . .

December 22.

Lay excessive Cold & uncomfortable last Night—my eyes are started out from their Orbits like a Rabbit's eyes, occasion'd by a great Cold & Smoke.

What have you got for Breakfast, Lads? "Fire Cake & Water, Sir" . . .

December 25, Christmas.

We are still in Tents—when we ought to be in huts—the poor Sick, suffer much in Tents this cold Weather . . .

"Quickly jot your thinking." I gave students a minute to jot and then said, "Turn and grow your thinking with a partner."

Ask students to think about the kind of thinking they just did, comparing it to the thinking they did when they read a particular passage from *The Tiger Rising*. Project that passage.

I called students back together. "Readers, I heard a lot of great conversations about this text. Will you think a moment about the *kind* of thinking that you were doing? For example, you might compare it to the thinking you did earlier this year, when we read this scene from *The Tiger Rising*." I projected this passage under the document camera for children to see:

> *"Hey," said Billy Threemonger, "you know what? This ain't Kentucky. This is Florida."*
>
> *He followed Rob and sat down right next to him. He pushed his face so close that Rob could smell his breath. It was bad breath. It smelled metallic and rotten. "You ain't a Kentucky Star," Billy said, his eyes glowing under the brim of his John Deere cap. "And you sure ain't a star here in Florida. You ain't a star nowhere."*
>
> *"Okay," said Rob.*
>
> *Billy shoved him hard. And then Norton came swaggering back and leaned over Billy and grabbed hold of Rob's hair with one hand, and with the other hand, ground his knuckles into Rob's scalp.*
>
> *Rob sat there and took it.*

"How is your thinking about the nonfiction text the same—and how is it different—than your thinking about the passage from *The Tiger Rising*?" I gave the children a quiet moment to think. "Talk about the similarities and differences in your thinking with your partner."

Tell children that you asked them to make this comparison because their work lately has been a bit mechanical. Talk up the importance of bringing imagination to nonfiction reading.

After a few minutes, I said, "I asked you to compare your thinking about these scenes, because it seems to me that sometimes you are reading nonfiction quite differently than you read fiction. As I watched some of you during reading workshop yesterday, I couldn't shake the feeling that once in a while what you were doing was mechanical and a little—dare I say it?—boring! As you gathered facts and put together information, it was like you were robots reciting the information, and not the passionate, excited class I'm used to! You'd record a fact such as 'People were killed in the Battle of Bunker Hill' without even wincing at the human cost of that.

"I began to worry if, when you are reading history, you have sometimes been leaving out . . ." I paused dramatically, letting the anticipation build, "imagination!

"Albert Einstein, who is one of the greatest scientists who ever lived, said, 'Imagination is everything.' And certainly, if we are to understand history, we need to read with imagination. We need to put ourselves in the shoes of the people we are reading about, just like we do with the characters in our fiction books, imagining their experiences just as we imagine Rob and Sistine's experiences."

❖ Name the teaching point.

"Today I want to teach you that the important thing about reading history is that it requires both imagination and factual knowledge. Readers need to use their factual knowledge to help them do the imaginative work of envisioning, of putting themselves into the historical scene."

TEACHING AND ACTIVE ENGAGEMENT

Share a quotation about the envisioning and empathy that is essential to fiction reading, pointing out that readers must also envision when reading nonfiction.

"Readers, John Gardner, one of the greatest fiction writers of our times, has described reading this way":

> It creates for us a kind of dream, a rich and vivid play in the mind. We read a few words at the beginning of the book or the particular story and suddenly we find ourselves seeing not words on a page but a train moving through Russia, an old Italian crying, or a farmhouse battered by rain. We read on—dream on—not passively but actively, worrying about the choices the characters have to make, listening in panic for some sound behind the fictional door. . . . In great fiction, the dream engages us heart and soul. (2010, 30–31)

"Gardner was describing fiction reading, and I know when you read *The Tiger Rising* earlier this year, you did all this. You pictured the characters, the setting, and the mood, and you tried to experience the story as though it was real life. But what I want you to know is that Gardner's description of reading applies to a great deal of nonfiction as well."

Set students up to listen to a primary source—a speech—putting themselves in the shoes of the people who were the original audience.

"So let's try this. I'm going to read another text—a speech that George Washington gave to his troops. As I read, use your best acting abilities and your best envisioning skills to pretend you are one of those troops that Washington is addressing. When he finishes talking, I am going to ask you to turn to each other and talk as if you are right there, in that moment. Don't talk about what you *would* have thought or said—actually *be* one of the soldiers." I read the speech aloud dramatically.

> The General wheeled his horse about, rode in front of the regiment, and addressing us again said, "My brave fellows, you have done all I asked you to do, and more than could reasonably be expected; but your country is at stake, your wives, your houses, and all that you hold dear. You have worn yourselves out with fatigues and hardships, but we know not how to spare you. If you will consent to stay only one month longer, you will render that service to the cause of the liberty, and to your country, which you probably never can do under any other circumstances. The present is emphatically the crisis, which is to decide our destiny."
>
> The drums beat a second time. The soldiers felt the force of the appeal. One said to another, "I will remain if you will." Others remarked, "We cannot go home under such circumstances." A few stepped

Coach kids to refer back to the character chart used in the previous unit to remind them of the work you have done in envisioning and walking in the characters' shoes.

Again, read aloud in such a way that you help your students to envision. You may want to have the "Envisioning" strand of the Narrative Reading Learning Progression available.

forth, and their example was immediately followed by nearly all who were fit for duty in the regiment, amounting to about two hundred volunteers. An officer inquired of the General if these men should be enrolled. He replied, "No! men who will volunteer in such a case as this need no enrollment to keep them to their duty."

"Let's stop here for a moment and think about your role. What are you wearing? How are you feeling? What's going through your mind as this is occurring?" I paused for just a moment to give them time to picture themselves in the scene.

"Now, let's start this again from the beginning, and this time I'll read it all the way through, and you'll *be* the soldiers. Put yourself right there, with General Washington, and act out what's happening." I read through the text a second time.

"Now, turn and talk as if you are one of those soldiers right there, in that moment." Students jumped into action, and I knelt down on the rug to coach into a few partnerships.

Debrief. Compliment children on their acting and envisioning skills.

After the children role-played, I called them back together. "Readers, you rose to the occasion. I saw you acting out this incredible turning point of this time period. You were filling in all the details—what you were wearing, what you saw, how you felt and why—wow! You really brought these texts to life."

LINK

Explain that texts cue readers how to read them and that only some history texts cue readers to read them as they read fiction.

"Readers, the texts you are reading—-like all information texts—are a mix of narrative and expository texts. Some passages are written in ways that signal to you that as a reader, you should be gleaning boxes-and-bullets outlines. Other texts are written in ways that signal to you that you should be reading them almost as if they are fiction—only in addition to walking in the shoes of characters, you will be learning information about the times.

You might want to remind students to use what they know of narrative and informational text to make an informed decision. Is it main idea we are reading for or is it story structure?

"For today, will you make a point, before you read, to think, 'How does this part of the text want to be read?' and then decide if the text is calling for you to read it as you read *The Tiger Rising* or if the text is calling for you to read it in a way that allows you to cull out the main ideas and the supportive details? You may want to use your Post-its to flag places where the text shifts, if that helps you figure out what the text is asking you to do. Make a choice that matches the text that you are reading.

"You and your research team and your partner may need to take a minute to decide on what you *are* reading. Are you continuing to read about the same topic, only filling in the details? Will you instead tackle another subtopic, with each member of the team reading up on it? Or is there a book you've gotten interested in that you want to read straight through? Part of being a researcher is deciding what you are going to read next, why, and how. As you make that decision, know that many nonfiction texts need to be read in ways that are similar to the way in which you read great fiction."

Supporting Students' Fluency, Comprehension, and Analytical Skills

EARLIER, you asked students to select a passage and to read that passage to each other, working to lift the level of that reading. At the time, you gave them the "Fluency" strand of the Informational Reading Learning Progression. Today, you may ask students to retrieve that progression, and to coach each other to progress from one level to another.

Support students with complex sentences.

You may want to help them specifically with the challenge of reading longer sentences. You might bring some sentences around with you as you confer or work with small groups, showing students how you would read those sentences, and then ask them to apply those same skills to their information texts. For example, you could carry sentences like this one with you, and talk to students about why they are hard to read:

> Because of the complexity of academic texts, the density of factual information and the frequency of unfamiliar vocabulary, books become hard.

> Books (even ones like this one) can become hard (well, perhaps not hard but complex), and people need to work harder (much harder) to read them.

Channel readers to read with prosody and fluidity.

Many people have found that it is effective to ask students to spend a bit of time engaged in repeated readings of some texts—and of course, those repeated readings need to be purposeful and engaging. One of the best ways to create conditions which allow for this is to suggest that readers perform some selected texts, and to ideally give them access to texts that are written in ways that beg to be read aloud. There are gorgeous speeches associated with the American Revolution, for example, and you might encourage students to imagine performing one of those speeches as part of their final presentation to the other groups. You could give them access to a professional rendering of the speech, and suggest they could listen to that enactment of the speech over and over and then try to do the same sort of thing. As students listen to and discuss powerfully read passages, they come to understand that the meaning is not solely carried in the words, but also in the way those words fall on the ears and the minds of readers.

MID-WORKSHOP TEACHING   Bringing Scenes to Life

"Readers, I'm going to ask you to choose a passage to bring to the share today that is one which you find yourself reading a bit like you read fiction—picturing the scenes, imagining the character's feelings. So locate that passage, if you can.

"Will you plan to read this passage aloud to your research team during the share, adding in gestures and actions as you read it? To do that, it will help if you think about what you know from all the research you have done that can help you imagine the content of the passage you read. For example, if you are reading that Sam Adams put on his coat and left the courthouse, and if you have a memory of the picture of the coats people wore back then from some of the videos you have watched, draw on that mental picture. (I'm picturing his coat has tails in the back, are you, and little gold buttons?) And if you read that Sam Adams walked down the streets, you bring in pictures you have from reading. Are the streets cobbled streets? Are there ditches on either side for the rainwater? Bring anything you know into your interpretation of the passage you select.

"So be sure you locate the passage that you will share and reread it, thinking 'What do I know from other passages that can help me bring this scene to life?'"

Of course, to do a similar reading of a famous speech, your students would need to read the speech many, many times themselves, and to think about the changing intonation that could make it come to life.

Help students adjust their reading strategies based upon genre.

As you confer with your students, you will want to notice the genre that a given student is reading and help that student to adjust his or her reading strategies based on the genre. Encourage a reader to think about the text that he or she is reading, asking, "Is this mostly a narrative? Or is it mostly expository?" If it is a narrative, for example, it will be organized by time: first, then, next. There will be a main character—a person, a group of people, an animal. Students who are reading narrative should be developing theories about the people in the text—about the *he*, *she*, *it*, or *they* around which this true story (or fictionalized fact-based story) revolves. And they should be thinking about ways the characters are meeting the challenges of their lives. If students are reading texts that are mostly narrative, then they'll profit from bringing a story frame to those texts.

If students are reading texts that are expository/informational, then they will be organized more by categories, in an all-about way, perhaps with subheadings. If there are no subheadings, readers can sort of supply their own headings that capture what a section was mostly about. They probably need to think about gathering main ideas and supports.

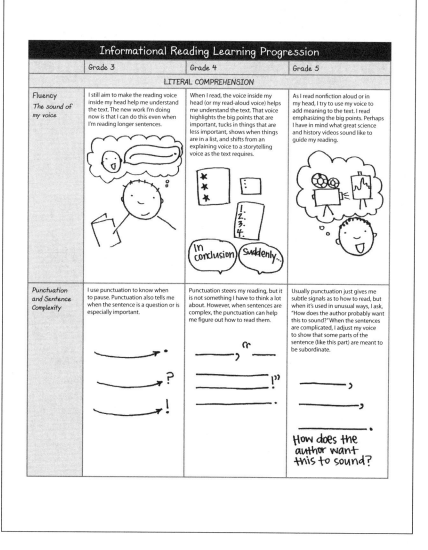

Dramatizing Nonfiction and Preparing to Teach Others about a Topic

Channel students to meet with their research teams, bringing selected passages with them, and to do an oral performance of those passages to each other.

"So readers, get with your research teams and take turns reading aloud the passage you brought. As you read, act out the part. Focusing on all of the details will help you bring the scene to life. Then discuss everything you were trying to show in your acting. Then read it a second time, trying to bring it to life even more. You probably won't get to everyone's scene, but taking the time to work on one or two scenes will be worthwhile."

Ask children to sign up for a topic to teach others during a future symposium.

Before class ended, I asked students to sign up for the topic they were willing to teach each other during an upcoming symposium. I explained that at that time, a group of children who felt knowledgeable about a particular topic—say, the causes of the American Revolution—would together, teach a small class on that topic, and a group of children who were knowledgeable about the Boston Tea Party would teach that topic, and so forth. I gave students a few minutes to revisit their notes, consider subtopics they were willing to teach, and form into small groups with other students interested in teaching about the same subtopic. "Right now, make a plan with your group. What will you teach tomorrow? What will you need to research tonight to get ready?"

 ## PLANNING TO TEACH

Readers, tomorrow you will be teaching others about your subtopic. You will work in small groups with others who have studied a similar subtopic. Plan: who will be teaching each part? How will you teach your part? What are the main ideas and the supporting details that are the most important for others to know?

When you teach, be sure to add enough details to make your subtopic come alive. The details remind us that these were real people, living in uncertain times. Try to make your audience feel that, too.

Session 9

A Celebration of Learning

 ear Teachers,

We've left this session for you, as the details will need to come from the particulars of your setting. If, in your writing workshop, your students have been writing a book about the American Revolution alongside their reading, today may actually be a day on which they share their publications. If they haven't written such a book, then today probably should be a time when they assemble all they know into some coherent form and do the best they can do to teach it to others. The important thing is that your students feel a drumroll approaching today, so they take time to review all they have read in preparation for teaching their classmates (or perhaps others, if you organize that) in a thoughtful, organized fashion.

Before your students teach each other, you may want to give them some pointers. Your teaching point could be this: "Today I want to teach you that when you teach someone all you have learned about a topic, your oral teaching needs to reflect all that you know about good information writing. Above all, information writing is structured—and that structure is clearly evident to your students, your 'readers' if you want to call them that."

You might then refer to a good piece of information writing as a model, and talk through four or five important points about effective information writing. You could ask students to research the qualities of good information writing by studying an informational text from their research bins, so that after you talk about the topic, they could think about their own notes and teaching ideas on the American Revolution subtopic, thinking, "Am I set, so far, to teach this in ways that show what I know about information writing?" If not, they can make some fast improvements.

Your first point will likely be that information writing must, above all, be organized. You can point out that your model information text has a table of contents of sorts, raising the notion that your children will need a similar plan for the teaching they'll do. You may also point out that in your model information text, there are ways the author clues readers into the structure to follow. The text may have a "tour-guide overview" such as "There were ways to follow the war. The first is . . ."

Again, students can consider whether their teaching plans include a way to let listeners know the plan for their teaching.

You will probably also want to talk up the importance of elaboration, and you may point out that there are a few main ways that authors of information texts elaborate—and these are all things that your students can do as they teach. They can cite a quotation. Your students might say something like, "As Patrick Henry says . . ." and then read from his words. They can also elaborate with examples, in which case they will need a transitional sentence like "One example of this is . . ." Or they can elaborate with a description, in which case they could launch that description with a phrase such as "Picture the scene . . ."

This amount of information is probably too much already, so you'll choose the parts that will help your students. Give them ten minutes or so to revise and rehearse their teaching in their small groups, and then set them up to teach each other.

Before your celebration of Bend I is over, you will also want to rally students to use the checklists to self-assess their work, and the easiest way to do this will be to ask them to assess the teaching they do for each other. Once children have taught each other, call them together for a serious conversation. This may well need to be done on another day altogether. Say to them, "Class, I need your help. Jose and Sophia have just taught their research team what they have discovered about Paul Revere. As they do this for us can we watch as their research team uses the checklists to assess the information that they are hearing and then advise them or asks questions."

As you finish this bend, you will begin to see their preliminary understanding of the American Revolution. No matter the gaps you may feel your students have in their understanding of the Revolution, take some time to recognize the independence and deliberation on the part of your fourth graders. It will be worth its weight in gold.

Best wishes,
Lucy, Janet, and Grace

Preparing for Debate BEND II

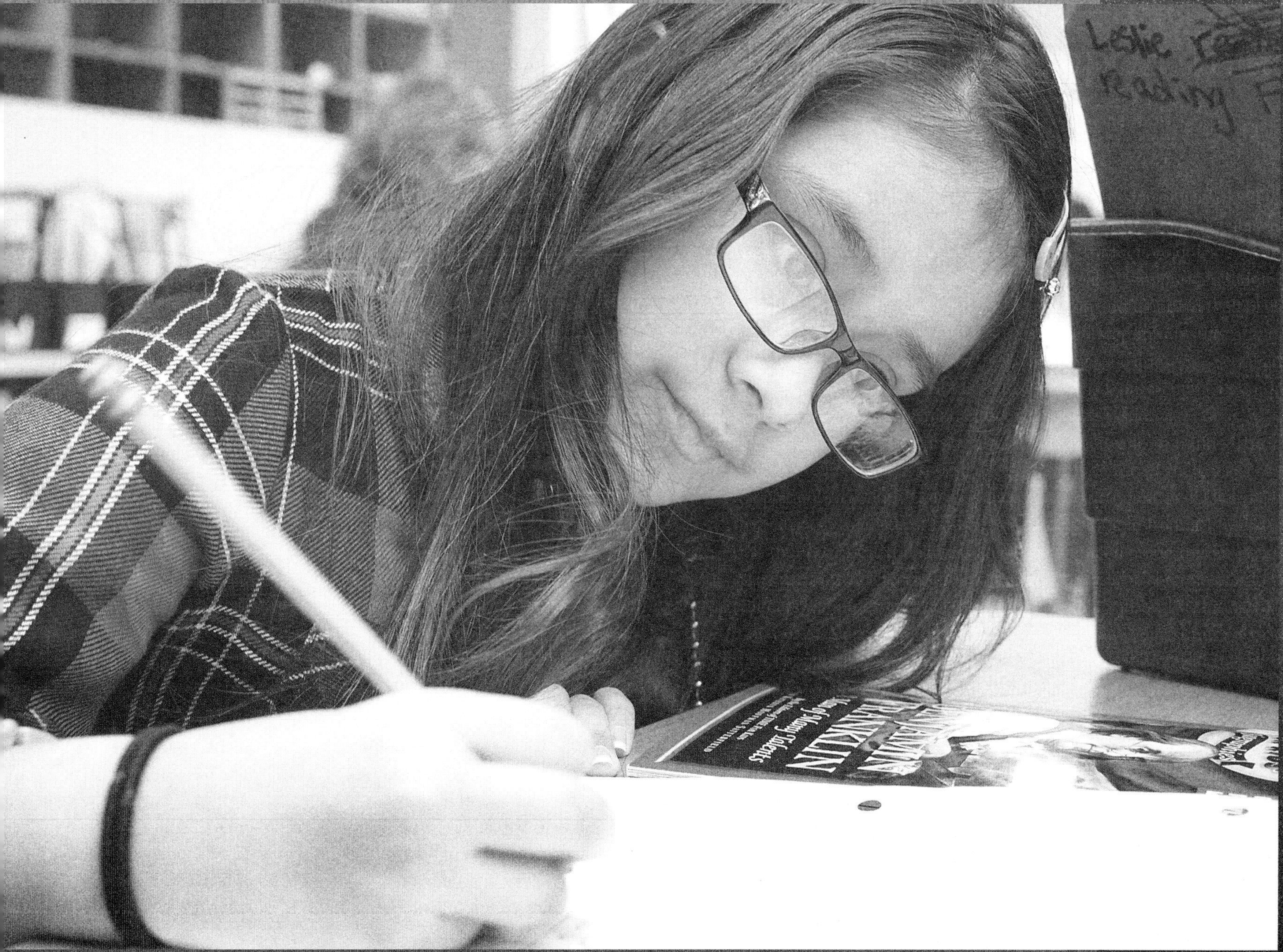

Recognizing Different
Perspectives

IN THIS SESSION, you'll teach students that historians pay careful attention to multiple points of view, so that they can try to form a more complete understanding of what happened in the past.

GETTING READY

✔ Display Paul Revere's engraving of the Boston Massacre. A link to the engraving is available in the online resources (see Teaching).

✔ Display Captain Preston's testimony about the Boston Massacre. A link to the testimony is available in the online resources (see Teaching).

✔ Project a copy of "Boston Riot" from page 7 of *The Split History of the American Revolution/British Perspective* for students to analyze for perspective (see Active Engagement).

✔ Gather primary and secondary sources depicting the British viewpoints of the events leading to the American Revolution. Be sure to select sources at accessible reading levels, and make them available for students to choose from and study. (see Link).

✔ Find an object, such as a fireman's helmet, that you can use to demonstrate different perspectives (see Mid-Workshop Teaching).

✔ Provide each student with a copy of the "Analyzing Author's Craft" and "Analyzing Perspective" strands of the Informational Reading Learning Progression, a copy of the article "Tea Troubles: The Boston Tea Party," and access to *Tea Drinking in 18th-Century America: Its Etiquette and Equipage* (see Homework).

I N THIS BEND, you point out to your students that any one account of an event—whether current or past—will have been constructed by a person who speaks from his or her own viewpoint, which will inevitably reflect that person's position and ideologies. Proficient readers are aware of the perspective from which a text is written, and they think, "What views are represented, what voices are heard, in this account? What voices have been silenced? Whose views haven't been revealed?"

Until now, your students will mostly have been reading the mainstream story of the American Revolution. Some texts may have presented two sides of a controversy—after all, that the British wanted to levy a tax to reimburse themselves for expenses caused by the French and Indian War—but your students will probably have identified wholeheartedly with the colonists' story, and won't have taken other perspectives to heart.

In this bend, you will teach your students that responsible historians go in search of as much information on a topic as they can—seeking to gather up all the facts they can before weighing in and taking a stance of their own. In this way, you will send a clear message about the importance of being active, not passive, readers of nonfiction. Use the strands "Analyzing Perspective" and "Cross Text(s) Synthesis" to help you push students. Remember that fourth-graders can recognize if an author is writing as if he or she were present at an event (a firsthand source) or not present (a secondhand source), and use that knowledge to help them see the resulting difference in points of view.

In the world of 21st century literacy, students must learn to be critical readers, giving careful consideration to alternate points of view and understanding that any one account of a topic or an event will be limited. Standards emphasize that students in fourth grade must compare and contrast first- and secondhand accounts of events or topics. Today's session will seek to help students with this work.

During Session 13, students will draw on the skills you teach them today, and over the next several days, as they debate whether or not the colonies should declare independence. We've designed Session 13 as a celebration, where families and administrators are invited in to experience the debate. You'll want to look ahead to this session to start planning for the logistics of this event.

Recognizing Different Point of View

CONNECTION

Share an anecdote about a time in which you only heard half of a story because you only listened to one person's viewpoint. Encourage kids to think about why that could be a problem.

"Readers, I overheard a big argument in the cafeteria yesterday between two of my former students, Nikki and Peter. Peter told me all about it. 'Nikki was being totally greedy, taking food from my plate,' he said. I glared at Nikki. She tried to speak but I stopped her. 'You don't need to explain, Nikki. I heard *all* about it. I know *exactly* what happened because Peter explained it to me. I've made up my mind what I feel about the whole thing.'"

I looked at the class and said, "What would the rest of you say to that?"

From all corners, students pitched in: "No fair! You can't just listen to Peter. You need to listen to Nikki too." "You should ask others who saw the argument too. They could tell you what they saw."

I nodded. "Exactly. So here is my question to you, and I'm going to ask you to think and not talk about your answer. Why did I start not just a minilesson, but an entire bend in our unit, with that story about an argument during lunch?"

I left some silence.

We picked this anecdote because most children will identify with having a grown-up not understand their side of a story. Use your tone and gesture, as you narrate this story, to make obvious how your judgment was unfair to the unheard Nikki.

❖ **Name the teaching point.**

"Today I want to teach you that historians always keep in mind that every account of history is told from a particular perspective, highlighting a particular side of the story. Just as we needed to seek out all sides of the story about the argument in the cafeteria, historians seek out all sides of the stories they research, and they realize there are always multiple points of view."

When you let students in on the rationale behind your teaching once in a while, it makes your teaching even more memorable.

TEACHING

Tell about visiting an art class, seeing many artists paint the same still life differently, using this as a metaphor to reinforce your point about the role of perspective in history.

"I recently walked into a high school art class. The students were busy at their easels doing what is called a still-life sketch. This means they put some objects on a podium in the center of the room, and everyone sat around those objects and sketched what they saw. So there were about twenty artists, sitting around a collection of a pear, a red apple, and a green bottle, quietly sketching.

"But here's the strange thing. As I tiptoed around the room, eyeing every artist's easel, even though everyone was drawing the exact same apple, pear, and bottle, they saw different sides of the same thing—because they were sitting in different spots. And it wasn't just that. Their sketching style, the shadows they noted, even the size and scale of each person's sketch was different. One artist had shaded brown, orange, and green into the red of his apple, another had managed to make that ordinary green bottle look a bit spooky."

Stress that every historical account is told from a particular perspective. Encourage readers to notice when they read only one side of the story and to seek out the voices they have yet to hear.

"Noticing how each of those artists saw the same subject differently reminded me that whenever any of us have been reading an account of a historical event, it is crucial that we pause, and think, 'What is this person's unique perspective? Who else might share that same perspective?' Then if we realize that some of our sources leave out one or more perspectives, we can deliberately set out to hear the voices of people we haven't been listening to, to imagine the viewpoints of people whose shoes we haven't stood in. My thought is that this is exactly the state of affairs for much of the research you have been doing.

"Think back to the presentation you made at the end of Bend I about what you have learned this far. How much weight did you give to the Loyalists' point of view on the American Revolution? Talk to someone near you about what you are thinking."

Channel students to examine a second account of the Boston Massacre, one that shows the event from a very different viewpoint than the one they examined earlier.

I showed the Paul Revere engraving students had seen in Session 7. "Let's start by returning to the engraving of the Boston Massacre that Paul Revere made. For just a second, will you think about what you know of Paul Revere? Think about how Revere's perspective might have influenced the way he depicted the Boston Massacre. Talk with each other about your thoughts."

I overheard some kids say that they knew Paul Revere rode to warn the colonists that the Redcoats were coming, but they weren't sure how that influenced his image of the Boston Massacre. Then I said, "I'm going to read aloud a different primary source about the Boston Massacre. This one is an account made by Captain Preston, a British officer who

To refresh your students' memories about the Boston Massacre, you may wish to have them read (or reread) "The Wigmaker's Boy and the Boston Massacre," available in the online resources. This article will give students a good overview of the Boston Massacre before they begin to examine different perspectives. (Indeed, the book this article is from, Short Nonfiction for American History: The American Revolution and Constitution, *by Anne Goudvis and Stephanie Harvey [Heinemann: 2015], is an excellent resource for lessons and primary sources throughout this unit.)*

was arrested after the Boston Massacre and charged with murder." I put a copy of Captain Preston's testimony on the document camera.

"It's now October 1770, more than seven months after the Boston Massacre. Captain Preston, a British army officer, begins to give his account in court. Let's listen to his words, then think about what his perspective on the Boston Massacre was."

> *At this time I was between the soldiers and the mob, . . . [trying] to persuade them to retire peaceably, but to no purpose. . . . While I was thus speaking, one of the soldiers having received a severe blow with a stick, stepped a little on one side and instantly fired. . . . I was struck with a club on my arm, . . . [that if it had] been placed on my head, most probably would have destroyed me.*
>
> *On this, a general attack was made on the men by a great number of heavy clubs and snowballs being thrown at them . . . All our lives were in imminent danger, some persons at the same time from behind calling out, . . ."why don't you fire?" Instantly three or four of the soldiers fired, one after another, and directly after three more in the same confusion and hurry. The mob then ran away, except three unhappy men who instantly [died] . . . one more is since dead, three others are dangerously, and four slightly wounded. The whole of this melancholy affair was transacted in almost 20 minutes. On my asking the soldiers why they fired without orders, they said they heard the word fire and supposed it came from me. This might be the case, as many of the mob called out "fire, fire," but I assured the men that I gave no such order; that my words were, "don't fire, stop your firing."*

"So, how did Captain Preston, a British officer, see the Boston Massacre? Who did he think was at fault?" I modeled looking closely at the text, giving students a few moments to think.

Jose spoke up, "It's not really clear. He said he didn't know who ordered the soldiers to fire."

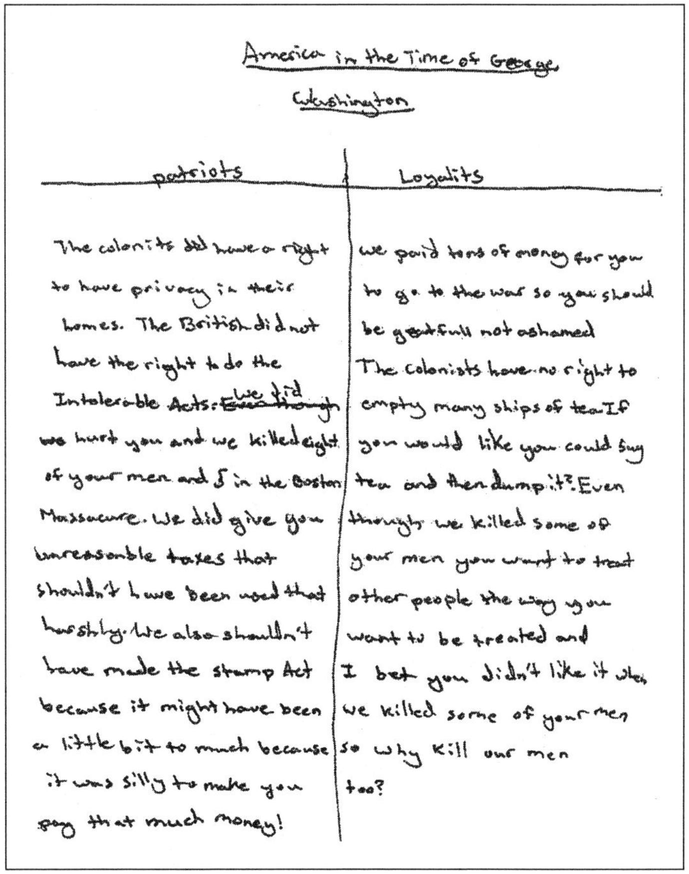

America in the Time of George Washington

patriots	Loyalits
The colonits did have a right to have privacy in their homes. The British did not have the right to do the Intolerable Acts. ~~Even though~~ we did we hurt you and we killed eight of your men and 5 in the Boston Massacure. We did give you unreasonble taxes that shouldn't have been used that harshly. We also shouldn't have made the stamp Act because it might have been a little bit to much because it was silly to make you pay that much money!	we paid tons of money for you to go to the war so you should be gratfull not ashamed The colonists have no right to empty many ships of tea. If you would like you could buy tea and then dump it?. Even though we killed some of your men you want to treat other people the way you want to be treated and I bet you didn't like it when we killed some of your men so why kill our men too?

FIG. 10–1 Student work that shows two different points of view

Maria replied, "But I think he blames the colonists. They were the ones hitting the soldiers with clubs and snowballs. He said he thought his life was in danger."

"What words did Preston use that suggest he thought he was in danger?" As kids called out phrases, I underlined them: *received a severe blow with a stick*, *probably would have destroyed me*, *our lives were in imminent danger*.

"And how did Preston show that he thought he wasn't to blame?" Kids called out phrases, and I underlined them in a different color: *trying to persuade them to retire peaceably*, *I gave no such order*; *my words were, "don't fire, stop your firing."*

Conclude by reiterating the importance of considering multiple perspectives.

"So researchers, my bigger point is that there is always more than one viewpoint of an event or a situation. When you are examining a primary source, you read it first for the main ideas. But once you have established those ideas, it is also helpful to reread, as we have learned in prior lessons, and to pay attention to the details that reveal the point of view of the author of that primary source. After all, if you only understand one side of a story, you may only understand half the story."

ACTIVE ENGAGEMENT

Display another account of the Boston Massacre, written from the British perspective, and channel students to analyze the viewpoint in this account.

"Researchers, you just analyzed an account of the Boston Massacre that provides a different viewpoint than Revere's image did. Will you now read this accounting of the Boston Massacre, and see if you can use this account, combined with Captain Preston's account that you just studied, to construct what the British might have said about the Boston Massacre?" I displayed a copy of "Boston Riot" on the document camera.

Boston Riot

From the beginning, the British soldiers were met with hostility by many Boston residents. Soldiers were insulted or beaten on the streets. These actions angered the soldiers, who only wanted to be let alone to do their jobs. Some retaliated by harassing the colonists.

On the night of March 5, 1770, things came to a head. In front of the Customs House, a crowd of people were yelling and throwing rocks, sticks, and icy snowballs at several soldiers. Someone yelled, "Fire!" which the soldiers took as an order, firing on the crowd. Five Boston residents died, and six others were wounded.

I gave students a few moments to talk about how this account was similar to Preston's account. Jose mentioned, "This account says that colonists were hostile to the soldiers and treated them badly, which is what Preston said, too." Nikki agreed and added, "And both accounts say that no one knows who gave the order for the soldiers to fire."

I said, "You'll remember that at the start of this minilesson, I suggested I could learn all about the problems between Nikki and Peter in the cafeteria by talking to Peter and getting just his side of the story. You reminded me that I needed to talk to Nikki as well, and to bystanders. By examining Paul Revere's image of the Boston Massacre and Captain Preston's account, plus reading this new account of it, you are beginning to understand more than one side of the Boston Massacre story."

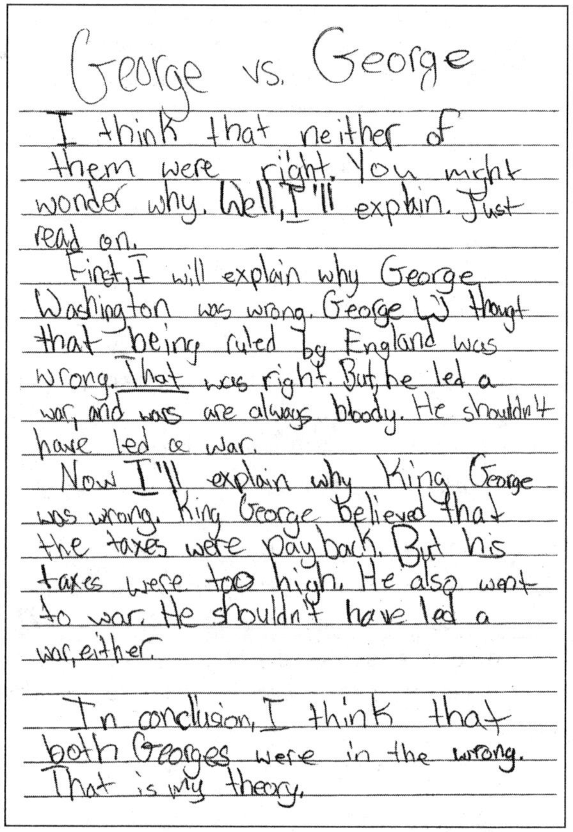

The work here supports the work of the Common Core standards as well as the National Social Studies Standards. Both of those standards address the importance of readers looking at two sides of a story—in other words, multiple perspectives. You are also helping readers see the relationships between texts. This is challenging work and will continue to be the focus of a good deal of instruction over the upcoming year. So we do not expect students to become experts at this yet.

George vs. George

I think that neither of them were right. You might wonder why. Well, I'll explain. Just read on.

First, I will explain why George Washington was wrong. George W. thougt that being ruled by England was wrong. That was right. But he led a war, and wars are always bloody. He shouldn't have led a war.

Now I'll explain why King George was wrong. King George believed that the taxes were payback. But his taxes were too high. He also went to war. He shouldn't have led a war, either.

In conclusion, I think that both Georges were in the wrong. That is my theory.

FIG. 10–2   A student considers two points of view to come up with her own theory.

Give students a way to consolidate the contrasting stories of the Boston Massacre as told from the perspectives of the colonists or the British soldiers.

"Right now, just to pull this together, will you and your partner list across your right hand, what the colonists' story was of the Boston Massacre? Contrast that with, on your left hand, the perspective that a British soldier might have."

Around the room, children held up their right hands and started counting off. "The British fired without warning. The British were plotting a massacre, colonists were killed, Captain Preston is in jail because of this." Then on their left hands, they listed, "A mob of colonists attacked the soldiers with clubs. The colonists threatened the British with names and snowballs. Captain Preston did not order the British to fire. Nobody knows who fired first."

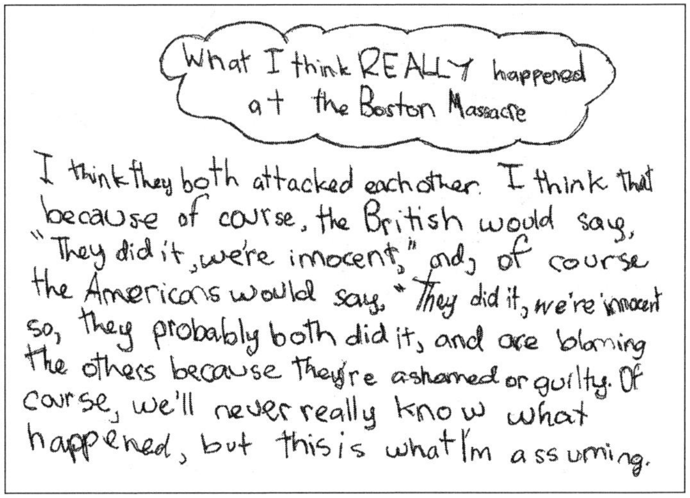

LINK

Spur kids on to continue their reading, this time with a focus on the British perspective on the Boston Massacre.

"So researchers, today what I have done is to set out some resources that you can read—and I am asking you to have one objective in mind. This is it: piece together the other side of the story.

"You can decide if you want to read secondary sources—that is, chapters and articles that tell about the British perspective—or if you want to continue reading primary sources that reflect the British point of view. Or you may decide you want to return to texts you already read and this time, reread them, deliberately trying to hear the rationale that may have been hinted at for the other point of view."

What I think REALLY happened at the Boston Massacre

I think they both attacked each other. I think that because of course, the British would say, "They did it, we're innocent," and, of course the Americans would say, "They did it, we're innocent." So, they probably both did it, and are blaming the others because they're ashamed or guilty. Of course, we'll never really know what happened, but this is what I'm assuming.

FIG. 10-3

Allow your readers to make the choice from the multiple resources you have selected. Make sure the resources you pick are on reading levels the students can comprehend and understand.

Recognizing How Word Choice Reveals Perspective

YOU CAN REMIND STUDENTS that when they were studying weather, they thought about the author's point of view or perspective, noticing that it can found in the words the authors chose, the examples they selected, and the ways they used text features and illustrations to make a reader think or feel a certain way about a topic. All of this is true for depictions of historical events as well.

You might convene a small group to analyze a short text together. You could work with the students' own topics, or you could continue to take the Boston Massacre as a case in point. For example, you might distribute this description of the Boston Massacre. You might ask that when students read it, they note the word choice, realizing the author could have used different words. "Will you think about why the author used the

MID-WORKSHOP TEACHING   Understanding How Perspective Can Shape a Primary Source

"Readers, I want to remind you that when you read primary sources, one of the first questions you need to ask is, 'Who wrote this? What perspective or point of view did that person bring to the topic?' As fourth graders, you really need to understand perspective or point of view. I've got something behind my back. I'm going to position three of you differently, and ask you to tell us, from your perspective, from your point of view, what you see."

I positioned one student straight in front of me, one off to the side, one directly behind me, and I held a fireman's hat behind my back, letting just the red lip of it poke out on the side of me. I called on the child in front of me. "From your point of view, from your perspective, what do I have behind my back?" The child had no clue. The child to the side of me guessed "something red." The person behind me pronounced that it was a hat.

"Researchers, do you see how simply by changing the position people were viewing an object from, they had completely different ideas about what that object was?

Right now, think about the last day of school—and tell what people feel about it. Tell your perspective, your Mom's perspective."

Kids did this, quickly, and then I said, "It is important for you to know if the primary source you are reading was written by a man or a woman, by a colonist or a Native American or a British person.

"That is important for you to know because there were lots of different people who lived during the time of the American Revolution. You could ask, 'Whose revolution was it?' And what you will find is that depending on who these people were and what their positions were, they saw different parts of the American Revolution—and those different parts had different meanings to them.

"Right now, will you tell your partner the point of view or the perspective of the text you have been reading today? Then wrestle with this important question. 'How would the text be different had it been written from a different point of view?'"

words she did? How did the author's word choice reveal something about her overall purpose?" you can say.

A Massacre in Boston

At times citizens and soldiers fought. The worst violence came March 5, 1770. In front of the Custom House, British guard Private Hugh White was arguing with colonist Edward Garrick. Soon a crowd of angry colonists gathered in support of Garrick, hurling taunts of "bloody lobster back" and "lousy rascal."

The Americans didn't just toss insults at the guard on duty that cold March night. The growing crowd pelted the soldier with chunks of ice. More soldiers rushed to the scene, and the crowd threw snowballs and sticks at them. Someone shouted, "Fire!" and the soldiers fired their guns into the shouting mob. Three men fell dead to the ground. Two of eight others who were wounded died later in what the Patriots called the Boston Massacre. Eight British soldiers and a captain were arrested and later tried on murder charges. All but two were acquitted.

You might ask the reader to notice how the events are described. Perhaps one of them will point out that the way the event is described, it seems that the citizens started it.

They might say, "It's interesting that the author tells all about all of the bad things the citizens were doing—like yelling bad names at the soldier and pelting them with chunks of ice." You could suggest the readers look at the precise words that the author uses. For example, you could point to the phrase *chunks of ice*. You might say, "I wonder why the author didn't say they were throwing snowballs?" Students will agree that *chunks of ice* makes what the citizens did sound intentionally hurtful.

Suggest students continue reading, paying attention to every little detail. When they finish reading, you can channel them to analyze it with their partners. "What did you notice in our second read-through?"

Some of them will have noticed that the author uses words like *taunts* and *pelted*—words that suggest the colonists were very aggressive. The fact that the text says that someone called out, "Fire!" which then caused the soldiers to fire their weapons makes it sound like the soldiers are just following orders rather than like they were firing on unarmed citizens. You might ask, "Why might the author want you to think the soldiers were just following orders? How is that part of the author's overall purpose?"

Reading to Think about Two Sides of a Story

Ask students to share ways their research now has made them have new understandings of the events leading to the American Revolution.

"Will you share your research and how your thinking is changing as a result of your research?" I said, and organized the students into five or six discussion groups, so that kids could talk with students outside of their own research teams.

After students talked for a bit, I convened the class. "I'm hearing some of you say, 'I've been thinking about how differently I see things now. Before, I'd thought that Britain was just a bully, but now I'm coming to realize that there were two sides to that story. I'm thinking that I need to really weigh both versions of this time period, thinking about who really was the bully—or even if there was a bully. And I'm also wondering if there could have been a way to settle the conflict peacefully.

"Will you take a few minutes and jot your thoughts in your notebook?"

SESSION 10 HOMEWORK

 IDENTIFYING AND COMPARING PERSPECTIVES

Readers, as you've been reading primary and secondary sources, you've noticed some connections between them. You've also begun to notice some contradictions. Sometimes, the most significant differences are in the perspectives of the authors. Tonight, you'll have an opportunity to look more closely at differences of perspective.

Read both "Tea Troubles: The Boston Tea Party" and *Tea Drinking in 18th-Century America: Its Etiquette and Equipage*. Then look at them side by side, and think, "Do these authors have similar points of view? Do they have different ones? And how do I know?" Use your copy of the "Analyzing Perspective" strand of the progression to identify and compare the perspective of each author. Can you do that at the fourth-grade level? Can you stretch to do it at the fifth-grade level?

Also, keep reading your independent books. You want to keep your reading volume high! Be sure to record how much you read on your reading log.

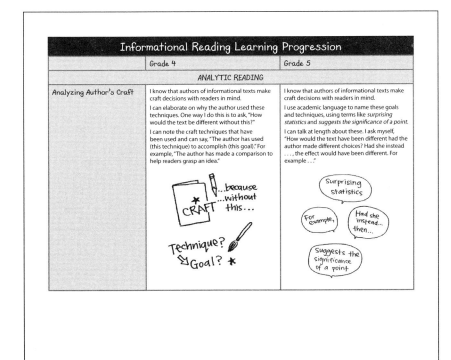

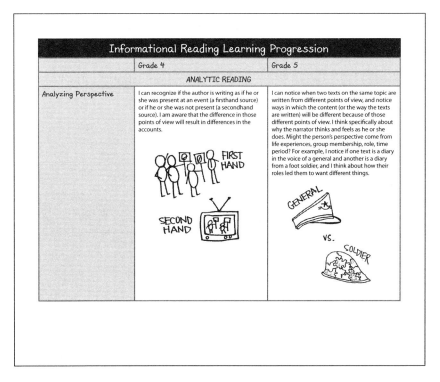

Readers Find—and Angle—
Evidence to Support Their Claim

IN THIS SESSION, you'll teach students that readers study historical evidence to determine their own point of view, and then they analyze the evidence to figure out how to make it support their point of view.

GETTING READY

✔ Display the image of *King George III in coronation robes*. A link to this image is available in the online resources (see Teaching).

✔ Prepare a template to help students figure out how to spin evidence to support their argument, "Ways to Spin Evidence to Fit Your Argument" (see Teaching).

✔ Project the **image** of a woman hugging her husband as he heads off to war for students to analyze for perspective. A link to this image is available in the online resources (see Active Engagement).

✔ Create a chart of prompts that support students explaining why evidence seems important (see Conferring and Small-Group Work).

✔ Display Benjamin Franklin's "Join, or Die" cartoon. A link to this cartoon is available in the online resources (see Conferring and Small-Group Work).

THIS SESSION BEGINS a two-day progression of work that culminates in your students reenacting the Second Continental Congress debates about independence. In May of 1775, delegates from the thirteen colonies convened in Philadelphia. Their meeting was prompted by the outbreak of military encounters between Patriots and the British army; the Battles of Lexington and Concord took place less than a month before the meeting began. Your students will step into history and become delegates to this Congress. At the Congress they will debate the question "Should the colonies become independent from Great Britain?" Just as at the Continental Congress itself, you will have students who come down on either side of this issue.

Starting today, students will read with their role in mind—Patriot or Loyalist. Even though the previous lesson allowed students to revisit the causes of the revolution from the point of view of the Loyalists, most of your students will likely be inclined to side with the Patriots. To ensure that enough students argue from a Loyalist perspective, explain that the most skilled debaters are those who can argue from a point of view not necessarily their own. Then, ask for volunteers to take on the role of a Loyalist. If not enough students volunteer, counsel them into becoming a Loyalist through a conversation during lunch or at recess. You may choose to encourage your strongest readers to take on this role. Though they may be initially reluctant to take on the side of the British, the engaging work of debate, argumentation, and stepping into character will soon overshadow their momentary reluctance.

After you have assigned roles, you will need to teach students to read with their role in mind, gathering evidence that supports their case. Today's minilesson begins this work. Students will need to look at primary and secondary sources asking of themselves, "Can I use this to support my argument?" or "How can I angle this document to support my idea?"

Some might say that teaching students to spin evidence to make a case means teaching them to engage in slippery practices. Yet in the digital age, where students are flooded with information from innumerable sources, students must learn that even seemingly unassailable statistics are employed to support the stories that authors wish to tell. By teaching students to read with the goal of supporting their argument, you will make students more discerning about what they read in the world around them.

"Students must learn that even seemingly unassailable statistics are employed to support the stories that authors wish to tell."

You will want to carefully evaluate how far your students have come by the conclusion of today's session. By the share of Session 12, your students will be asked to debate the question they begin researching today, providing strong reasons and evidence to support their position. You may find you need to add in an additional day between these two sessions for students to continue research and angle evidence to support their claims. This additional time will be particularly beneficial for your students who are arguing as Loyalists, as they are likely newer to researching this position.

Readers Find—and Angle—Evidence to Support Their Claim

CONNECTION

Introduce students to the Second Continental Congress, and suggest that they'll need to be looking for information with their role in mind.

"Readers, today is an exciting day for us. I want to announce to you that two days from now, we will be staging our own Second Continental Congress. Each of you is going to become either a Loyalist or a Patriot and debate the question, 'Should the colonies become independent from Great Britain?'

"To do this, you're going to need to take up the role of either a Loyalist or a Patriot delegate to the Congress. It will be challenging to argue the side of the Loyalists. Can I see some volunteers who are willing to do that challenging work?" After half a dozen students volunteered, I channeled a few others to join them, so soon half the class had agreed to argue for each side of the debate.

"Preparing for the Continental Congress will be almost like a crash course of law school.

"Most people think that lawyers just stand up and speak eloquently. But the true secret to winning cases—as all great lawyers know—is knowing what to do with the evidence. They kind of look at something—maybe it's a scrap of hair stuck to the wall, or a fingerprint and first think, 'Geez, this is never going to help me!' But then they stand back for a moment, and ask themselves the key question: 'How can I use this itty-bitty piece of evidence—this scrap of hair—to make my point? How can I make this fit the argument I'm trying to make?'"

♣ Name the teaching point.

"Readers, today I want to teach you that readers look at historical evidence and ask themselves 'What does this tell me? What can I make of this?' And if you have looked at enough evidence to decide on your point of view, the question becomes: 'How can I use this to support my point of view?'"

Deliver this introduction with both enthusiasm and gravity. If you do, expect that students will be turning to each other with smiles of excitement. They may even begin chanting "Go, Patriots!" If they do, let them exult for a moment as you smile at their delight, then motion when it's time to return to the task at hand.

At this point, you might straighten your back, to make the lawyer character come alive for the kids.

TEACHING

Use an anecdote to show how readers might angle evidence to support their idea, then demonstrate how they might do this with a primary source document.

"Readers, when reading fiction, you developed theories about the characters and the books, and then you read on with that theory as a lens. If your theory was, 'Rob learns that he shouldn't hold things in, he should talk about them,' then you'd read a bit of the story—say about the rash that he had—and you'd think, 'Could this rash relate in any way to my theory that it is toxic for Rob to hold his sadness in? *Might* the rash be a way to show that the sickness a person holds in ends up coming out in other ways?'

"When you did that work, you took something—the rash—that definitely didn't at first glance appear to be about Rob holding in his sadness, and because you were looking through the lens of that theory, you thought, '*Might* this possibly go with my theory? Could I use this as evidence?' People even word that a little differently, saying, 'Could I *spin* that as evidence?' to acknowledge that the reader has to make the evidence fit the argument.

"I'm telling you that because for the next two days, you'll be reading material that includes primary source materials about the American Revolution. You'll be reading with your theory in mind—which for some of you is that the colonies *should* declare independence from Great Britain, and for others, your theory will be, 'No, we should ask for other things, but remain as part of the British Empire.' Now here's the challenge: The materials you read won't come tagged 'This is evidence for the Patriots' position' (or the Loyalists' Position), any more than the rash in *The Tiger Rising* came tagged as evidence for the theory that Rob needed to stop holding in his grief. Your job will be to read the material through your lens and to think, 'Might I be able to use this as evidence in my side of the debate?'"

Channel readers to study a seemingly irrelevant picture and to look from a particular angle. Show that you can spin material to turn it into evidence for your side of the debate.

"Right now, let's study this image as if we are all looking from the Patriots' point of view. Think about what you see and think, and about what I see and think. You'll notice that I keep my argument in mind and look for ways I can make the image fit my argument."

I displayed an image of King George III, wrapped in coronation robes made of mink.

"Hmm," I said to myself, studying the image intently. "Let's see. This is King George III. I know he's the King of England at the time of the American Revolution. So I guess that image is not for me, since it's the Loyalists who want him as their king, not me. I'm on the Patriots side." I started to take the image off the document camera. Then I paused, my hand in midair for a moment, clutching the image.

"Hang on," I said. "I need to remember that often the material doesn't come with a sign on it 'Good for This Side' or 'Good for That Side.' It sometimes depends on how the material is spun. Let me look again and think some more. How can I use this to support my point of view?"

Remember to channel students to consider both sides of the event when they pick the evidence that helps them prove either the Loyalists' side or the Patriots.

> The Colonies should have stayed with England because they would be weak because the Colonies were nothing compared to England without the british The indian attacks could start again they would get captured and become slaves and things would just get worse they could starve and other countries might try to invade the 13 colonies and the patriots wouldn't be able to protect themselves. Thats why I and the British think the colonists would be weak without the British

FIG. 11–1

Again, I looked at the picture. "I notice something about King George III here. He's wearing these fancy robes on his shoulders. I think they could be mink, and that is *expensive*. The robes also have gold trim. I'm trying to prove that the British don't actually need the colonists' money, that the French and Indian War hasn't destituted them, and that they just want to tax the colonists so they can spend more money on themselves. So I'm beginning to wonder if I could use this image to support my point. . . ."

I looked up into the air, thinking and leaving time for kids to think. In short order, kids' hands were shooting into the air. I asked for their input and one said, "You could show the photo as an *example* of the British spending lavishly on themselves, and say that's why they needed to take money from the colonies."

Debrief in ways that accentuate the replicable and transferable nature of what you and the kids have been doing.

Nodding, I recapped for the students what we'd done. "Did you see how I almost let that image go, because at first glance, it looked like evidence for the other side? But then I realized that I could spin it to fit an argument I want to make *against* the British. You'll want to look for opportunities do similar work with whatever you read. "Here is a template that you can follow to help you figure out how to spin the evidence to support your argument."

ACTIVE ENGAGEMENT

Channel students to analyze a second image, this time from the Loyalists' perspective.

"Now it's your turn to try this without any help from me. Here's another image. Will you try thinking from the Loyalists' perspective?" I said and displayed another image, this one which showed a woman hugging her husband as he heads off to war. "If you were a Loyalist, how would you use this in your argument against splitting up from Britain? Use the template I made to help you structure your thinking."

As students talked to their partners, I called out reminders. "Remember, keep your argument in mind as you study this image," and "Use the smallest details to your advantage," and "Try thinking, 'They could have . . . but instead they . . .'"

LINK

Invite students to continue their research, considering how each piece of evidence they examine could support their argument.

"Readers, when you head off to do your research today, know that you have just today and tomorrow to prepare for your side of the debate. You'll want to make sure to have plenty of evidence to support your argument. As you are reading your texts, always keep in mind the perspective of the people you are representing. Remember to use the template I made to support you in this work. At the end of today, you'll be able to caucus with others who share your same perspective and show each other some of the evidence you have collected for your debate thus far. Get started!"

> *Ways to Spin Evidence to Fit Your Argument*
>
> This (document type: painting/letter/ advertisement) shows _____.
>
> I notice that _____.
>
> It could support my argument because _____.

Searching for Evidence to Support a Position

THE WORK OF TODAY'S SESSION is very challenging. Not only are students reading densely packed primary and secondary sources, trying to glean their meaning and purpose, but now we are asking them to extract evidence from these sources to support a particular viewpoint. So you may find that some students need reminders about how to read these difficult sources to understand them, while others might benefit from support in reflecting upon the significance of details.

Have students do close reading and analyzing of primary sources.

Remind students that they can apply what know about close reading of texts to primary sources. To build their knowledge of their subtopics, students have been rereading and reexamining a variety of texts carrying different lenses, such as rereading to find main idea and author's purpose. As they look closely at their primary sources, students could also reread looking for information, then reread the same text looking for patterns. Each time they read the texts students are learning to see more than if they just read the text through once.

If students struggle to understand the content, purpose, or perspective of a primary source, remind them about the questions they need to ask of a primary source, to understand the meaning and significance of the document. This is true for visual sources as well as for text sources. I pulled a chair next to George, who was looking at a political cartoon with a puzzled look on his face, clearly having trouble trying to figure out what it meant. "I see you have an old political cartoon. What do you notice about it?" I asked. He said, "It's a snake cut up into pieces, and it says 'Join, or die.' But I don't know what it means, or which side of the argument it goes with."

"I can see why you might be puzzled. But look carefully at the details. What are those letters on each segment of the snake?" George replied, "I see N.Y. and N.J. Are those New York and New Jersey? Maybe that means these other ones are the other colonies."

MID-WORKSHOP TEACHING
Readers Build Their Case with Plenty of Evidence

"Readers, can I have your eyes and ears for a second?" Once students were attentive, I continued. "I want to tell you about a bit of news I just heard." I removed a note from my pocket, and read it aloud. "Dear Colleague," I read, "Tomorrow, there are going to be record rains in the area. It will be the greatest rainfall since 1920."

The kids looked startled for a moment. I said, "What do you think is the best thing to do next?"

"Think about the risk of flooding," suggested one student. "Cancel school," suggested another. Finally Joselen said, "I'd find out who said that and if it is true."

"Good call," I said. "There is a lot of misinformation flying around this world. So how would you find out if this is a credible forecast?"

"I'd ask you where you got that information?"

"I'd ask my mom if she heard the same thing," Angela said.

"I'd go to weather.com," mentioned Jose. "Or maybe watch the weather report on TV."

"What you've just done," I said to them, "is that you have recognized that researching the credibility of a source is key. And one thing many of you are saying is that just reading something in one source isn't reliable. To make a strong argument, you need to speak with the power of many sources behind you. As you continue your research today, keep that mind as you gather sources to make your case."

FIG. 11–2

"I think you're on to something. So if all of the parts of the snake represent colonies, what does the caption 'Join, or Die' mean?" I said. George replied, "Hmm, . . . I think it means the colonies need to join together, that they won't survive if they don't."

"Good thinking. Now remind me, who made this cartoon?" George looked back and said, "Ben Franklin. And I know he's a Patriot, so this is definitely some evidence I can use for my side of the debate."

I left George with a quick reminder of the transferrable work he had done. "Remember George, anytime you're studying a primary source, it helps to ask questions about what you see and who made the source. These questions can help you understand the significance of the source."

Challenge students to reflect on evidence found in primary sources.

As students study their primary sources, you will probably see them becoming more skilled at noticing the details in primary sources, whether they are studying images, letters, or paintings. So the challenge for them may not be so much in what they see, but in reflecting on the significance of the evidence they find in their primary sources, especially in the ones that seem at first one sided. If this is the case, you can teach students that one way to develop a key point is to find direct quotes in primary sources that highlight, support, or illustrate the key point.

Remind them that it is important to explain why that quote, image, description, or word seems important. You can also encourage them to do this by offering additional prompts to help spark their thinking:

- This fits with my theory because . . .

- Most people might say . . . but I say . . .

- Could it also mean . . . ?

- What you just said is making me realize . . .

- Another way to look at this is . . .

- At first I thought . . . but now I'm starting to think that actually . . .

Your students will probably need you to prompt them to reread their primary documents to make their case using the evidence they find. For more support you might have partnerships do this work together.

Readers Select Their Strongest Evidence

Channel students to review all of their evidence, selecting the strongest pieces of evidence to support their position.

"Readers, a strong position is bolstered by lots of evidence. It is also bolstered by selecting the strongest evidence. These are the pieces of evidence that will knock your opponents socks off and drive the decision in your favor. You can do this by looking over your notes and selecting the *best*, the most compelling, pieces of information to support your position.

"Lay out all the pieces of evidence that you have to support your position." I gave the students a moment to do so and then continued, "Now rank them from strongest to weakest. You might think of it as a race. Which piece of evidence would take first place? Second? Third?" Some students moved their notes around, creating a line of evidence going from strongest to weakest. Others added numbers to their notebook pages. "Turn and explain to your partner why you put your evidence in that order. You might think, 'What makes this piece so compelling?'

"Once you evaluate the strength of your evidence, you decide what to include in your argument and what to leave out. With a partner, talk about which of the pieces you would keep and which you would leave out. Remember you want to select the strongest pieces of evidence to ensure your position is compelling." I gave the students time to turn and talk, listening into the conversations and then reconvened the class.

"Tomorrow you will debate. Remember that you'll want to state a strong position and support that position with several pieces of strong, compelling evidence. If you think you need to find stronger evidence than what you have now, you have tonight to research."

Loyalists side
colonists should remain loyal to england
• No trading system without england
• England has better army
• makes them weathey en
• well known power
"slaverys is the same thing as liberty"-

   I think this means that when your not conecteel with england you don't just get things you have to work for it. (like slaves)
• treaty wouldn't be true
• fair because

FIG. 11–3

Patriot Side
colonists should be independent from england

• shut down the boston harbor
• how can you rule someone from far away
• treaty's would be gone
• doesn't let colonies have voice in desitions
• unfair laws

"Even animals do not eat their young"-

   I think this means that england is like an animal and it's devoring the 13 colonies money.
• saposed to be place for freedom

FIG. 11–4

PLANNING TO DEFEND

Readers, today you learned how to select evidence from your sources to support your position. You remembered that there are always at least two sides to every story. And you remembered that everyone has their own viewpoint on events—even people who lived long ago, in the past.

Tonight, continue to think about the arguments that can be made for your side in this debate. Whether you are representing a Patriot or a Loyalist, how would the people on your side have viewed the coming conflict? What was their perspective? And how can you represent that perspective with the evidence you have gathered? In our next session, you will be speaking out. You will use your evidence to try to convince others to take your side.

Don't forget to keep up with your independent reading tonight. Be sure to log your reading when you have finished.

Session 12

Rehearsing a Debate

I N THE FIRST UNIT of this series, students debated *The Tiger Rising*, looking at the complexity of Rob, Sistine, and their relationship. During that work, they learned to form debatable, provocative ideas, take a position, and support that position with evidence—in particular, evidence that was most compelling. Today's session will build upon that work. For today's debate, the idea has already been developed and posed, and students have already taken a position and conducted research to support that position. Therefore the work of today will be to carry what they have learned about debate into nonfiction, organizing their evidence by reasons, and then thinking about the order in which they will present those reasons. Tomorrow's session extends this work, and you'll ask students to bring their strongest reasons and evidence from their initial debates with a partner into a whole-class debate. This work is high energy and incredibly powerful, but it requires some advance preparation, so we recommend previewing Session 13 prior to today's workshop.

To engage in debate, one must know a lot about the topic. Your students have been researching the American Revolution for a couple of weeks now, and those who are taking the side of the Patriots should have the information at their fingertips to successfully put forth a strong and compelling argument. Those who are taking on the side of the Loyalists, however, are in earlier stages of their research and might need some additional time to gather evidence. You could use your read aloud as a time to bolster their knowledge base, or, you might decide to add in an additional day of research and preparation prior to this session.

When you and your students are ready, think strategically about your timing. While you will want students to have ample time to reread their sources and notes to prepare, the main event is the debate itself, so you'll want to be sure that you get to the share with plenty of time to do so. This will likely mean that your share will be longer than usual.

IN THIS SESSION, you'll teach students that debaters research both sides of an issue to present their position effectively with reasons and evidence and rebut the position of their opponent.

GETTING READY

✔ Display the "Tips for Being a Great Debater: Moves that Pay Off in Arguments" chart to help students finalize their debate plans (see Teaching).

✔ Have read-aloud texts and familiar images accessible to model studying texts to determine evidence (see Teaching).

✔ Display the "Phrases to Use in Debates" chart to help students acquire the language to structure their debate (see Active Engagement).

✔ Use markers and chart paper to record the major arguments in a "Loyalist and Patriot Arguments" chart (see Share).

Rehearsing a Debate

CONNECTION

Channel students to reflect on their experience with debate from an earlier unit, then tell them that readers can use many of the same techniques for a debate about nonfiction as about fiction.

"Readers, let's think back to the start of this year when we read *The Tiger Rising*. Do you all remember that?" The students nodded emphatically. "As we read the text, all of you had different ideas about Rob, Sistine, and their relationship. Some of these ideas were quite compelling, so much so that you had to debate with your clubs and defend your thinking. Take a minute and think back on that." I paused.

"Readers of nonfiction can also debate their research topics. There are multiple perspectives inside of a topic or issue, just like there are multiple sides to a character or a relationship. When you see different perspectives, it can be helpful to take those into a debate, stating positions and supporting them with evidence, aiming to persuade the other side."

✤ Name the teaching point.

"Today I want to remind you that when you are debating, you want to be compelling. As a good debater, you'll state a position, give reasons to back up that position, and give evidence to support each of your reasons. A good debater is never wishy-washy!"

TEACHING

Situate today's debate work in the historical context of the American Revolution and remind students of their positions.

"As you know, debates begin with a provocative idea that can be argued from both sides. Our forefathers were confronted with just such an idea. The Second Continental Congress was confronted with the idea that the colonies should become independent from Great Britain. Skirmishes, demonstrations, and massacres were breaking out in the colonies. Tensions between the British and the colonists were at an all-time high. But not all colonists agreed about what needed to be done. A line started to be drawn between those who wanted to work with King George III and Parliament to mend

---

◆ COACHING

Allowing students to recall an activity they've already experienced will help set the tone and expectation for the similar work of today.

Tips for Being a Great Debater: Moves that Pay Off in Arguments

- Take a clear position

- Give reasons to support your position

- Back up each reason with multiple pieces of evidence

the relationship and those who wanted to sever all ties with Great Britain. Both sides fought for their positions through speeches, pamphlets, and even songs.

"Today, you are going to transport yourselves back to that time. You are going to become those colonists and you will debate this idea: 'The colonies should become independent from Great Britain.' Half of you will take the position of the Patriots, arguing in favor of breaking free from Britain. The other half will take the side of the Loyalists, arguing that the colonies should remain part of the British Empire. You already know your positions. Raise your hands if you are a Patriot." I paused as they did and then called out, "Raise your hand if you are a Loyalist." The other half of the class raised their hands.

Provide tips for debate, and demonstrate how to create an evidence-based argument.

"Whether you are a Patriot or a Loyalist, today, you are going to want to put forth your most powerful argument. I have a few tips to help you do this work. These aren't new for you. You used these same moves when debating *The Tiger Rising*." I put up the "Tips for Being a Great Debater: Moves that Pay Off in Arguments" chart.

"It has been awhile since your last debate, so I am going to do this work right now in front of you. I'm going to transport myself back in time and take a position, supporting it with reasons and providing evidence for each reason." I paused and thought for a moment.

"I am a Loyalist, so I take the position that the colonies should remain with Britain." I patted my palm and repeated, "I take the position that the colonies should remain with Britain."

I held up my forefinger and said, "My first reason for this is the British army and navy offer support." I grabbed the read-aloud text and several images and began flipping through them searching for evidence to support that claim. When I found one I looked up and, still holding my first index finger, said, "My evidence for that is the British protected the colonies from certain takeover by the French and Native Americans . . ." I looked back in the text and found another example then said, "Also, it says in *Liberty!* that the British were worried about the colonists and needed the money to help provide the protection and support they needed.

"Jump in and do the second one with me." I put up my second finger and nodded at the class to do the same. Then I said, "My second reason is that the colonists wouldn't be here if it wasn't for the British." I gestured to my notes and the students started flipping through their own. I gave them a minute and then signaled for them to come back together, "My evidence for that is in the book *Liberty!* it clearly states that the colonists were grateful to Britain for bringing them to America and providing them with the protection they needed to survive in a strange new world. Also, . . ." I began and then trailed off. "Turn and talk! What else did you find? Give it a go!"

If your students are not yet aware of their positions, you might need to take some time now to set that up. We recommend setting your stronger students up to take the side of the Loyalists, because it is a more challenging position to defend. Of course, if your students were already assigned roles they could use their evidence gathered for today.

In deciding on the position that you will take in this debate (or any debate you do with your students), try to remember that you want to leave the low-hanging fruit for the kids. Usually one side of the debate will be easier to defend than another, and your instinct will be to take the most obvious position as your own. Don't do that—leave that one for the kids. In this instance, I'm taking the British side, because this was the side that fewer students were apt to see.

While you will want to model looking across texts and notes in the moment to demonstrate what you hope students will later do, you'll want to have several examples at hand and ready to use to keep the teaching tight and lean.

Debrief in a way that accentuates the replicable and transferable nature of what you and the kids have been doing.

"Readers, did you catch those moves? I got us going by stating the position clearly, without any wishy-washy language. Then we worked to name reasons and provide evidence for each reason. And not just one piece of evidence, but several examples directly from the texts to support each reason."

ACTIVE ENGAGEMENT

Set children up to practice stating and supporting positions. Give them phrases that they can use to state and defend their positions.

"Okay, now you're going to give this a go. You've got your position, and you spent yesterday gathering evidence and weighing that evidence to make sure you were picking the strongest, most compelling information. Now, you are going to present your position, reasons, and evidence. There are some phrases that will help you do this work." I pointed to the chart where I'd written some key phrases on chart paper.

After a few minutes I reconvened the class and asked students to share what they had done. "Friends, let's gather together. Right now we're going to listen to Emmanuel as he shares his position. Eyes on him!"

Emmanuel launched into his argument, "I take the position that the colonists were correct in declaring their independence. My first reason for this is that they were taken advantage of, treated as children, and abused by Britain. My evidence for that is that according to history.com, the colonists still loved Britain but realized that they were being taken advantage of. It also said the taxes forced some of them into homelessness and the British government ignored them. In the book *Revolutionary*, it clearly states that the colonists tried to talk to Britain and negotiate, but Britain wouldn't negotiate with the colonists. It also states that Britain began to be more and more aggressive."

LINK

Send students off to read, take notes, and prepare for a flash debate at the end of reading workshop.

"Readers, at the end of today, you are going to debate. You will face your opponent and you will state your position. Remember that you don't want to be wishy-washy! You want a strong position. To do that, you state your position, support it with reasons and provide evidence for each reason.

"You'll want to do plenty more reading and research to ensure that you have your good, solid reasons and evidence ready to go. You may also want to reread notes from yesterday. Make sure you have taken notes in a way that helps you be ready to debate. Head off!"

Phrases to Use in Debates

"I take the position that..."

"My first reason for this is..."
"My evidence for that is..."

"My second reason for this is..."
"My evidence for that is... Also..."

Debate is something that you will see referred to again and again throughout this reading series and across the grades. We thank Kelly Boland for her progression that allows us to see how debate changes and grows throughout the grades. For further information look in the fifth-grade reading series book on argument and debate.

Preparing for Debate

AS YOUR STUDENTS SET OFF to prepare for today's debate, take a moment to observe your students at work. This will give you insight into the small-group work that you will need to lead today. As the debate question has already been formed, and the students have already staked their positions, you will likely find that the majority of your teaching is around the usage of evidence and the structure of argument.

The key to a strong argument is the evidence to bolster it. If students are lacking that evidence, you'll want to spend some time working with them on finding it. You might begin by modeling how you reread parts of a text, using your position as a lens, looking for details that stand out. When you find one, model pulling out words or phrases or quoting direct lines, showing students how to take the information presented directly from the text. Then, push students to do this same work, looking across their texts with their position as a lens, identifying not only parts that support their position but exact facts, lines, or phrases.

For students who have a singular piece of evidence, remind them to look across their sources. You might say, "Readers, remember that you want to bolster your position with multiple pieces of evidence. The best way to do that is to read across all your sources, thinking, 'What can I pull from each one?'" Set the students up to look for information they might use. You might find it helpful to pull upon yesterday's teaching during today's small groups, showing students how to return to images as much as print, thinking about how they can spin what they see to support their position.

You might notice students with lots of evidence who need to sort and categorize that evidence. For these students, you might ask them to sort their evidence into piles. "Think about which pieces of information fit together, then stack them." With stacks formed, they could work with partners to explain why they put each one together. They could say, "These go together because . . . And these go together because. . . ." Once

they create their categories, or reasons, you might prompt them to do a quick round of boxes and bullets in their reading notebooks so they can refer back to it during debate.

You might find that several students would benefit from building off the work done in yesterday's share around ranking evidence and selecting the most compelling. Some students might need additional practice with this skill, laying out their evidence and justifying their rankings to a partner.

For those students who quickly form their reasons and select their pieces of evidence, you might work with them on structuring their argument. You might pull them aside

---

MID-WORKSHOP TEACHING **Anticipating the Counterargument and Planning for Rebuttal**

"Readers, one way to strengthen your position is to anticipate what your opponent will say, and then find ways to debunk, or talk back to, those points. Look back at your texts and your notes to identify what your opponent might say. What reasons might she give? What evidence might she use? Then think about how you could convince someone that your argument is stronger. You might use phrases such as 'Others might say . . . but I argue . . .' or 'I know you are thinking . . . but that isn't as important as . . . .' In just a few minutes you're going to debate. Make sure that you have a strong argument. You'll want a clear claim, as well as strong reasons and evidence. If you're ready, you might plan for your rebuttal as well."

and tell them that when making an argument, a debater must precisely choose the order of his or her points. You could offer two possible structures for their arguments saying, "Readers, you'll want to put forth your strongest argument during the debate. To do this, think carefully about the order of your points. You might decide to start with the most compelling and then go in descending order, ending with the least compelling. Or, you might start with the least compelling and then work up to the most compelling. Think about whether or not you need to hook your reader right from the start or clinch the deal in the final points." Students could then work with partners to rehearse their arguments, saying their points in one order and then another, comparing which makes for the strongest argument.

Debating with a Partner

Quickly review the parts of a debate and coach students through each part.

"Readers, the time has come for you to debate just as the Second Continental Congress did. Like the founders of our nation, you will break down into sides. Each side will present their position, stating their reasons and evidence. Each side will have time to present their side without interruption. Then, you will meet with your team and plan a rebuttal. After your caucus, you will give your rebuttal.

"Those of you taking the position of the Loyalists, move to the right side of the meeting area. Those of you taking the side of the Patriots, move to the left side of the meeting area." I gave the students a moment to move. "Members of the Second Continental Congress came together to plan out their talking points. You're going to do that right now. You are going to caucus—meet with the members of this Congress who share your position—and you are going to plan out the most important points and pieces of evidence, the ones that you know will bowl your opponents over. Remember to use your notes and your texts. The language of argument will also help." I gestured to the chart with language to help them argue and then set them up to talk.

While the students planned what they would say with their same-position classmates, I rotated between the two sides doing some lean coaching. "Plan it across your hands," "Use more evidence," and "Look back at your notes" were several of the most common coaching notes.

"Colonists, now it is time to debate. The founders of our nation elected representatives to share the position of their compatriots. But in this room there are so many voices that would beautifully represent each side that you are all going to face off. Please make two straight lines." The students moved into two lines facing each other. "You are going to face off against your direct opponent. Please find the person right across from you and shake his or her hand." The students did so and I continued, "Position A: 'The colonies should remain under British rule' will go first. You will have two minutes to state your position. Go!" The room erupted into chatter.

After two minutes, I called the students back together, "Position B: 'The colonies should declare independence' will now have two minutes to present. Go!"

Phrases to Use in Debates

"I take the position that…"

"My first reason for this is…"
"My evidence for that is…"

"My second reason for this is…"
"My evidence for that is… Also…"

When the Patriots had completed their argument, both sides returned to their caucuses to plan their rebuttals. Then students returned to their lines and faced off against their opponents. This time, they talked back to the points each opponent made.

Conclude the debate, restating the key points that each side made.

"After a powerful debate, it is important to reflect on what each side said and to restate the major points made. This is particularly important, because when we debate again in our next session, we'll want to have the strongest arguments at our fingertips. Right now, return to your side and caucus with your team yet again. Reflect on your argument. Which points were indisputable? Which points did your opponent struggle to rebut? Which points felt most critical to your argument?" I gave students time to talk with their teams.

"Another important part of debate is to give credit where credit is due and consider the compelling points that your opponent made. Again, talk with your team. Which points did your opponents make that made you reconsider your position? Which points were particularly powerful?" After a few more minutes of talk, the class came together to highlight the key points on both sides, creating a chart.

Loyalist and Patriot Arguments

Loyalists	Patriots
The Sons of Liberty are too violent.	The British have no right to tax us. They are forcing some to lose their homes and their livelihoods.
The colonists need to be grateful.	The British are forcing us to fight for our rights. They will not listen to us.
The Boston Massacre could have been avoided if the colonists would not have attacked the soldiers.	The British shot six men and injured others without provocation.
Why shouldn't the colonists pay taxes? They are British citizens.	The British are forcing their rule on us.

SESSION 12 HOMEWORK

PREPARING FOR A NEW ROUND OF DEBATE

Readers, today you presented your arguments at the Second Continental Congress. You stated your arguments clearly, got feedback on which of your arguments was most persuasive, and presented your rebuttals of your opponents' arguments. This practice will be invaluable when you prepare for a new round of debate.

The night before they go to court, lawyers often sit in bed thinking "I have collected lots of evidence, but what is the exact order I should present it in?" Tonight, you are going to do the same type of work. Look over your notes, and think to yourself, "Should I present my best evidence first or last? Where should I put my least convincing evidence?" You may want to make a little list for yourself that you keep in your pocket, which reminds you what evidence you will present first, second, and last. For when the time comes to step to the podium, you will want to make sure your argument flows so well that it leaves the audience ready to applaud.

Session 13

Staging a Second Continental Congress Debate

ear Teachers,

Your students have done a lot of important learning. They've learned to read and understand point of view, to uncover important details and facts, to begin to angle evidence to fit an argument, and to begin to think about who side is right, which do I believe and why?

The debate that you are staging today—a reenactment of part of the Second Continental Congress—is a culmination of that work. From the moment your students stepped into the roles of Patriots and Loyalists, they have probably been looking forward to this day. We recommend that you build on their excitement and make today a day that will stand out in their minds at the end of the year and for years to come.

PREPARING FOR DEBATE

With this in mind, it is of the utmost importance that today's session feels different from all the rest. You might face your students across from each other, so the Patriots take one side of the room, the Loyalists another. The lines of chairs, with the two sides facing each other, might create a heightened sense of tension and excitement as you stage the debate. Alternately, you might also decide to set up the room in a way more akin to the way in which many historians believe the Continental Congress set up their debates, with all of the delegates sitting side by side, regardless of their position. Though of course the original members of the Continental Congress did not wear specific colors, you could encourage the Patriots to wear blue and the Loyalists to wear red for this day, to visually delineate the sides of the debate. Or you might let them wear what they feel represents their side.

Recent research has revealed that kids learn more from what teachers *do* than from what they *say*. Therefore, it is important for you to step into the past just as you are asking your kids to do. One way to do this is to take on the role of John Hancock, the President of the Second Continental Congress. You might set up a table in front of the chairs so that you can preside over the debate. You might find a gavel with which to call to order the session. You might obtain a quill and parchment, and take notes on the kids' arguments. These small flourishes will mean the world to your kids.

To give your debate even more grandeur, you may want to invite people from outside your classroom community to attend today's session. Administrators can become part of the congress or view it from the audience box. This will add to your students' engagement. Your students' former teachers will delight at seeing the kids step into the past, and parents will also enjoy seeing their kids present the work they have done. These observers could take on a variety of roles, from neutral observers, as we have suggested with the administrators, to delegates who ask questions after each argument is presented. Or they could become the third party present during this congressional meeting.

HOLDING THE DEBATE

This debate is intended to be staged as a whole-class event. While you may be a bit reluctant to have one student present at a time, there are a few distinct advantages to staging the debate in this whole-class format. First, it is historically accurate; on the floor of Independence Hall, delegates from the thirteen colonies presented their statements one at a time, with many interruptions as controversial statements were vociferously contested. (If your students do the same, take heart—they are acting just as our founding fathers once did!) Second, world-class speaking standards ask fourth-grade students to "report on topics using . . . relevant facts" and "differentiate between contexts that call for formal English and situations where informal discourse is appropriate." Debating in a whole-class format will provide your students a golden opportunity to learn from the formal tone of your class' most skilled public speakers. Finally, a whole-class debate provides an opportunity to create a shared text that you will carry with you throughout the year, just as your read-alouds become part of your classroom culture. You might take the chance to share impressions and reflections about the debate the day after it happens, and months down the line your students will probably say "Remember the 'Give me Liberty or Death!' speech Jose gave at the Second Continental Congress? That was so persuasive!"

Fourth-grade readers and writers are asked to attend to the setting of the novels they read and the narratives they compose. This debate is a perfect opportunity to model that work. While your students have pored over texts which support their side of the debate, they might not know much about the Second Continental Congress itself. Therefore, you might give them a bit of the history of the First Continental Congress, and the events that precipitated the Second Continental Congress. This information can be found in the online resources.

The text that follows is an interpretation of John Hancock's speech that a teacher piloting this unit wrote as a way to begin the opening session of congress. This is an adaptation, not the actual opening speech, but you might find it useful to set the scene before students launch their debate.

John Hancock
Second Continental Congress Teacher Opening Statement

Welcome speakers, welcome arguers, welcome delegates, and welcome observers. My name is John Hancock, and I am going to give you a bit of the history of Second Continental Congress and the First Continental Congress before our debate begins.

It is July of 1776, and we are sitting in Independence Hall in Philadelphia, Pennsylvania. You have come here from Georgia and Rhode Island, from Pennsylvania and Virginia, and some of you are from New York.

But this is not the first time you have met here in this very room. In 1774, you met in the First Continental Congress. There, you passed a resolution warning Great Britain that it must stop its abuse toward the colonies. But Britain did not heed your warning.

In May of 1775, just after shots were fired in Lexington and Concord, you reconvened for the Second Continental Congress. You have been meeting here since May of 1775, for more than a year.

Now it is time for a decision. Will the colonies remain loyal to Great Britain, the most powerful nation on earth? Or will the colonies be independent from Britain?

I have heard that you have differing opinions on this question of independence. Remember the rules of this body. We will speak one at a time. We will not interrupt the speaker, and we will hear out the argument, the rebuttal, and a one-sentence response to each rebuttal.

Gentlemen, who would like to begin?

When you debate in a whole-class format, the debate's structure and timing will be important. You might begin by allowing each side to give an opening statement and closing statement. For the body of the debate, you might have the Patriots present one of their arguments for two minutes, followed by the Loyalists' two-minute rebuttal, and the Patriots' one-sentence response to the rebuttal. By repeating this format for each of the Patriots' and Loyalists' arguments about independence, your debate will have a clear structure, move along efficiently, and provide plenty of opportunity for many children to contribute. Alternatively, you might want to give the students numbers and have the president call them to speak, as some say it was done historically. You need to think about the structure that would work best for you and your students.

The most difficult and perhaps most important work of teaching is anticipating students' struggles. Accordingly, you will want to think about what problems may arise during your debate. Some students may get stage fright, so you will want to coach each side to support their team members, and coach the opposing sides to have patience with nervous presenters. If need be, students can step in and present statements that their team members have written. Remember that this debate is only a culminating celebration, and that even

Bryce's Argument: The British did everything they could for the Colonies.

My Counter: I disagree, because of the Quartering Act. The Quartering Act had the Colonies under strict military rule. We weren't given the right to vote, we had the military governors choose. Soldiers could stay in our homes, if we liked it or not. What if our house was crammed? And, what if, there was a very poor family, with not much food. We would have to give out more of our food, and it might resort to giving the soldiers ALL of our food! They even closed the Boston Harbor, where all the Bostonians made their money by fishing. Their entire economy would cripple! Then, they couldn't afford your taxes! How, would they even, afford things for daily life like food, since the fish was probably their food, too, not only their economy. That, too me, does not seem in any way that the British did everything they could for the Colonies.

FIG. 13–1

Isaac's Argument: The Colonies would become poor.

My Counter: I disagree, because actually, I think we would become poor when we pay those taxes you put on us. If we are independent, we don't have to pay your taxes, and it will be the opposite; we'll have money. I understand that there might be some poor people in the country, but there are poor in every civilization. I bet even in "Mother England" there are some poor. Not everybody is able to be as corrupt as King George III! So, actually, I think that we would not become poor, but wealthier instead.

FIG. 13–2

students who don't speak during the debate have done the important work of collecting and synthesizing evidence. You may also have students who leap out of their chairs in outrage at the point that another side just made. Respond with calm, and their protests will soon subside. Yet don't be afraid to give kids nonverbal signals to move their presentations along; while the Second Continental Congress met for over a year, a brisk pace to your debate will make it all the more lively. You may also have too many speakers, and in that case you might want the students to pick representatives from their sides to talk.

REFLECTING AFTER THE DEBATE

After the debate is over, the spectators have gone home, and your teaching has won admiration from the administrators and teachers present, you will want to have your students reflect on their experience. You might want to give your students time to write what they did well (glow) and why they still need to do (grow). For example, kids might point out strategies they have learned, reflect on their presentation—the language they used, or their body language. They might even reflect on their notes to think about which one is stronger for their argument. *Remember to keep the reflection short.*

Homework

In the next class meeting, you and your students will move forward to begin a new bend. Students will launch a new research project focusing on what happened after the Second Continental Congress. To launch this new project, they will need to identify subtopics on the American Revolution after 1775, so for tonight's homework, you might suggest that they look at an overview text on the American Revolution to get an idea of the big subtopics important in this time period. You might have them jot down a list of subtopics that authors write about all the time and be ready to share that list at the start of the next lesson. Also, you might remind students to continue their fiction reading by reading their independent book, working on their reading plans, and logging their reading.

Building the Prior Knowledge that Makes Texts Accessible

IN THIS SESSION, you'll teach students that readers often read much easier texts to get background knowledge on a topic before tackling harder texts.

GETTING READY

✔ Prepare baskets for the students on subtopics related to the American Revolution after 1775 (see Link).

✔ Remind kids how to start a new project by reviewing the "Launching a Research Project" chart from Session 5 (see Connection).

✔ Display the "Subtopics on the American Revolution after 1775" chart (see Connection).

✔ Prepare several texts on a subtopic for students to study, ranging in complexity. Be sure to include at least one easier text. (see Teaching).

✔ Make copies of the "Main Idea(s) and Supporting Details/Summary" strand of the Informational Reading Learning Progression for grades 4 and 5 (see Conferring and Small-Group Work).

✔ Distribute copies of the "Comparing and Contrasting" strand of the Informational Reading Learning Progression for grades 4 and 5 (see Mid-Workshop Teaching).

✔ Prepare to write some prompts on chart paper to help students think about the product of their research and the audience (see Share).

✔ Be ready to project a website to show students how to check the credibility of a source. We used www.ushistory.org. A link to this site is available in the online resources (see Share).

THIS BEND BEGINS as third bends often do, with an opportunity for children to restart the process they learned earlier in the unit. During the upcoming bend, students will engage in a focused investigation of a particular subtopic, ideally one which takes place after the Second Continental Congress. Most of them will probably work with a partner on a topic of choice, selected during this session. You may need to do some behind the scenes manipulation to be sure that students who struggle as readers work with a topic for which you have an abundance of more accessible resources. During this session, students will select a subtopic for deeper investigation with a partner. You may wish to guide your struggling readers toward subtopics for which you have a plentiful supply of easily accessible sources, both texts and videos.

Teachers who are teaching both this unit and the sister writing unit, *Bringing History to Life*, will note that the writing unit allows for some students to continue pursuing a study that is already underway. We suspect that if your students are reading about the American Revolution as well as writing about it, devoting at least two periods a day to that work, they may have exhausted most of your accessible resources on their first subtopic, and that you'll therefore want them to pursue a second topic. We also anticipate that you may want their focus to shift toward topics that take place after the Second Continental Congress, just to maintain a chronological feel to the unit. That, of course, entirely depends on your resources, because the most important thing is that students have accessible reading materials and are researching topics of interest to them.

In any case, in this session, you will ask students to launch their upcoming research, and you teach them the importance of doing so in ways that allow them to handle the challenging texts they'll need to read. They need to know that as they go forward in life, there will be times when the sourcebooks on a topic will be very challenging. When that is the case, instead of trudging through too-complicated texts, students would benefit from being proactive about the problem. They can find texts that are far more accessible on the topic and read those in preparation for handling the others. That is, prior knowledge on a topic is the one thing that gives readers a leg up on reading texts that would otherwise be too complex. It is important for students to realize that they can take action and create the prior knowledge that they need.

Trust us. This seemingly simple session is one that can make a dramatic difference to your students. It can change your teaching, too. In an effort to enable students to tackle increasing levels of text complexity, all too often teachers are "scaffolding" students to inch through texts that are miles beyond anything those students can begin to handle independently. And sure, if we devote a week to a page of text and walk students through the text word by word, defining and digesting every phrase, then students will get through that text. But the goal is not for a teacher-student pair to be able to work in unison for days to read a tough passage. We won't go off to college with the young people who are our students. The goal needs to be independence.

This session provides the answer. "Go find an easier text on that topic, and read that easier text with intensity," you can tell students.

A few words of caution. When we have seen teachers teaching this session, all too often the text they pull out as an "easier text" is actually written at grade level. This session teaches kids the power of developing their own prior knowledge—but for that to actually happen, you absolutely do want to move kids into a text that is as low a level text as you can find, as long as it will still teach some new knowledge of the subject.

Because this session asks students to set themselves up with a collection of texts on a topic, it will probably make sense for you to schedule a trip to the school library and ideally to the local library to give students more opportunities to find those sources. If your school has a media specialist/librarian, recruit that person's guidance in provisioning this portion of the unit.

Building the Prior Knowledge that Makes Texts Accessible

CONNECTION

Set up the work for the upcoming bend. Remind kids that although the temptation is to dive in, it is helpful to take time to plan.

"Today begins an exciting new bend, because you'll start a new research project focusing on the war. In our last session, we left off with the Second Continental Congress debating the question of independence. Now it's time to move forward and find out: what happened next?

"When you start a new research project, I know the temptation is to just dive in and get going. But remember, you have already learned that the most efficient thing to do is to take some time to make a plan for your research.

"Right now, will you and the person sitting next to you list across your fingers five things that you know to do, early on in a research project?"

The room was filled with the buzz of conversation. I called kids back, and, pointing to the bullet points on the "Launching a Research Project" anchor chart, quickly reviewed the major steps in starting a new project.

◆ COACHING

Recalling work that students did in the reading and writing unit demonstrates to them that the skills they learn are always important. It shows that reading and writing are inextricably linked and that skills they have learned across any unit could always be used.

> **ANCHOR CHART**
>
> ### Launching a Research Project
>
> - Gather sources on the topic to preview.
> - Generate a list of subtopics that frequently appear.
> - Choose an accessible book to read for an overview.
> - Identify the text structure to help determine what's important.
> - Pause at the ends of chunks to recall the text in a structured way.
> - Record only the important things.
> - Read more texts on the same topic and synthesize notes on them.

Create a chart of the subtopics authors often write about related to the American Revolution after 1775. Rally students to select a subtopic to study across the bend.

"Last night for homework, you looked at an overview text to get an idea of what the big subtopics are. So today, let's start by brainstorming a list of the subtopics that authors write about all the time. What did you find?" I displayed the kids' suggestions.

"Take a look at this list, and think carefully. What subtopic would you like to research for this bend?" I jotted down the subtopics the kids selected, and made sure that each child had a partner to work with on this new research project.

Point out that if students find themselves trying to read texts that are too hard, the thing to do is to find easy texts on the same topic and to study them to build a platform of prior knowledge.

Then I said, "Before you proceed, I want to talk with you about a problem I am pretty sure most of you will encounter. Most of you will open up the resources on your topic, and you'll get started reading, and you'll quickly realize the texts are hard. For me when that happens, the words almost swim in front of my face. I can read the same paragraph five times and still not 'get' it. Has that ever happened to any of you?"

The kids agreed, and so I pressed on. "The important thing is that you realize that there will be times throughout your life when this happens. You'll be at college and the professor will assign you a topic and some texts to study, and you'll sit in front of those texts and think, once again, 'Whoa. This is too hard.' When that happens, you need to be a strategic problem solver."

❖ **Name the teaching point.**

"Today, readers, I want to tell you that when researchers find the texts on a topic are just too hard to read, they can get some other texts that are *way* easier. If you read an easier text first—really studying the words, the ideas, so that you master them—those easier texts can give you the prior knowledge you need to handle the hard texts."

TEACHING AND ACTIVE ENGAGEMENT

Tell students about a time when older students read a "baby book" to give themselves prior knowledge. Help them feel it is acceptable to revert to extremely easy texts.

"This is a true story. Recently, I worked with some eighth-graders who were totally stuck on a text about black holes. It was too hard. So they went to a book that was written for *second-graders*. At first the text practically looked like a baby book, but they read that text with their minds turned onto full power. Those eighth-graders really grasped what that very easy text said about black holes. Then they went to a somewhat harder text—maybe it was written at a third-grade level. It was almost like those eighth-graders were climbing the stairs of text complexity. Eventually, they were back to the original text, but this time, they knew enough about black holes that they could make sense out of that text."

Subtopics on the American Revolution After 1775

- Declaration of Independence
- Battles
- George Washington
- Strengths and weaknesses of both sides
- Life as a soldier in the Continental Army
- Life as a Loyalist
- Setting up a new government

Choose the subtopics you chart strategically, listing subtopics on which you have readily accessible resources. You might choose to combine several smaller subtopics, such as the Battle of Trenton and the Battle of Valley Forge, together into a larger category—Battles—that will yield more resources for research. Alternatively, you might ask students to turn and talk about the lists they generated for homework. Then, calling the students back together, you could say, "I heard you say . . ." and jot down the list of subtopics on which you already gathered resources.

Give students a dense text to read on a subtopic.

"Let's try it. Let's say your topic is 'Battles,' and you sit down to read a text on the Battle of Bunker Hill. You go to read a text, and it is a bit dense. Try reading this," I said, and distributed a two-sided page, with the first passage below on the top side, and other easier rendition on the reverse side. The students read this silently:

In third grade, students were encouraged to preview texts to gain knowledge of text that was complicated and difficult.

Battle of Bunker Hill: June 17, 1775

On June 17, some 2,200 British forces under the command of Major General William Howe (1729–1814) and Brigadier General Robert Pigot (1720–96) landed on the Charlestown Peninsula then marched to Breed's Hill. As the British advanced in columns against the Americans, Prescott, in an effort to conserve the Americans' limited supply of ammunition, reportedly told his men, "Don't fire until you see the whites of their eyes!" When the Redcoats were within several dozen yards, the Americans let loose with a lethal barrage of musket fire, throwing the British into retreat.

After re-forming their lines, the British attacked again, with much the same result. Prescott's men were now low on ammunition, though, and when the Redcoats went up the hill for a third time, they reached the redoubts and engaged the Americans in hand-to-hand combat. The outnumbered Americans were forced to retreat. However, by the end of the engagement, the Patriots' gunfire had cut down some 1,000 enemy troops, with more than 200 killed and more than 800 wounded. More than 100 Americans perished, while more than 300 others were wounded.

Battle of Bunker Hill: Legacy

The British had won the so-called Battle of Bunker Hill, and Breed's Hill and the Charlestown Peninsula fell firmly under British control. Despite losing their strategic positions, the battle was a significant morale-builder for the inexperienced Americans, convincing them that patriotic dedication could overcome superior British military might. Additionally, the high price of victory at the Battle of Bunker Hill made the British realize that the war with the colonies would be long, tough and costly.

"Turn right now and retell what you just learned," I said, and listened. Many of the students had gleaned a few bits of information, but hadn't gotten a good grasp of the sequence of events.

Explain that if students read simpler accounts of the same event first, and eventually return to the original text, they'll find it more accessible. Coach students through this process.

I spoke up. "It's not the easiest thing to read, is it? Even if you grasped the content to some degree, you'd be wise to read an easier accounts of that event first and then to reread this. Right now, flip the page over, and read the two easier accounts, trying to grasp exactly what is going on. Talk to the person beside you after you have read these to make sure you understand what they are saying."

The Americans learned that British troops planned to take over the hills around Boston. That would give the British an advantage in battle. Knowing that, the Americans secretly moved their troops onto Breed's Hill. This unoccupied hill was located in Charlestown, just outside of Boston. The Americans built up fortifications during the night and prepared for battle.

The next day, the British realized what had happened and attacked. Their commander William Howe led three charges up Breed's Hill. The Americans fought back the first two charges. But they started to run out of ammunition and had to retreat at the third charge. The British gained the hill, but their costs were great. Around 226 British were killed and 800 wounded. However, the Americans did not suffer nearly as many casualties.

Students did that, and then I said, "Now, try an experiment. Go back to the original text, and this time, try to read it in a way that allows you to fully comprehend it. Bring all you know and your full brain power to rereading that original text."

After the students reread the original text, I said, "Now readers, will you talk about what you know about this event?" For a moment, the kids talked about the event itself and their understanding of it in their groups. I moved among them, listening in on their conversations as a quick, informal way of assessing their understanding. Patrick said, "Oh now I get it—the 'fortifications' are also called the 'redoubts.' They are the guys fighting against the British." Another student said, "Yeah and now I get that when they said 'ammunition' they were talking about the shots bullets." I congratulated them for how they were using the easier text to support their understanding of challenging vocabulary from the harder text.

Note the order of the texts: we began by giving students the harder text, then followed with the easier one. We chose this order deliberately, so that kids would see for themselves that reading an easier text can help them understand the harder text. From here forward, however, you hope that students will read the easier text first, as a way of orienting themselves to the subtopic.

LINK

Name the ways in which you've set children up with resources—accessible texts—to support their comprehension of harder texts about their subtopic.

"Readers, in life, you will often need to find your own accessible texts when you encounter hard ones, but I've done three things to help. First, we have a shelf of easier books on the American Revolution—and remember, a book that overviews the whole revolution and has just a little paragraph on your topic will tend to just highlight the main things about your topic. Next, I've put an easy text on each of your subtopics into your resource bin. And finally, I have a bibliography of videos that I have put into your resource bin.

"You can start by using these resources. You'll still need to line them up carefully so that you read an easier text on the exact topic that your harder text addresses first, and then you can go between the easier and the more challenging text.

"You will want to read these texts in a super-intensive way, making sure you *really* grasp the vocabulary words and the concepts. So don't just skim over these texts, and don't settle for a general loose sort of comprehension of them. Okay, readers, head off to research!"

Remember that students need to start with texts that are easy and accessible then move up to harder levels of text complexity. You might add leveled books on the subtopics, primary sources, articles, maps, website suggestions, video suggestions, bookmarks to help them read through a text.

Using the Learning Progression to Lift the Level of Summarization

ONE OF THE MOST IMPORTANT SKILLS readers need to read expository non-fiction is the ability to find and understand the main idea. Earlier you have used the learning progression to assess and set goals working to lift the level of your students' work on main idea. Today, you may ask students to bring out the learning progression to help them see where they are now and help them set goals to progress from one level to another.

Support students with naming a main idea in their own words.

You can show students who can summarize chunks of text to do higher-level work by saying the main idea of one part of text and linking it to related points. As you confer or work in small groups, you can tell students that often times in easier nonfiction texts, the main idea can be stated quite obviously. Often times the main idea is stated in a sentence embedded in a paragraph or a section of the text. You can coach students as they are reading to see if they can find a sentence that seems to capture the main idea. Help them to recognize that sentence as being important, and coach them to use their own words to name the main idea. As you listen to students using their own words, you may prompt them to have a few tries, and then choose the one they think best names the main idea.

Move readers to name multiple main ideas in their own words.

For your students who are pushing themselves to name multiple main ideas in their own words, help them to remember that if they come upon a sentence that seems to capture one or another of those main ideas, they can recognize that sentence as important. They can use that sentence to help them name multiple main ideas using their own words. Holding onto the main idea, they will need to identify details from the text that best support each idea. In your conferences or small groups, you will want to teach them that there may be parts of the text that feel somewhat extraneous to the main ideas, and the new work for them will be to think and talk about the relationship of those parts to the main ideas. These extraneous parts may include background

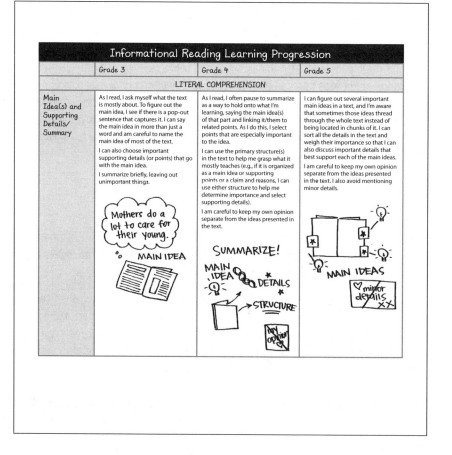

"Readers, can I have your eyes up here? I know it's early in your study of your subtopic, but I had to stop you now, before you go any further. We know that the reason why readers often turn to an easier text first is because that easier text gives them some prior knowledge, almost a little boost, that can help them understand a harder text on that same subtopic. What I want to remind you is that when you go to the second text, you read it differently, constantly thinking about similarities in the information being taught and the new information you're learning. You've done this work before, in our earlier nonfiction reading unit, and I want to be sure you're doing everything you know that readers do when you read across texts.

"I'm going to give you and your partner the 'Cross Text(s) Synthesis' and 'Comparing and Contrasting' strand of the Informational Reading Learning Progression. Can you and your partner take a few minutes to read through the fourth- and fifth-grade levels of the checklist? Notice what stays the same from level to level and what's new." I gave students a few minutes to read independently and jot notes, and then I channeled them to talk.

Calling the students back, I said. "Now that you remember what's expected of you as fourth-graders, and now that you have some ideas of what's expected of fifth-graders, can you and your partner take an honest look at the work you've been doing so far? Where do you see evidence that you've tried this work? Point to specific places in your notes or in your books to show what you've done. What goals can you set moving forward?

"Keep reading, and working on your goals."

information, implications for the future, or conflicting perspectives on the issue. As you coach students in this work, you may ask questions such as, "How does that relate to the main idea?" or "Does this part support the main idea?" to help think about the relationship between the parts and the main ideas.

Readers Anticipate What They Will Teach Others and Find New Resources

Challenge children to imagine the main points they will include in their research presentations, and display ways to make plans for these.

"Researchers, by the end of next week, you'll be acting like professors, teaching kids from other classrooms, as well as your parents, what you are learning from your research. So during this week, keep in mind that you are learning for that larger audience. Right now, even though you are at the start of your research, pretend your research time is over, and it is time to teach others what you have learned. What do you think will be the main parts of your presentation? What are the main chunks that you'll teach others about? If you don't know, use terms like 'Probably we will . . . And also we might . . .' Start talking!"

As students talked, I displayed some added ways to think about their eventual product and audience:

> They're going to need to know about . . .
>
> We'll probably have to explain a lot about . . .
>
> The most interesting stuff might be . . .
>
> If we can, it would be good to include stuff on . . .

TOPIC IDEAS for AMERICAN REVOLUTION		
PEOPLE	**EVENTS**	**PLACES**
• John Hancock	• Boston Massacre	• Carpenters Hall
• Paul Revere	• Boston Tea Party	• Fraunces Tavern
• Patrick Henry	• Battle of Trenton	• 13 Colonies
• The Continental Congress	• Taxes (Sugar, Stamp, Tea, Navagation etc.)	• Philadelphia
• Nathan Hale	• Battle of Saratoga	
• Sons of Liberty	• Declaration of Independence	
• British Army (Redcoats)	• Battle of Concord and Lexington	
• Military Leadership Colonies	• Battle of Yorktown	
• Military Leadership British		**ISSUES**
• Crispus Attucks	**Broad Topic Ideas**	• Taxes
• General George Washington	• American Revolution and Native Americans	• Taxation w/o Representation
• Continental Army	• American Revolution and Women	• Impact of war on N.Y.S & N.Y.C.
• Thomas Paine	• American Revolution and African Americans	
• Mary Katherine Goddard	• Spies of the American Revolution	
• Margaret Corbin		
• General William Howe		

Invite children to research online resources to add to the books they have, and explain how to assess the credibility of websites.

"I think that many of you have realized that the materials in your bins are only a start, and you'll need to get some added resources. One place to look for resources is the internet, and I want to encourage you to use that as a resource. But meanwhile, I want you to be especially ready to assess the credibility and relevance of materials you encounter on the internet.

"For example, Atif and Patrick, who are researching the Battle of Valley Forge, located a website called UShistory.org. That's a helpful research site. It is also what researchers call 'credible,' which means believable, trustworthy. To measure the credibility of a site, you need to be a bit of a sleuth. You figure out who the author is—which is not always very apparent and may be an organization, not a person—and then you stop looking at the site itself and instead do a background check on the person, just as if you were a hiring office and you were checking out whether this person is a researcher you'd like to hire. You have to see if the person has credentials that make you trust that he or she is an expert."

I projected the website to show students how I could assess its credibility. "If I click on the 'Who We Are' tab, it brings me to information about who runs this website. Sometimes this section is called 'About Us' or something similar. Here, it tells us about the Independence Hall Association, which was founded in 1942 to help create Independence National Historical Park in Philadelphia. They describe themselves as a nonprofit corporation, which tells us that they're not making money, or a profit, off of the work they're doing. That seems trustworthy, though it might not mean that they're experts. What else do you notice?" I asked students to turn and talk, and I knelt down to listen.

"It says that their mission is to educate the public about the Revolutionary and Colonial eras. So they would need to know a lot to teach others about American history," Patricia noticed.

"Yeah," Joyce chimed in, "and it says they're an 'independent group of private concerned citizens.' That seems like they really care about this topic, and they're independent, so they're not listening to what other people say."

"Great thinking! So remember, we can't always trust the credibility of everything we read on the Internet. It helps to act like a sleuth, looking around for clues to who wrote it, asking ourselves, 'Do I trust this person or organization? Are they an expert?' or 'Why might this person be writing about this topic?' Keep that in mind as you discover new resources for your research."

SESSION 14 HOMEWORK

 ## GATHERING RESEARCH MATERIALS

Readers, for homework, begin to collect information and materials to support your research projects. I'll make sure you have plenty of resources in class, but anything you can add to your team's basket would be great! If you do some Internet research, will you think about the credibility of the sources you find and be able to talk to your partner about that? Here are a few suggestions for gathering materials:

- Go to the public library, our school library, or a bookstore to get a book or two on your topic.
- Conduct internet research using a kid-friendly search engine like awesomelibrary.org, kids.gov, or revolutionarywar.com.
- Find maps, primary sources, documents to help you in your research.
- Look for illustrations and political cartoons.

Last, don't forget to continue doing your additional reading, and to log it.

Strategies for Tackling Increasingly Complex Texts

IN THIS SESSION, you'll teach students that readers use special strategies for making sense of a complex text. They begin by previewing the text closely, and then they read a section, paraphrase what they just read, and notice whether it goes with what they've read before or introduces something new.

GETTING READY

✔ Display a passage from a summary of a popular television series, to demonstrate how to make sense of a short complex text (see Teaching and Active Engagement).

✔ Prepare a chart, "Transitional Phrases to Help Talk about the Texts" (see Mid-Workshop Teaching).

✔ Carry the "Monitoring for Sense" and "Main Idea(s) and Supporting Details/Summary" strands of the Informational Reading Learning Progression with you as your confer (see Conferring and Small-Group Work).

Y OU MAY FEEL as if this session is going backward five steps. In it, you teach readers to recognize when a text is too hard and to shift strategies accordingly. You explain to readers that if they decide to persist with a too-hard text, they essentially need to break down the text so that it *is* accessible, translating it down a notch as they read so they can grasp what it is saying. That is, when necessary—which should be rarely—readers can make their way through texts that are too hard by reading chunk by chunk and stopping often to paraphrase.

Earlier you taught students to decide what is important in a section of text so they can take effective notes on that content. You also taught students to ascertain the structure of a text to take notes in a text structure that mirrors the one in the text. Both of those strategies require that students can first read and comprehend a passage, and that won't always be the case. When a text is really too hard, the first thing that readers do is to shift gears and read the text in a stop-and-go fashion, alternating between reading and digesting—or you could say, between reading and paraphrasing.

This session acknowledges that some of the time, kids will be reading texts that are too hard for them, and that they'll need special strategies for coping.

Today you'll support students in the critical skill of monitoring for meaning. As fourth-graders, your students should come to an informational text expecting the parts of the text to work together so they teach main ideas. It's crucial that students learn to monitor for when their understanding breaks down. You'll show students strategies they can turn to in these situations, moving through the text part by part, paraphrasing, and considering how parts of the text fit with the whole topic. You might chose to study the "Monitoring for Sense" strand of the Informational Reading Learning Progression to anticipate the supports your students might need as they take on this important work.

Strategies for Tackling Increasingly Complex Texts

CONNECTION

Acknowledge that kids will be "reading up" on their focal topics, and point out that they will literally read up levels of text complexity.

"Readers, I know you'll be reading up on your subjects today. That's an interesting phrase: *reading up* on your topics, because that is exactly what you'll need to do. You'll need to read *up* levels of text difficulty. The work with easy texts will have helped you somewhat, but you may still probably need to read some texts that are really hard.

"Today, and whenever you read anything, you need to do something that reading researchers call 'monitoring for sense.' Many reading researchers think that is the first and most essential reading strategy anyone ever uses. You read, keeping an eye on whether you are gleaning meaning from the text, whether it is making sense to you. When meaning falls apart—and it will for any reader, some of the time—the important thing is that you can feel that. It's like you just dropped the thread of the story: 'Whoops,' you go. 'I didn't understand that last part.' And then the key thing is that you *do something*. Sometimes you just read on, really alert to finding the thread again, to picking up what you dropped. That may work—but often doesn't. Often you stop, go back to where you dropped the meaning, and reread from there. That often works, but doesn't always.

You're reminding youngsters that they have not one but several strategies to tackle complex texts.

"Sometimes, you need to take more extreme measures. I think of it as you need to shift your reading into four-wheel drive to go up this big mountain of hard text."

✤ Name the teaching point.

"Today I want to teach you that if you make a choice to persist in reading a text that is too hard, you will want to *really* preview the text, and then to read a chunk, pausing to paraphrase what you have just read. As you read the next chunk, ask, 'Does this go with what I just read or is this something new?'"

TEACHING

Tell about a time when a text was challenging, but you used a strategy to help tackle it. Channel students to read the dense passage with you, then show how you read a bit and paraphrase.

"Readers, last night when I got home, I wanted to watch the second season of 'The Sopranos' on Netflix. I needed to read up on what happened in the first season, so I found a summary of that season on the Web. I looked over it for a bit, and then started to read it. It said this . . ." and I showed the passage and read it aloud, not trying to make it comprehensible by the way I read it:

> *The mob is besieged as much by inner infidelity as it is by the federal government. Early in the series, the greatest threat to Tony's Family is his own biological family. One of his closest associates turns witness for the FBI, his mother colludes with his uncle to contract a hit on Tony, and his kids click through Web sites that track the federal crackdown in Tony's gangland.*

"Whew," I thought. "That's supposed to help? Are they crazy?" I paused. "But I really did want to get the background I needed to watch my show, so I decided to reread that hard passage and work on understanding chunks of it. What I did is the exact sort of work you need to do when your books get tough. I read in smaller chunks than usual, stopping often to paraphrase it—using easy language to retell each chunk.

"Let's try that together. We'll stop extra often, just for practice." I reread the below:

> *The mob is besieged as much by inner infidelity as it is by the federal government. Early in the series, the greatest threat to Tony's Family is his own biological family.*

"Okay, now I'm going to paraphrase, putting it into a simpler text. So far, this says that the mob, the mob that Tony Soprano is part of, is besieged, is surrounded on all sides by infidelity. Infidelity? Oh yes, that is a lack of loyalty. Tony is surrounded as much by a lack of loyalty as by the main enemy, the federal government. The greatest threat to Tony's Family is his mob family. Huh? The greatest threat to his family is his family? I think they mean the greatest threat to his Mob Family is his actual biological family. Okay, I think I got that."

Debrief what you just did.

"Did you see what I just did? I broke that paragraph into chunks and used easy language to retell each chunk. I paraphrased it."

ACTIVE ENGAGEMENT

Channel students to read the remaining part of the challenging text and to paraphrase it to their partner.

"Will you read on in that summary of 'The Sopranos' with your partner and see if the two of you can continue to do as I did, translating it into easier language, paraphrasing it? As you read the next sentence or two, think, 'How does this add on to what we just read?'"

When telling an anecdote such as this, you'll need to use your best judgment in terms of the example you use. Obviously, "The Sopranos" is a show intended for adults, and we are not advocating that children watch it. But because this is a series that has been enormously popular, we feel that this example gives life to this anecdote. If you feel that this example would not fit with local sensibilities, of course, please feel free to substitute another example.

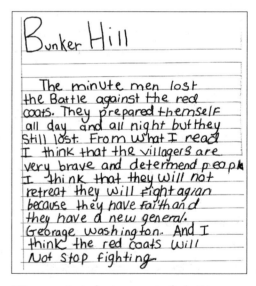

FIG. 15–1   A student account of a battle during war

One of his closest associates turns witness for the FBI, his mother colludes with his uncle to contract a hit on Tony, and his kids click through Web sites that track the federal crackdown in Tony's gangland.

The kids worked, and I voiced over a few tips to lift the level of their work. "Think about what each part of the sentence teaches you," I said. "They're all important." A minute later, I added, "I hear some of you saying a part doesn't fit. Reread to see if you missed something."

Then we agreed on an understanding of the passage. That understanding of the upcoming portion of the text began with restating the first portion. "So Tony is worried about loyalty even from his own family. For example, his own mother and uncle hire someone to kill Tony. . . ."

Debrief in a way that makes the work you have just done applicable to students' research—now and always.

"So researchers, I have a big question. Why are we studying about 'The Sopranos'? What does this have to do with the American Revolution?" I gave the students a minute to brainstorm in partnerships.

I summed up our understanding by saying, "Whether the text you are reading is about a television show or about the surrender at Yorktown, if it is really too difficult for you to read easily, the wisest recourse is to inch through it, paraphrasing as best you can. When you move from one part of the text to the next, it helps to ask, 'Does this fit with what we read earlier or is this something new?'"

LINK

Remind readers that they have several strategies to deal with hard text, including "paraphrasing" chunks.

"Readers, I know that today you'll be reading more texts and harder texts about the subtopic you are studying. You'll bring background knowledge to that reading, and that will help you, but you will sometimes still feel like the text you are trying to read is hard. Know that when this happens, one possible solution is to break it up into smaller chunks and paraphrase each chunk.

"We didn't have a lot of text features or photographs to support our work with the passage about 'The Sopranos,' but the texts you are reading may provide lots of supports to readers. Use those supports.

"You will want to decide how best to use your partner. It may be that you and your partner want to read the same text together—one person might read a part, then you pause to paraphrase, then the next reads a part, and so on. Or you may want to read different texts and get together after a bit to talk. You decide on the best way to proceed."

Teaching students to paraphrase is not as easy a task as one might think. Students first need to understand the information they are reading and then be able to recall and say it in their own words. It will take practice and patience.

Coach students to check their paraphrasing with the information given in the text.

Supporting Children as They Tackle Complex Concepts and Texts

A S YOU CONFER TODAY, you will naturally be on the lookout for the various ways in which children respond to increasingly complex texts and concepts. You may find that today, especially, you need to adapt the whole-class instruction so that it is more accessible to some students and so that it offers a greater challenges to others.

Of course, the work you've taught today isn't entirely new. Students will have done synthesis work in prior fiction and nonfiction units, as well as earlier in this one. You can anticipate, however, that some children may need reminders as they try this work now with more complex texts. Look to the "Monitoring for Sense" and "Main Idea(s) and Supporting Details/Summary" strands of the Informational Reading Learning Progression for suggestions of how to support this work. Meanwhile, others will be ready to do more than just summarize texts and monitor for meaning.

Challenge advanced readers to engage deeper with the content they're reading.

Advanced readers will benefit from the push to go past making sense of one chunk of text, to reach back further, synthesizing this section with earlier sections. Or they might embrace the challenge of noticing more than just the text as they do this work, looking also at the information they can gather from diagrams, photographs, maps, captions, and illustrations. That is, they might synthesize and make sense of *all* the information on the page, not just the words. Or they could think how this one chunk of text prompts them to have ideas, or to revise their thinking. This was the case for Mia.

When I sat down next to her, she started telling me about the work she was doing in the book, *Reporting The Revolutionary War*. She'd read a big portion of the book and was obviously excited. I asked her to tell me about her experience and she said, "Last night, as I was reading, I was like, 'Whoa! How did I ever think this book would be boring?'"

As I scanned the book, Mia showed me her notes, which she had created as the same kind of timeline that we had developed during Bend I of the unit. "First there was the article on the French and Indian War. Then there was the idea that the British were

MID-WORKSHOP TEACHING
Encouraging Text Citations in Conversations

"Readers, can I stop you for a second?" I said, and waited until I had their attention. "When you meet with your partner to talk about your subject, keep the texts you have been reading open in front of you. Use as many opportunities as possible to say, 'For example, in this text it says, . . .' or "I want to add on. This author reports that . . .'

"You should be able to refer to your texts a dozen times within a five-minute conversation. Use these transitional phrases to get you talking about the texts":

Transitional Phrases to Help Talk about the Texts
- For example, the text says . . .
- For example, according to the text . . .
- For example, early in the text, readers learn that . . .
- For example, in the beginning, we hear that . . .
- (So-and-so) claims that . . .
- (So-and-so) writes that . . .
- (So-and-so) describes this, saying . . .
- One thing to note is that, toward the end of the text, readers learn that . . .

"Get started talking." I listened as children began to do this work. Jose started off, saying to Sophia, "Early in my text, it says that the Congress voted for the Declaration of Independence on July 4, 1776, but that didn't really make the colonies free. They had to finish the war before they were truly free."

Nodding, Sophia added, "That's right—just because they said they were free, it didn't mean that they really were. One thing noted in my book is that nobody had done this before. No colonies in America had broken free from a European empire before. So what the colonists were doing was new and uncertain, and probably scary."

At that point, I moved on to listen to another partnership.

afraid to lose the land. They thought it was going to go back to normal, the colonists said. Then, boom! Here come the soldiers! What nerve. Then one of the taxes began and the law to buy from England . . ." Before Mia could continue retelling the book in all its detail, I jumped in to celebrate the fact that rather than putting the book down, she had kept going. "Many readers are unwilling to read on, when they think a book may be dense or dull, and they miss so much!" I said. "I'm so glad you recognized the value of giving a book a try, and that you used a strategy that works for you.

"Can I give you a tip?" Mia nodded, so I continued. "As I listen to you retelling all this book's details, I'm thinking that I need to revise my earlier instruction. I suggested that you read a big chunk, then capture the main ideas on the page, and I can see from your timeline that you've done that. But Mia—my thought is that it would help you even more if you recorded not just what the book says, but also your ideas about those facts."

I tapped her book and said, "I can tell that you're really excited about what you are discovering. But your timeline doesn't really show that."

Mia looked at me, a bit defensively. "I remember *everything* I've read. I can list all the facts for you."

"I love what you did, Mia, and that you used a tool you learned earlier this year. But I think you're ready to do even more than I've taught. This isn't something I've taught yet—but I'm suggesting that when you pause in your reading to think, 'What are the main ideas of this part?' you can also think, 'What are *my* ideas about that? Why are they important?'

"Right now, try this. Spend a little time jotting your thoughts—after all, writing is one of the most important tools readers have to think, to respond to a text, to come up with ideas." I stayed with Mia as she got started with the work, coaching her to say more about her ideas, and then I moved on to confer with other readers.

Help readers who struggle to move past empathy to engage with complex concepts.

If you see kids who are having a hard time with complex concepts, use your conferring to teach them more about nonfiction reading and about how to deal with these concepts. You will also want to share more strategies with them.

This was the case for Sophia and Jose, who were reading books on a higher level than their usual ones. I asked what they'd learned about the causes and effects of the revolution.

Jose answered, "I'm reading about the people who couldn't afford British products and how that made them feel bad. I think they look worried. I thought that, because they said they needed to board up their windows and to hide buying cheaper stuff from others. Sophia was just saying that she wished someone could help the people. We thought it would be kind of cool, but also kind of scary, if others would rescue these people. You know, like give them food and security."

I got the impression that Jose and Sophia wanted to transport themselves within the pages of the book and help the colonists. They showed a lot of empathy, but an inability to push past emotion to more complex thinking. I said, "Remember last month, and across last year when you were reading fiction, you stopped some of the time to retell what you read? Can you retell what you have learned about the time period to say more about what was really going on here?" Then, counting on one finger, I started them off. "The colonists were taxed on most of their products."

Sophia gave it a go and added on, "Umm, then they were told they couldn't buy from anybody else even if they were poor and couldn't afford British merchandise, but I don't understand why?" I was impressed with Sophia's effort to understand the idea that life is complicated, that the poor often suffer more than anybody else, and to make sense of her book. I complimented her, "That's it! You're starting to tackle some important issues that occurred during the revolution—poverty, unfairness, taxation—these aren't your everyday, easy concepts. Great work."

Then, shifting to the teaching part of my conference, I said, "I want to give you a tip. When you get to complex concepts such as these, it helps to change how you read. You know how when a roller coaster goes up that slow steep hill, it shifts gears to get to the top? It's the same thing with reading. When you read concepts dense with meaning, your thinking needs to shift into second gear. Right now, think about things you've learned that you can do to help. For example, you might decide to use your toolkit of charts or you might get a graphic organizer or read a section of a text more slowly. Or you may decide that you need to flip back a few pages and reread to see how the new information you are learning about your topic connects to the information you read earlier. Ready to give it a try?" I stayed and watched them as they began, before moving on to other kids.

Readers Plan the Subtopics They Are Researching

Remind students to be mindful about *what* they read, as well as *how* they read. Remind them to think about the subtopics within their topic, and to read with density about one, synthesizing across texts.

"Readers, we have talked a lot about *how* you are reading so that you understand the text, and that's important, but you also want to think about *what* you are reading: about the portion of your topic that you are researching.

"Remember that every topic has parts to it, has subtopics. Earlier, you were reading about the American Revolution before the Second Continental Congress, you divided your learning into parts, into buckets: problems between Britain and the colonists, the Boston Tea Party, the Boston Massacre, the Sons of Liberty. . . .

"Now you are studying subtopics in more depth. You may be researching something new to you—such as the Declaration of Independence, the battles, the role of George Washington—but that one subtopic still has parts. If nothing else, you can divide the topic up chronologically and write about the early part, the middle part, the later part. For example, if your subtopic is George Washington, you can write about the early part of his leadership in the years before the war, the middle part of his leadership during the war, and finally, his leadership at the end of the war and the building of a new nation.

"You need to divide your topic up, to bucket it, so that you can read a bunch of things about one part, synthesizing information across texts as you read about that one part."

Set partners up to make sure they have divided their topic into parts and decided which part they are researching at any given time.

"So will you work with your partner and make sure you have divided your subject into parts, and make sure you choose what to read based on the part of your subject that you are studying at any given point. Talk with each other about that, and make a plan for moving forward."

Research

When Concord & Lexington Battle accourd

On april 18 1775, 800 brittish troops left boston to make way to concord

warning
Head of Patriots Dr. Joseph Warren alected Paul Revere & William Dawes that the Brittish are coming

people that fought
Minuteman and John packer Blocked town of lexington
First shot of American Revolution was fired here

No one knows who fired the first shot in Lexington

Patriots and Red coats continued on to concord

Patriots took an early lead on the brittish at concord

Major John Pitcarn sent

FIG. 15–2   Student research from Bend III

TEACHING WHAT YOU LEARN

Readers, you will want to continue reading and researching tonight, as you did in school today. As you take in more and more information, one thing to remember is that brains are a bit like stomachs. Brains need to digest, just like stomachs do!

To digest all that you are learning, after you read tonight, have a conversation with someone about what you are learning. You could talk with a family member, or you could talk over the phone with a classmate.

Start by teaching that person what you are learning. When you teach, remember to think about the big points you want to make. List them across your fingers or jot them down. Develop one point before jumping to the next. Also, actually open the text and to read specific parts aloud. Become accustomed to saying things like, "So-and-so explains, saying . . ." or "So-and-so writes. . . ."

After you have taught about your topic, spend some time talking about your ideas. See if one or two of these prompts can help you get started talking and thinking:

- This fits with what I learned before because . . .

- This is different from what I read earlier because . . .

- This is making me realize that . . .

- This is starting to give me the idea that . . .

- This is helping me understand why . . .

- Now, I'm wondering . . .

All of this talking will make it very likely that the reading you do tonight stays with you for a long time.

Readers Study All Parts of a Text to Determine Main Ideas

IN THIS SESSION, you'll teach students that nonfiction readers know that there are specific places in a text where an author often reveals important information related to the main idea: introductions, conclusions, and text features.

GETTING READY

✔ Project the pages of the "Don't Fire until You See the Whites of Their Eyes" section of *Liberty! How the Revolutionary War Began*, pages 30–31 (see Teaching and Active Engagement).

✔ Carry the "Main Idea(s) and Supporting Details/Summary" strand of the Informational Reading Learning Progression as you confer (see Conferring and Small-Group Work).

✔ Project the "Analyzing Author's Craft" strand of the Informational Reading Learning Progression (see Mid-Workshop Teaching).

✔ Display page 6 from *Liberty!* and page 11 from *The Revolutionary War* to compare how text features can reveal important information about the main idea (see Share).

W HEN WE WERE WRITING *Bringing History to Life*, this unit's sister writing unit, we decided that in the second bend, students would embark on a second study about history, this time with increased independence. But we knew we couldn't just set them to work on a second book without clarifying how specifically we would help them to ramp up the level of their work. We had to figure out what this bend would really be about. In other words, we had to figure out the main idea of the bend. What we soon came to realize is that fourth-grade writers (and readers!) need to consider not just how facts are strung together on a page, but how an author uses structure and text features to highlight what is most important about the information.

This session, then, is one in which readers are asked not only to consider the most important ideas in a section of text, but also to do some interpretation to figure out the central message. This session closely follows the teaching in *Bringing History to Life*, and its primary purpose is to help your students to make connections between the writing about history they may be doing and the reading they are undertaking in this unit. In short, this session is designed to help your students to read like writers. Whether or not you are teaching the companion writing unit, this session will stand your students in good stead when they are attempting to determine how authors clue readers in to what matters most.

You will teach students to read a section of a text, then pause and study certain parts of it more closely, thinking, "What clues is the author giving me about what is most important here?" Sometimes those clues can be found in the introduction or the conclusion of the section, in the text features, or even in the outside sources that the author quotes or references.

One of the ways in which we guide students to determine main ideas is by studying text features that supplement the text in their nonfiction books. An important lesson when reading nonfiction is that text features matter. They are there to teach additional information that may not be present in the words alone. An extension to this teaching, for which your students are likely ready, is that text features are also there to help spotlight what the author deems to be especially important.

You may realize right away that a large part of this session's focus is on finding main ideas, in other words, what the author is teaching. Certainly, that is a goal of this session. Particularly as text difficulty ramps up, students need a variety of entry points to figure out main ideas, as these become increasingly implicit and unstated as texts get harder. Then too, the work students need to do to determine main ideas gets more complex as they have to synthesize larger chunks of text to determine what is most important. This session offers a few more ways students might begin to understand more about the message the author is sending and what his or her main points are.

Additionally, this session supports students in interpreting information from the whole page, from the visuals and other text features as well as the entire body of the text. Main idea as we all know comes across in many different parts or chunks of text as well as across the whole book. Global standards state that fourth-graders should be able to not only find main idea in the whole text, but also in parts of the text.

As you confer, we suggest you carry the "Main Idea(s) and Supporting Details/Summary" strand of the Informational Reading Learning Progression with you to help you assess whether your students are growing in understanding and complexity as readers—whether they can look within and around the text to come up with more complex comprehension of the text they read. This is the time when students should move from literal readers to interpretive readers.

The homework will give students time to map the text using the words and features together to find and discover the right direction. It will be as if they are going on a big road trip, using the features as signposts and seeing how the larger chunks of text fit together.

Readers Study All Parts of a Text to Determine Main Ideas

CONNECTION

Using an anecdote, highlight the importance of knowing where to look when trying to figure out what is most important in a challenging text or lecture.

"When I was in college, I took a course called Finite Mathematics. It was incredibly challenging for me! I didn't have a great background in the topic, and I was confused by a lot of what the professor was saying. So, I had to come up with tricks to figure out the most important things to learn for the exams. I figured out that the professor would often start his lectures by naming and describing two or three things that he was planning to discuss that day. Even though his lectures tended to meander all over the place, I realized that the two or three things he named at the start of his lectures were the things that were most likely end up on the exams.

"Also, the professor used the white board as he lectured to illustrate his points. He didn't use the white board all the time, so when he did, I paid especially close attention. It turned out that the kinds of math problems he demonstrated on the board were often the ones he tested us on. It was as if he were using his visuals as a highlighter, pointing out the main ideas—the parts of his lecture that were the most important for us to pay attention to.

"Remembering this story from my college days got me thinking about the work that you are doing as nonfiction readers, trying to determine what is really important in the texts that you are reading. You are doing this work not just in simpler texts, where figuring out what is most important can be easier, but in harder texts as well.

"Readers, we have done a lot of work thus far on how to figure out the main ideas in the texts we read. For example, we talked about pausing after reading a chunk of text to consider the main ideas. We talked about a note-taking as a way of capturing the main ideas in a text. What I want to teach you today is one more way you can figure out the main ideas in the books you are reading."

A story such as this underscores the importance of reading strategically when the going is tough, and also positions you, the teacher, as a learner. We encourage you to tell your own story about a time that navigating a text or lecture was difficult for you. Students recognize and appreciate their teacher's willingness to share authentic struggles.

❖ **Name the teaching point.**

"Researchers, what I want to teach you today is this. There are specific places that a nonfiction reader can look to figure out the main ideas that the author of a text deems to be the most important. These places include the introductions and conclusions to a section, and any text features that go with the information."

TEACHING AND ACTIVE ENGAGEMENT

Channel students to study a page in the demonstration text, asking them to consider ways that certain parts of the text can help them to determine main ideas.

"I thought that we could try this together today, studying a part of a nonfiction text to think about the main ideas. Let's study a page from *Liberty! How the Revolutionary War Began*. The section called 'Don't Fire until You See the Whites of Their Eyes' tells about the beginnings of the American Revolution. I could skim this first page and notice lines such as 'American militiamen had worked all night to build a fort,' and 'Swarms of redcoats arrived from Boston, crossing the river by boat,' and I could think, 'Oh, this part tells all about the first battle of the Revolution and what happened there.'" As I said this, I projected the page on the document camera and pointed to the lines I mentioned.

"But let's look a bit closer and see if we can figure out what the author might really think is important about this topic. As I mentioned earlier, three places to particularly study are the introductions, conclusions, and text features.

"Right now, will you and your partner try this? Study the beginning and the end of this section, and then think, what might Lucille Recht Penner think is really important about the Battle of Bunker Hill?"

As students began to talk, I projected the pages of the book, drawing their attention to the beginning and ending sections.

A great way to teach the value of a new strategy is to demonstrate a less effective strategy first.

Don't Fire until You See the Whites of Their Eyes!

When the sun rose over Boston Harbor on June 17, 1775, sailors on the British warship Lively *awoke and stretched. Suddenly, one of them shouted in surprise. On a hill across the Charles River from Boston loomed a fort. It had not been there yesterday!*

Whistles blew and gunners raced to their battle stations. Soon the Lively's *cannons were spitting fire and black smoke. Other British warships joined in.*

When the Americans were gone, the British counted their dead. Almost half the soldiers who had set out that morning had been killed or wounded.

The Battle of Bunker Hill showed both sides how terrible war would be. But it was too late to turn back. Even deadlier battles lay ahead.

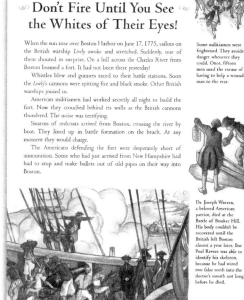

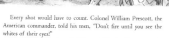

Coach with lean prompts, then convene the class and ask students to share their findings.

Partnerships leapt into discussion, and I moved among them, coaching into their work. To Jerry and Patricia, I said, "You are getting some interesting theories going based on the introduction. Now, study the conclusion and see if what's there matches your theories."

Some partnerships were getting hung up on details from both sections, and weren't making the inferential leap to consider how these details might relate to the main idea. I coached, "Readers, there are some rich details in the sections, details about the British gunners springing into action and about the numbers of soldiers who died. Why might the author have included these details? What might she be saying is important about this battle, and about the war in general?"

I whispered to another partnership, loud enough so others could hear, "Remember, authors choose their words carefully and include everything for a reason. Why might this author have decided to begin and end this part with the British perspective, instead of the American?"

After a few minutes, I called students back. "What do you think? What are some of the most important things the author might want us to know about this part?"

George said, "Grace and I thought maybe she wants us to think that the British were really scared, and that made us think that maybe what is important is the war was scary."

I nodded, "The war was scary, even for the side with more power. That could certainly be something the author considers important about this part."

Joyce chimed in. "We were saying she wants us to know that war is terrible, and this war was really deadly."

Explain that readers also study text features to determine what the author thinks is most important. Give students time to study text features, then highlight key ideas that are shared.

I nodded. "Readers, I think you're on to something here. There's another place I was telling you about that nonfiction readers can look to try to figure out what's most important. Are you game to try looking there as well?"

The students nodded, and I continued. "In addition to studying the introduction and conclusion of a section, readers can look at the text features to determine importance. We are starting to grow some ideas already, based on the introduction and conclusion. Now, study the text features with your partner and ask yourselves, 'What does the author think is most important about this information?'"

I projected the pages, zooming in on the text features as the students talked.

You'll notice that the method of teaching in this minilesson is not the usual demonstration. Instead you are providing students with guided practice.

After a few moments, I shared some of what I'd overheard. "Readers, I heard a few of you talking about the image and caption, saying that many American militiamen were afraid and avoided danger whenever they could. Based on this, you guessed that the author thinks it's important that many of the Patriots might not have wanted to go to war. The other images and captions tell about American and British soldiers who were killed. You were saying these show that the author thinks it's important that both sides suffered many casualties.

"I'm getting the sense that you are starting to think that there are two main ideas the author wants to get across on this page. One, the war was terrifying and dangerous, and two, neither side was really happy about going to war."

Debrief, naming the replicable work that the students did that you hope they will continue to do as they read.

"Readers, what a leap in understanding you just took. We started out thinking that this part was mostly about the Battle of Bunker Hill, and that perhaps the most important things the author wanted us to know were details about the battle, like how it started, who was there, and that kind of thing. But after studying the introduction, conclusion, and text features, you are starting to think that actually, what the author might really want us to know is that neither side really wanted to go to war, because war is terrible, for any reason. Do you see how studying certain parts of the text helped you to figure out the main idea the author might want to get across in this part?"

LINK

Launch students into their independent reading and research, reminding them that the work they just tried can help them to determine the main ideas in the texts they are reading.

"Readers, this work of determining what the author wants us to think or to know about the information isn't just something to try once and then forget. This is really crucial work to do from now on, anytime you read a nonfiction book, or a website, or listen to a lecture. You can study the beginnings and endings and text features to think, what are the most important ideas here?

"You'll have lots of choices to make today about what to work on. But would you try this work of using parts of the text to determine main ideas at least once? Off you go!"

For many young readers of informational text, text features can feel "separate" from the main body of text. This teaching will allow children to connect everything on the page to forge a cohesive "main idea."

Predictable Challenges with Determining the Main Idea

TEACHING STUDENTS to determine the main idea is no small feat, particularly with the added angle of considering what the author deems to be most important. Getting kids to attempt this work is crucial to their development as nonfiction readers. You won't want kids to brush this teaching aside, thinking, "I know how to do that." Therefore, chances are good that much of your conferring and small-group work today will be in supporting kids to apply the teaching of the minilesson.

You might gather a small group of students and explain to them that the strategies they learned today, studying certain parts of a text to get ideas about what the author deems important, can be helpful not only when reading a text for the first time, but also as a way to take a fresh look at a text you've already read. Explain that you recently went back to reread and rethink a section in *The Revolutionary War*, by Josh Gregory, and you were surprised at what you found.

We recommend you draw on the "Main Idea(s) and Supporting Details/Summary" strand of the Informational Reading Learning Progression as you consider ways to support your students with this challenging work.

One expectation is that students are able to summarize the main points that the author makes and to link these to related points. Another expectation is that students are able to differentiate between the details that are important to the idea, and not just details that are interesting to the student. Likely, you'll notice that many of your students could use support in either one of these trajectories.

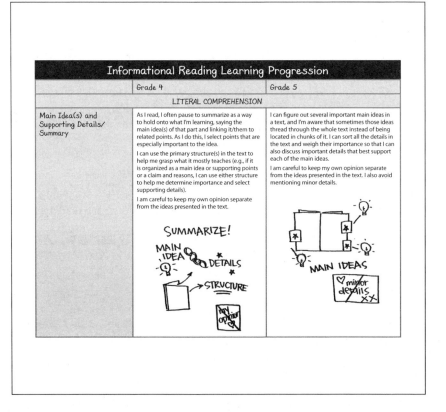

I placed the "Analyzing Author's Craft" strand of the Informational Reading Learning Progression under the document camera, then I called for the students' attention. "Readers, would you turn so you can see the screen? Let's take a moment to study part of our checklist together and think about what this part, 'Analyzing Author's Craft,' might mean for us as readers. This part describes some work that many educators think is really important for kids to be able to do, which is thinking about the choices that the author of a text might have made. To do this work well, and to be an even better *reader* of information, it helps draw on all you know about being a great *writer* of information. Would you read the third-grade section, and talk to your partner for a moment about the work third-graders are expected to do?"

I waited for a moment, and then repeated some of what I'd overheard students saying. "I heard some of you saying that in third grade, kids are expected to notice decisions the author has made, decisions like ways to begin and end, and parts to say a lot about. You also were saying that in third grade, kids are expected to think about times that an author made something in particular stand out.

"Now, would you and your partner study the fourth-grade portion together? See if you can find the parts that are different from what is expected in third grade, and talk especially about those parts."

After a moment, I called for the students' attention. "It sounds like some of you are thinking that in fourth grade, the new expectations are for you to be able to talk about ways that the author's choices affect you as a reader, and to name some of the craft moves the author has made.

"As you read on, would you give all of this a try? Make sure you are doing the third-grade work, so notice parts that really stand out. Then, try the fourth-grade work. Write or make plans to talk about the how those parts made you feel or what they

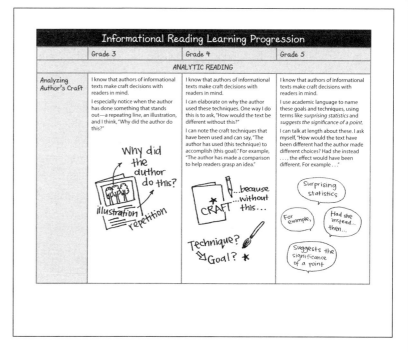

made you think. If you can, name some of the craft moves the author made to make you feel a certain way, like repeating a line, or using a quote from another source, or including a particular text feature. In information books, even craft moves like the size of the font in certain parts are often designed to evoke certain feelings in readers."

Support students in finding the main idea.

For texts that are in the lower text bands, you might teach students who struggle with main idea to read to find the main idea in the text. This main idea is explicitly stated and can often be found by looking at the topic sentence the first sentence in the book or looking for recurring details. As students identify the topic sentence, the other sentences in the section provide the supporting details that fit with that sentence. So coach them to flag the topic sentence and the sentences that follow it.

Students at lower levels are probably reading texts that have headings. You can teach them to look at all the headings within a section and ask, "What is the main idea based on all these headings?" then you can move them from naming a topic to identifying a main idea. You might show students how you try this work by using examples from *Revolutionary War* by Josh Gregory. You might look at some of the headings in the beginning of the book: "A New Start in North America," "Seed of Rebellion," "The War Begins." You might show students that the headings tell a story already: colonists looked forward to a fresh start, but something went wrong that led to a war. You might tell students that in this case, the main idea for this section might be the causes for the war.

If you have students who easily notice facts, brilliant! You might teach these students that one way to find a main idea of a text is to start with the key details. You are likely to work backward. You'll likely to teach students to list out the important details they are learning and then ask, "What are the big ideas that these details are trying to show or support?" Students can do this work within one paragraph, noticing how the details all fit together.

Summarize details to come up with the main idea.

While reading fiction, you taught students to read chunks of the text, and then pause to summarize. You might show readers that they can do that again in nonfiction. Anticipate that they'll need reminders not just to summarize the parts they've just read but also to remember that when they summarize, they synthesize the information connected to the main idea.

The summary might not be from one text necessarily but many different texts. So you want to remind students to pause in their reading, asking themselves if the information they have gathered in the sections of text they read (including diagrams, excerpts, captions, and illustrations) fits with something they have read previously in another text. Ask children to think if the information connects to what they are thinking about at the moment, or perhaps causes them to revise their main idea. You can remind students that just as fiction readers pause often in their reading to summarize the events of the story, nonfiction readers pause often to summarize the important information of the text.

Focusing on Text Features

Ask students to examine the read-aloud text to discover how text features reveal important information related to the main idea.

"Readers, no two texts are exactly alike. Each text is so different, and you will never find two that provide totally the same perspective, text features, structures, or information. Let's take a look at our read-aloud text *Liberty!* asking, 'How do the text features reveal important information about the main idea?' Reread some of that text, then turn and talk." I displayed page 6 on the document camera.

I voiced over to lift the level of student work. I added, "Now, look at some of *The Revolutionary War* and ask yourselves the same question, 'How do the text features reveal important information about the main idea?' Then turn and talk." I displayed page 11 from *The Revolutionary War* on the document camera.

The students noted that in *Liberty!* the dialogue, captions, and talk bubbles helped identify what's important, and the pictures provided a contrast to what was said in the text. Students noted that in *The Revolutionary War*, the pictures, captions, and maps highlighted important information that supported the main idea.

"Remember that when you examine the text features, they will often reveal information to you that will help support the main idea of the section. This helps you know what's really important about the text you're reading."

TEXT FEATURES CAN HELP YOU ROAD MAP

Readers, today you discovered that authors often reveal important information in text features. Those text features often help convey the main idea of a small chunk of text. There were lots of ways in which that work was supported today. Today, you only read a tiny portion of the text, so you were really looking for the main idea of a few paragraphs not of a larger text. Tonight, read larger portions of text, maybe ten or twenty pages, and then determine the main idea of that whole large chunk of text, using the text features as we did today as a guide. Think of the text as a road map as if you going on a big road trip. The features are like signposts that help you see how the larger chunks of text fit together.

Readers Alter Their Strategies Based on the Kind of Text They Are Reading

ear Teachers,

By now, your students know a lot about many genres, and they have a lot of skills they can draw on for reading in a whole range of ways. But it is more common than you might think for students to forget to draw on what they know. And that is where this session comes to play.

Today, we suggest you teach students to access their prior knowledge of text structure as they preview their texts. Then, after they've identified the structure of a text or a part of text, you'll likely want to teach students that they can draw on all the strategies they know for reading that kind of text. To make this work especially powerful for students, you will want to pull out anchor charts you used in earlier units, highlighting strategies students know for reading different genres of texts. Across your teaching, you'll emphasize that readers make their way through texts differently, based on their knowledge of the genre they're reading.

MINILESSON

In your connection, you will probably want to remind students about the benefits of reading an easier text to develop the prior knowledge enough to be more able to handle denser texts. You could ask students to bring the texts they have been reading to the meeting area. Suggest they show each other the easier texts and talk about the enormous amount of learning they could do from texts that at first glance seemed simple, perhaps even baby-ish. Then again, you might display an accessible text that two of your researchers studied, pointing out that the really active, thoughtful learner can glean *so much* from one of those not-to-be-dismissed texts.

Your teaching point might be, "Today I want to teach you that just as it helps to bring prior knowledge of a *topic* to your reading of a complex nonfiction text, it also helps to bring prior knowledge of how this kind of text tends to go. To access that prior knowledge of genre, you need to preview a text (or part of a text,) thinking, 'What do I know about strategies for reading this sort of a text?'"

In the teaching part of your lesson, you'll perhaps remind students of the strategies they already know from reading narrative and expository texts, and within the latter category, for reading texts of various structures. You will presumably want to highlight anchor charts from earlier units that accentuate some of the strategies students have learned to use when reading other genres. For example, you might bring the "Reading Intensely to Grow Ideas" anchor chart forward from the first unit in your year.

Ask students to study it, asking "Which of the strategies that we use when reading fiction are relevant when we read biography and other forms of narrative nonfiction?" You can do the same with the "Rev Up Your Mind before Reading Nonfiction!" anchor chart from the Grade 3 *Reading to Learn* narrative nonfiction unit.

You might remind students that narrative nonfiction often shares certain elements with narrative fiction. Refer them to the "Story Elements" chart and remind them that they can draw upon their prior knowledge of fiction story elements when reading narrative nonfiction.

For your active engagement, you might want to give students the opportunity to practice previewing texts for text structure and drawing on the strategies they know for working with the kinds of texts they are encountering. For example, you might give them a passage from *Liberty!* which is structured in complex way, requiring them to shift from reading in one way to reading in another:

Spies!

What is a spy?

Someone who secretly watches and gathers information about an enemy's actions and plans.

A spy could be anyone. The young boy who held a British officer's horse might listen to a conversation and report it to the Sons of Liberty.

Some spies memorized the information they gathered so there would be no proof if they got caught. Others hid notes in their shoes, in hollow buttons, and even in bullets.

"Sympathetic ink"—a kind of invisible ink—was used by both sides. So were ciphers and book codes.

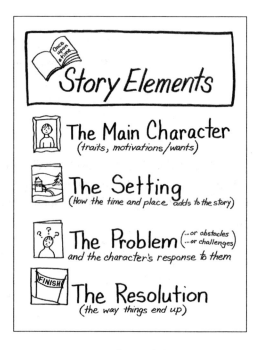

Ciphers were easy to write. You just substituted a different letter for each letter of the alphabet. For example, if you sent your friend a message saying T RGLPGB, he would be able to read it—as long as he knew the cipher you were using:

T stands for A
R stands for S
G stands for E
L stands for C
P stands for R
G stands for E (again)
B stands for T

T RGLPGB would mean A SECRET.

Ask students to talk to a partner about what they are picturing as they read the text. What sort of mental movie are they constructing? Are they constructing a mental movie of the text, picturing what they're reading as if it were real life? Or, are they creating their own text features in their minds as they read, almost drawing boxes and bullets or timelines and charts to capture the information they're learning?

For your link, you might send students off to read, encouraging them to draw on their prior knowledge of text structure to help them find strategies for reading these texts. You might decide to ask students to record the mental pictures they are creating as they read.

CONFERRING AND SMALL-GROUP WORK

By now, students should have read several texts on a particular subtopic, and so you will want to harken back to the earlier minilessons on synthesizing across texts. Remind students to read each new text on a subtopic thinking, "Does this add onto what I already knew? Change what I already knew?" Your hope will be that students will have read the sparser text on a subtopic first, taking notes from that one text, and then turned to a more detailed text, synthesizing the notes from the more detailed text into the broad outline of the first set of notes.

For your stronger readers, you may want to channel them to think carefully about the relationship between two texts on a topic. For example, students may read about the aftermath of the American Revolution from both Josh Gregory's *The Revolutionary War* and Rosalyn Schanzer's *George vs. George*. You might coach some of them to closely compare the two texts, noticing what each author has made important. You could say, "Readers, after you read a couple of sources on any topic, it is helpful to compare and contrast those sources, noticing how the texts portray the topic in similar ways and how the texts are different. You can then consider how each author made different craft decisions. You might think, 'Does the way the author wrote this relate to the big idea he or she is trying to get across?' *The Revolutionary War*, for example, seems to want readers to know that at the conclusion of the war, the country still faced many trials. Then,

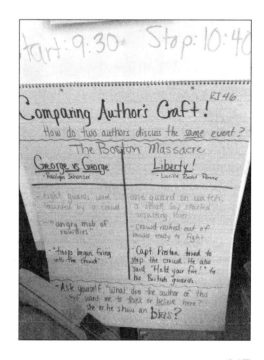

students might ask themselves, 'What information is in this account that is not in other accounts?' and 'What major points is each author making? What are the key details each other is including?'"

For students who need more support, you might consider leading a guided reading session. You'll probably want to work with any one of those groups for three days or so, with the aim that when the days are over, they will be able to continue reading texts at the level of difficulty that you supported without your help.

You'll want to decide whether to support the kids in reading one chapter of a book, a picture book, or whether to channel them toward a shorter text. If you decide on a longer text, you will probably read just a chunk of it in any one day's guided reading session, encouraging students to continue to read it on their own.

If you decide to work with students who could be reading level Q, with support, you might channel them toward the picture book *The American Revolution* by Don Nardo. In your text introduction, you might say something like, "You are about to read a book that shows the determination of the early Americans. The book celebrates the fact that despite many disadvantages, the American colonies were able to successfully defeat the large and powerful British military to form an independent country and give birth to modern democracy." You will probably want to help them think about the structure of the book, so you might say, "You'll notice that the book is structured as a narrative. It tells the story of the colonists and what they had to endure. There are parts of it that are written as informational texts, such as a little section that tells all-about the laws against the colonists or all-about a particular battle. But mostly this is a narrative, so read it, thinking about the colonists as a character in a true story."

You might say, "I left some Post-its in your copy of the book, and when you get to those Post-its, would you wait for the others to catch up and do some talking about what you have learned so far? I'll help in those spots." In this manner, you give your students an extra dose of prior knowledge not only of the topic, but also of the text structure, and that will help them read a text that was just a tiny bit beyond what they could handle with independence.

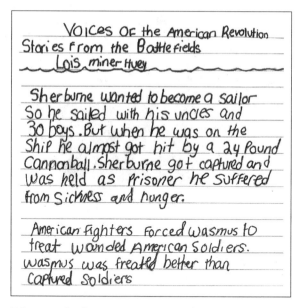

FIG. 17–1 Student summarizing and envisioning.

Mid-Workshop Teaching

In your mid-workshop teaching, you might focus kids' attention on envisioning a hybrid text—one that has both narrative and expository elements. You might highlight an example that you found from a student, such as Talia. "Readers, Talia just read a primary source, 'Stockbridge Indian Speech,' and she noticed that it also both narrative and expository parts in it. So how do you envision a text when it has elements more than one genre? Let's hear what Talia did."

Talia said, "'Stockbridge Indian Speech' starts with a story about how the colonists first came to America, and the Indians befriended them. But then the speaker says that over time, the colonists grew stronger and stronger, and the Indians became less powerful. I can really picture that part, like a movie in my mind.

"But then if I keep reading, I could almost make boxes and bullets in my mind. The box, or the main idea, is that the Stockbridge Indians wanted the colonists' protection. Then I can picture the bullet points: that the Indians would fight with the colonists against England, that the Indians would seek help from other tribes, and that all the Indians wanted was to be able to fight their own way, not like the English."

I said, "Okay everyone, so take a look at the texts you're reading. If you see that they have the structure of more than one genre, you can picture the narrative parts as a mental movie, and the expository parts as a diagram, like boxes and bullets."

SHARE

For your share, you might set students up to use the "Envisioning" strand of the Informational Reading Learning Progression for grades 3, 4, and 5 to assess their work. You might say, "Readers, I've asked you to record the mental movie you're generating about the texts you're reading. Look at your copy of the 'Envisioning' strand of the progression. I know you've seen this strand before, in earlier grades. I am showing you another level of it because it's important to always push yourself toward new goals. Will you and your partner use the progression to assess how you made that mental movie? And together, figure out some goals to push yourself higher."

Then, listen in and coach, interjecting some prompts that raise the level of what students are doing. After a few minutes, gather the class and ask a student to share work and goals that will benefit the rest of the class or highlight what you have heard. You might say something like, "Readers, I see you all deciding where on the progression your work falls, and setting some goals for yourself. Let me share with you what Emmanuel said, because I think it is very important. Emmanuel told Sophia that he thinks he is already doing some of the work at the fourth-grade level, because he has been careful to make a mental movie as he reads, just as he does for fiction. But he wants to push himself to do this work at the fifth-grade level, by making sure his mental movie includes details not just from that part of the text, but from earlier parts of the text as well. Sophia said that she's been picturing the events she's been reading about as a timeline, with one event following the other. This is work that you can be doing. Set yourself a goal, and read and reread with that goal in mind."

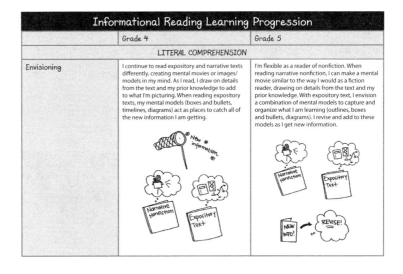

Homework

For tonight's homework, you might want to encourage students to work on volume. Urge them to read for as many pages as they can, perhaps even surpassing their last reading time entry in their log. Remind students to be aware that oftentimes nonfiction texts can be both expository and narrative, and that the envisionment work that they do for each genre will be different. You might ask students to find another scene in their book that feels particularly significant to the experiences people had during the American Revolution. Urge them to go back and reread that scene intensely, several times, and see how it connects to other scenes. Finally, you might ask them to find at least one other scene that connects to the one they have chosen and reread that second scene, as well.

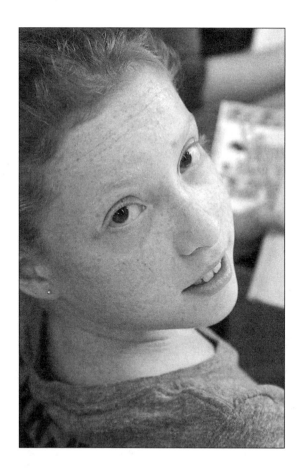

Session 18

Developing a Richer Conceptual Knowledge of Key Vocabulary

RESEARCH SUGGESTS THAT vocabulary becomes increasingly important as students become older and their texts become more complex. While easier texts often embed the definition of a word into the text so that readers need not bring prior knowledge of the word to their reading, as texts become more challenging, readers are increasingly expected to know many words beforehand. Even understanding definitions becomes increasingly difficult because often these new, hard words are defined by other hard, technical words.

Today, you will teach students that to know a word, to truly know it, it's often insufficient to just read the dictionary definition of the word and move on. The words students are encountering in these historical texts are nuanced and complex: *revolution, sovereignty, treason, repealed, subjects*. That means, students cannot encounter the word *pardon* in a text, look up the definition and see it reads "forgiveness of crimes" and say, "Yup, I've got it. I know this word inside and out." Your teaching today will bring this to life for students. You will teach them that in addition to figuring out how to say a word and getting the gist of it, they have to know words well. That means they should be able to give examples of the word, talk about its variations and the ways it is similar to and different from those variations, and give examples of how the word tends to be used.

To do this, students will have to read and think beyond the sentence in the text where the word initially appeared. You'll show students how they can generate an initial definition for a word and revise this definition each time they encounter the word in a text.

The muscles we're developing here are not new ones. Your students are used to growing initial ideas about their characters early in their fiction books and then holding those ideas loosely, looking for evidence that confirms their ideas or leads them to revise their thinking. They know that ideas take time to grow. Today, you will show them the same is true when they encounter complex vocabulary.

IN THIS SESSION, you'll teach students that when readers approach a new word, they not only learn the definition of it, but also work to understand the word and how it is used at a deeper level.

GETTING READY

✔ Display the "Figuring Out the Meaning of Unknown Words" chart from Session 6 of *Reading the Weather, Reading the World* (see Connection).

✔ Prepare an excerpt for students to read and practice their word-solving skills learned in the last unit (see Teaching).

✔ Display the "Knowing a Word Means You Can . . ." chart to help students understand new words at a deeper level (see Teaching).

✔ Distribute a challenging passage for students to read and name the strategies they used with a partner. A link to the passage we used is available in the online resources (see Teaching).

✔ Select four brief text excerpts that each contains the same unfamiliar vocabulary term. You will divide the class into four groups and give the partnerships in each group a copy of one of the excerpts. These excerpts are available in the online resources (see Active Engagement).

✔ Choose a student who has an effective system for keeping track of new vocabulary to share the system with the class (see Mid-Workshop Teaching).

✔ Create a short list of words historians often use to share with students (see Mid-Workshop Teaching).

Developing a Richer Conceptual Knowledge of Key Vocabulary

CONNECTION

Remind students about word-solving strategies that they learned in the previous unit.

"Readers, the other day when you helped me paraphrase a dense and difficult text about 'The Sopranos,' we could have gotten stuck on words like *infidelity* (which you may remember means 'not loyal'). I happened to know the hard words in that passage about 'The Sopranos,' but for me, and for every reader in the world, there are lots of times when we are reading along, and we come to words that we don't know.

"You've studied strategies for tackling complex vocabulary words already, and I thought we better start by reviewing those strategies. Do you remember this chart from our last unit?

"Remember that when you look *in* the word, you are thinking about the word parts. A root word can clue you in to the meaning. A prefix, like *anti-* or *dis-*, which both meant *not*, can change the meaning of the root word. And a suffix like *-ness* or *-able* changes the kind of word it is.

"And remember that you can also look around the word to help you figure out its meaning. Perhaps the author gave a definition, or the meaning of the whole section might help. You can also try turning your tentative definition into a synonym, and see if it makes sense if you substitute it for the tricky word.

"But is that all you need to do to really know a word?"

✤ **Name the teaching point.**

"Today I want to teach you that getting to know a word well is like getting to know a person or a character in a book. You don't meet the person and then say to yourself, 'I've got that person completely figured out.' It's the same way with words. Getting to know a word well, like getting to know a person well, takes time."

◆ COACHING

Figuring Out the Meaning of Unknown Words

Look in...
- *Root words*   hemisphere (½) (●)
- *Suffixes*   recycle
- *Prefixes*   antibody ✗

Look around...
- *What do you picture?*
- *What's happening?*
- *Is it positive or negative?* ☺⁺ ☹⁻
- *What type of word is it?*
  object   action   describing word

TEACHING

Give students a chance to practice the word-solving skills they learned in the last unit by reading a challenging passage and naming the strategies they used with a partner.

"Before we go on, I'm going to ask you to use those strategies to read a passage, trying to use the strategies you have already been taught to do this work." I distributed this passage. "Work on your own for a minute to figure out some of the tricky words."

> *Cornwallis, desperate for reinforcements that would never reach him in time, hatched a plan to try to escape across the York River. Bad weather, however, disabled his transport boats and Cornwallis was finally forced to surrender. On October 17, surrender negotiations began and were finalized two days later. As a result of the surrender, the Americans took more than 7,000 British troops prisoner and the entire Revolutionary War had nearly come to an end. According to legend, as the British soldiers formally surrendered, their drummers and fifers played the tune to* The World Turn'd Upside Down. *Yorktown would be the last major battle of the war.*

"Readers, in a minute, I'm going to ask you to talk to a partner about some of the tricky words that you found and the strategies that you used to figure out those words. Be sure to let your research group know what you did. Like you might say, 'I started off by looking *inside* the word and I noticed . . . and that made me think of . . . Then I looked *around* the word and I noticed some of the clues in the text including . . . so I thought maybe the word could mean . . . This helped me understand that. . . .'"

"Turn and talk."

Tell students that knowing a word well means more than simply knowing a definition, and give them a familiar example of a word they have come to know very well.

"Readers, I think sometimes kids grow up thinking that to get to know a word, all you have to do is learn the definition of the word. You learn a way to tell what the word means in about five or six words. And it is true that being able to do that is helpful.

"But think about the word *minilesson*. You could, if you needed to do so, come up with a four- or five-word definition of a minilesson. But you could also talk for a very long time about everything you know about minilessons." I then showed a list.

"Think right now whether you could give some *examples* of minilessons. Could you talk about how minilessons are *like and unlike* similar ways of teaching and learning? For example, could you talk about how minilessons are similar to and different from read aloud, for example? Could you talk about how they tend to go—what tends to happen at the start, the middle, the end of minilessons? Could you talk about varieties of minilessons—-say, about minilessons in writing, minilessons in reading?"

Academic vocabulary is one of the world-class standards that is talked about and studied by all the major reading researchers and yet students still have problems with vocabulary. One thing we suggest is to let your students learn to deal with complicated words and not give them the definition.

Knowing a Word Means you can...

- Give examples of it

- Talk about how it is similar to and different from variations

- Explain how it tends to be, or to go

- Talk about the various kinds of it

Ask students to test their understanding of a challenging word related to the American Revolution not just by defining it, but by explaining it well.

"It's pretty clear that you have really learned the word *minilesson*. But have you really learned words related to the American Revolution like *boycott*?

"Right now, with your partner, come up with a four- or five-word definition of *boycott*." I gave children a half-minute to do that.

"Now can you work through the chart and see if you can do these other things for *boycott*, as you can for *minilesson*. Get started."

The room erupted into conversation, and I traveled quickly from one set of partners to another. Not surprisingly, they floundered a bit. "Readers, I'm not surprised that you had some difficulty talking long about this term—and my hunch is that will be true for other terms that you have just begun to learn as you study the American Revolution. That's okay, because research shows it takes about twenty encounters with a word for a person to grasp the word at all. Many of you have only seen the term *boycott* a few times.

"But the important thing is not that you have mastered all the vocabulary words that you are encountering. No, the important thing is that you *don't* think getting a tiny little definition of a word is all you need. The important thing is that you realize that getting to know a word, like getting to know a person, takes time."

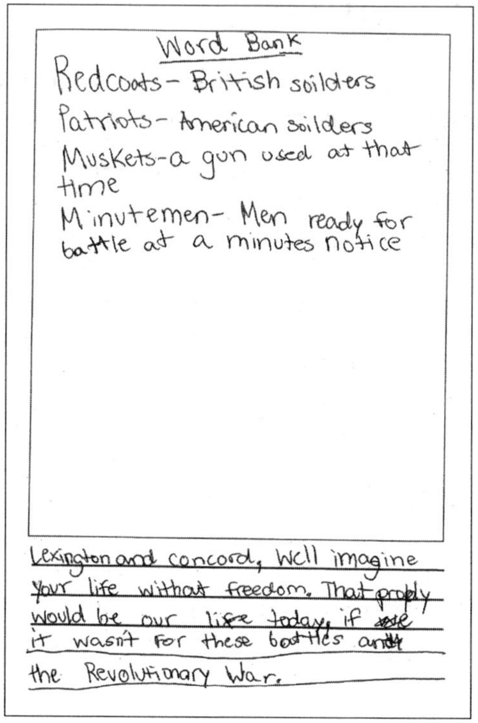

ACTIVE ENGAGEMENT

Divide the class into four groups, charging each group with the task of understanding the meaning of a word from a text excerpt.

"So let's work on at least starting to know the term *boycott*. We don't have time for us to read enough that we see the word in twenty places, so what I am going to do is to divide this class into four quadrants, and I'm going to give each partnership in each quadrant a small text that includes the term *boycott*. And I'm going to ask you to study your text for all it is worth and to glean everything you possibly can about boycotts from your text. Then you'll need to come together with the other partnerships sitting in your quarter of the meeting area, and see if you can piece together a deeper understanding of this term." I gave three groups new texts containing the word, and I gave the text we had just studied together to one group to revisit.

Text One:

> The Stamp Act was one of unfair laws women fought. To raise money, the British government passed a law saying that colonial citizens had to pay a tax on every piece of printed paper they used. Everything—from newspapers and marriage licenses to playing cards—was taxed. Many felt this Stamp Act tax was unfair.

Word Bank
Redcoats – British soilders
Patriots – American soilders
Muskets – a gun used at that time
Minutemen – Men ready for battle at a minutes notice

Lexington and concord, Well imagine your life without freedom. That proly would be our life today, if we it wasn't for these bootles and the Revolutionary War.

FIG. 18–1   Personal word bank.

In talking about academic vocabulary, world-class standards discuss the use of a word in several different ways. The students need to be able to recognize how the word is used and why. Listen in to the students and coach in when necessary as they explore the meaning of boycott *together.*

Text Two:

Many women—among them, those calling themselves "daughters of liberty"—agreed to boycott British goods to protest the Stamp Act. These women refused to use British cloth to make their clothes.

Text Three:

From 1764 to 1775, England enacted a series of taxes on the American Colonies . . . The men and women of Massachusetts particularly were opposed to England's policies. They formed political resistance groups, such as the Boston's Sons of Liberty and Daughters of Liberty, and boycotted the taxed goods. But whenever the British government repealed one tax in the Colonies, it quickly introduced another.

Text Four:

1764—In May, at a town meeting in Boston, James Otis raises the issue of taxation without representation and urges a united response to the recent acts imposed by England. In July, Otis publishes "The Rights of the British Colonies Asserted and Proved." In August, Boston merchants begin a boycott of British luxury goods.

I gave students a minute to read their excerpts and discuss what they learned about the word *boycott*. Then I continued, "Readers, eyes up here. You've all had a moment to read and think about the word *boycott*. Now let's see if we can really know the word *boycott*, based on all that you have learned from your reading."

I asked Jose to start. "Well, our quick definition was that a boycott is when people decide not to use or buy something. And now we know a bunch of examples of that."

His partner Sophie chimed in. "Yeah, one boycott was by the Daughters of Liberty and they boycotted buying cloth that was from Great Britain. And another one was from a Massachusetts court, boycotting goods like glass and lead and paint and paper."

I named the work Sophie and Jose had just done for the class. "That's one way you can get to know a word well, by learning and then giving examples of it."

George jumped in. "I think I can say how they tend to go. Boycotts tend to be started by some group—mine said they were often started by resistance groups. And they tend to involve a lot of people, not just one or two." He paused, glancing at his passage. "Oh, and they often lead to something else, like boycotting British goods would make the British angry, and they'd react."

"Readers, do you see how when we first encountered the word *boycott*, it was hard to say more than a few words about it? But then, as we encountered the word multiple times, our understanding became more nuanced. Now, I think we can safely say we're on the road to knowing this word."

A quick, appreciative debrief of the good work done by one student is great encouragement for all students to try the same thing.

LINK

Encourage students to pay particular attention to new unfamiliar words as they read today. Urge them to write those words down, define them, and work hard to really get to know them.

"Readers, as you go off to read today, I want you to pay extra attention to the new words you come across. Test yourself to see if you really know what they mean. When you see an unfamiliar word, jot it down in your word bank, or whatever system you have to keep track of your new words, and try first to define it in four or five words. Then as you read, see if you come across that word again. Think about all the ways you can get to know what word better so that you really, truly understand it.

"Off you go!"

Word Bank

Colonists	loyalists	intolerable acts
people that lived in the colonies	people that lived in the colonies but were still loyal to the king. Also called kingsmen or tories.	More taxes and acts put up after the Boston Tea Party
Red coats	Patriots	Militia
British soldiers. Also called lobsterbacks	American Army, the people in the militia, also called rebels	Army for ex. the American militia.
Minutemen	Smugglers	General
Soldiers that could be ready in a minutes notice.	people would buy goods from other countries to avoid paying taxes.	The leader of an army.

FIG. 18–2   Vocabulary

Keep the Unit Work Going while Supporting Vocabulary Development

YOU'LL WANT TO CONFER and lead small groups to support your students doing all that they know how to do as nonfiction readers. Some of your teaching today might focus on using the "Building Vocabulary" thread in the "Word Work" strand of the learning progression, which mentions *concept words*. Anticipate that your English language learners (ELLs) and struggling readers may not be able to *identify* which of the unfamiliar words they encounter are actually concept words. You might pull up a small group where you explain what these are.

It is tempting to tell youngsters that concept words represent "abstract" ideas but remember that the word *abstract* might not be familiar to many ELLs either. Your definition will have to be as basic as it can be. "Concept words are trickier than other words—they define something you can't touch or see. They don't describe a thing (like a rock or a dog—you could touch and see a dog and a rock), they describe an idea like democracy or a process . . . ," you might say. You'll want to use plenty of examples of concept words to help readers mentally categorize these. Your small group could help each other create a list of concept words associated with their topics. For example, *revolution*, *tariff*, *representation*, *rights*, and *authority* are concept words that would go with the American Revolution.

While dictionaries seem like a simple solution to word solving, watch out for children who require coaching in looking up a word. Many will skim over a "glossary definition" without really soaking in meaning so you might want to teach them to categorize words to create more nuanced understanding:

◆ What part of speech is this word?

◆ Is there a word we can use to substitute for this word?

◆ How does this word go with the bigger topic?

◆ Say the word out loud. Try using the word in a sentence.

MID-WORKSHOP TEACHING
Knowing Words that All Historians Use

"Readers, I know you are reading up a storm, but I just have to tell you that some members of this class decided, on their own, to make word walls. What a terrific idea! Will you and your partner make sure you have some plan for recording your vocabulary words? You can make a word wall, or a glossary, or some other system—but do something.

"You'll have to decide how to define the words. Sophia is drawing little pictures of each word as she comes to understand it (and some of those words aren't easily illustrated!).

"Whether you have a word wall of your own or not, I do want to make sure that you know a few words that are historians use a lot. They aren't specifically about the American Revolution, but they are words that all historians use. Will you and your partner see if you can come to a beginning understanding of these words? We'll come back to them several times over the next week. If you aren't sure what they mean, talk to each other.

"And remember that you'll be getting to know these words for a long time. If you get an early definition of them today, that's a start—but expect to continue learning about them for a while."

annotate	secondary source
context	perspective
primary source	chronological

After children worked together on the short list of words, I said, "Back to your research, and your word work!"

Readers Learn Vocabulary from Each Other

Ask students to set up a display, with visuals and definitions, of a few key words from their research. Give partners time to visit other displays and talk about the words they displayed.

"Readers, instead of us coming together today, I'm going to ask you and your partner to make a display of two or three keywords that you have learned as you do your research. The display can include sketches or definitions you have made for the words, passages in book you have earmarked that illustrate the words, work on prefixes or suffixes or root words. You have five minutes to set this display up, and then I'm going to ask one member of your partnership to go to other partnership spots and learn their words. The other partner, stay behind to talk to people who come by to learn from you. If you have more time before people come, work on your display.

"Get started!" I gave students a few minutes to create their display. While they worked, I coached in, reminding them that their display should show they really know the word well. Then, I said, "All right, decide which partner is staying and which partner is traveling to other displays, and then start learning from each other."

As children moved from one spot to another, I said, "I love that those of you who are traveling around learning words are recording those words. You will definitely need to bring them home to your partner and add them to your own word bank."

KEEPING TRACK OF WORDS WITH SPECIAL MEANING

Readers, tonight for homework you may discover that the words you are noticing have a special place in the books, or a reason for being there. These words may recur in many different ways. Tonight, if you notice a repeated word, can you put it on the shelf in your bank of words? Be prepared to share any words you find with your partner and to hold those words in a special place. Make it a goal to learn and then remember these words' meanings as you encounter them in other books.

Also, continue reading your independent book and logging your progress. Take a good look at your log. Have you read more this week than last week?

Session 19

Questioning and Hypothesizing to Reach Deeper Conclusions

ear Teachers,

We are choosing to write this session as a letter to you, to provide guidance on how you might plan your teaching to best meet the needs of your students. For the past several days, your students have been reading, researching, and note-taking in groups, aiming to cull the most important ideas and information about their topics and also to grow their own ideas about all they are learning. The latter skill, though often it is less emphasized than the former, is the one that is a critically important twenty-first-century learning skill.

Today, then, we emphasize the growing of ideas as students read.

Too often, students get the message that having a question about something isn't a good thing. Having a question could imply that they're confused, and being confused could imply that they aren't bright. But what many students don't realize is that it is actually the brightest students who ask the most questions.

Inquiry, as a process, continues to be the basis for great scientific discoveries and creative outputs. Many professionals, from advertising executives, to teachers, to physicians, do their best work when they engage in a process of posing and hypothesizing answers to meaningful questions.

In this session, you will launch students into their own inquiries, teaching them that while researchers sometimes ask questions that can quickly be answered, they also ask questions that don't have clear or quick answers. Then, rather than pausing here, you'll teach students that once researchers generate questions, they go a step further, considering several possible answers to their questions. As they do so, they draw on their growing body of knowledge about the topic. At the same time, you'll make clear the critical importance of this work in our society and in the lives of your students.

MINILESSON

You might start your minilesson by telling a story about a famous researcher who reached a grand understanding by asking and answering questions. You might tell the story of a familiar character, such as Benjamin Franklin, who loved to ask and answer questions. In addition to being remembered for his role in the American Revolution, Franklin is known for his inventions and scientific discoveries. All of his discoveries started with questions, and were fueled by Franklin's intense desire to find out answers. For example, he was dying to know whether electricity could be collected from lightning. He couldn't find an answer in any of his reading. But, he had done enough research about electricity to make a hypothesis, or a guess, that the answer was yes. Though we don't know all the details for sure about how Franklin made his famous discovery, the story goes that he held up a kite with a key attached in a thunderstorm, and when lightning struck the key, he got a small electric shock.

Then debrief, explaining that this story shows that many important understandings have been reached because people aren't afraid to ask and answer questions. You might also stress that Benjamin Franklin was able to hypothesize an answer to his own question, because he had done a significant amount of research on the topic.

Then, name your teaching point. You might say something like, "Today I want to teach you that researchers don't expect to quickly find answers to every question they have. Instead, they use what they know about a topic to hypothesize possible answers to questions without clear answers."

To illustrate your point, you might tell the story of a student who was at first stumped and frustrated at not being able to find answers to a question, but who then used what she knew about the topic to hypothesize an answer. "Readers," you might begin, "A few years ago, my students and I were studying ancient China. One of my students, let's call her Clare, had been reading voraciously about the Great Wall. Clare came up to me and said, 'I've been reading a lot about the Great Wall of China, but I can't figure out how long it took to build it. Do you know? How long did it take?'" You could explain that you were flummoxed, you didn't have a ready answer, and didn't know what to tell the student. But then, the student continued, saying, "In one book, it says that they started building it after the Ming Dynasty started in 1368, and they kept building it until the 1600s, so that would be more than 200 years. But then another said it took centuries, which is even longer. And one said there were lots of versions of the Great Wall and one only took nine years to build! So, I'm thinking what's hard about figuring this out is that there were lots of walls called the Great Wall over time."

Then, debrief, explaining that though the student never did find an exact answer to her question, she had read enough about the topic to come up with a hypothesis. Then, explain that the work of compiling what one knows from his or her research and formulating an answer to a question, is in many ways even more important research work than simply finding an answer. After all, without researchers who are willing to ask questions without easy answers, we never would gain new knowledge!

For your active engagement, you might draw on the work of a student who posed a question based on your class topic and then set out to find the answer. You might display a page from a student's notebook

160

with a question written, such as: "Why did women like Molly Pitcher risk their lives to help Patriot soldiers during their battles?" Rally students to generate possible hypotheses to answer his question, thinking about what they know, rereading their notes, and looking in sources to get ideas. After students study, you might choose to share out a few different hypotheses.

For your link, you might remind students that they can add this strategy, (or a text set) asking and answering questions, to the work they do today as they continue to read, take notes, and gather the final bits of information they need to be ready to share all of their learning with a larger audience shortly.

CONFERRING AND SMALL-GROUP WORK

The final days of the unit are fast approaching, and it's important that all readers feel ready to share and celebrate their learning by the unit's close. With topics as vast as the ones your students have chosen, it can be difficult to determine a clear stopping point. There is always another book that can be read, another page of notes than can be jotted, another conversation to be had with one's research team. Today, you'll want to make sure that all of your readers are on track to meet their goals for the end of the unit, and that they are clear what they plan to share on the day of the celebration.

As you confer today, we suggest you particularly lean on the "Growing Ideas" thread of the "Critical Reading" strand of the Informational Reading Learning Progression. You might notice that many of your students are doing the work outlined in the third-grade portion of the learning progression. However, they may not yet be reaching for the work outline in the fourth-grade section. Check to make sure that students are not merely growing ideas but also grounding these in facts gleaned from (preferably) more than one text on their topic. During conferences, you might ask them to defend their theories by citing from specific points in the text.

Another way to help students to ramp up the level of their thinking and hypothesizing is to teach them to move the ideas they are growing away from specific answers about the content and toward more universal theories about the topic and the world. For example, a student aiming to answer the question, "Why did some women choose to fight in battles in the Revolution, even though they weren't allowed?" might first hypothesize this was because they believed in the cause to gain independence from England.

You might coach this student to consider how what she could hypothesize about conflict in general, or about women, or those who are seeking to gain independence. With some guidance, perhaps the student could formulate a more general theory, such as: women have played an important role in history, even if their accomplishments aren't always recognized.

Informational Reading Learning Progression

	Grade 3	Grade 4	Grade 5
ANALYTIC READING			
Critical Reading *Growing Ideas*	When I talk or write about a text (or a text set) I not only summarize it, I also grow my own ideas. For example, I might ask a question and try to answer it. When I am asked to apply what I have learned to a real-world problem or situation, I can do so. I notice when what I'm learning doesn't match my prior knowledge/experience, and I think about what to make of that.	I develop my own ideas about what I have read. Those ideas might be about values, the world, or the book. My ideas are grounded in text-based information and ideas, and I draw on several parts of the text(s). I raise questions and larger theories about the topic or the world. I read and reread with those questions in mind, and this leads to new insights. My reading helps me to develop my ideas. I think and sometimes write things like "Is this always the case?" or "Could it be . . . ?" I am not afraid to think in new ways.	I can synthesize several texts in ways that support an idea of my own. I select the points that do the best job of supporting my idea(s). For example, "How will this author add to or challenge my argument?" I think and sometimes write things like "Is this always the case?" or "Could it be . . . ?" I can apply what I have learned and my own ideas to solve a problem, make an argument, or design an application.
Questioning the Text	When I disagree with an idea in a text, I still try to think about it, and I also talk back to it. I also notice if something is described positively or negatively, and I think about how it could have been described.	I think about what implications my theories and what I have learned might have for real-world situations. I can apply what I have learned. I'm aware that texts can be written to get readers to think and feel something about an issue or topic, and I can say, "I see what you want me to think/feel, but I disagree."	I consider what a text is saying about an issue, idea, or argument and whether I agree or disagree. I weigh and evaluate a text for how convincing and reliable it is. I consider who wrote the text and what the author might gain from the text. I can talk back to texts.

Mid-Workshop Teaching

To ensure that students continue to record evidence for their thinking in the form of details from their reading, you might want to remind them of the note-taking work they did toward the start of the unit. Draw their attention to the chart you created in Session 4 that supports students in recording details and growing ideas about information from their texts.

SHARE

As a way to celebrate the heady work that students undertook today, you might gather them in the meeting area and conduct a symphony share to showcase some of their best thinking. Ask them to study the writing they did today about their reading as they hypothesized answers to their questions. Ask them to circle a sentence or two that captures an idea of which they are especially proud.

After giving readers a few moments to do this, invite them to read their ideas aloud when you gesture toward them. At the end, summarize some of what you heard students doing in a way that captures their best work. For example, you might say, "Readers, you're doing powerful work growing your own ideas. You're reading across several texts to grow your own questions, not just about the American Revolution time period, but about some of the bigger themes in history, such as why people turn to conflict, and the lengths people will go to protect their rights."

Homework

For homework, you may choose to extend the work of growing ideas that students did today. To do this, you might send students home with the "Critical Thinking: Growing Ideas" thread of the Informational Reading Learning Progression for grades 4 and 5. Ask them to first study the progression, making sure they understand the work of each level. Then, channel them to study their notes, marking up their notebook where they see evidence that they've tried this work. Of course, you'll also want to remind students to continue reading their independent books and logging the reading they do.

Best wishes,
Lucy, Janet, and Grace

Taking Notes to Record Important Information and Explain it:

I learned that ________.

An important detail to support that is ______________.

This seems important because

____________________.

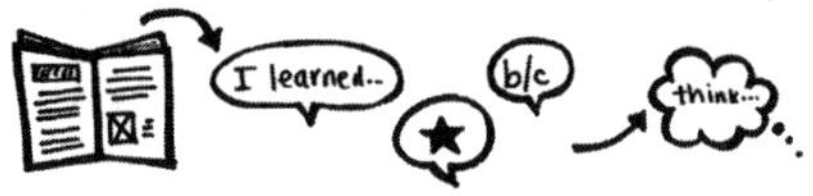

This makes me think _______.

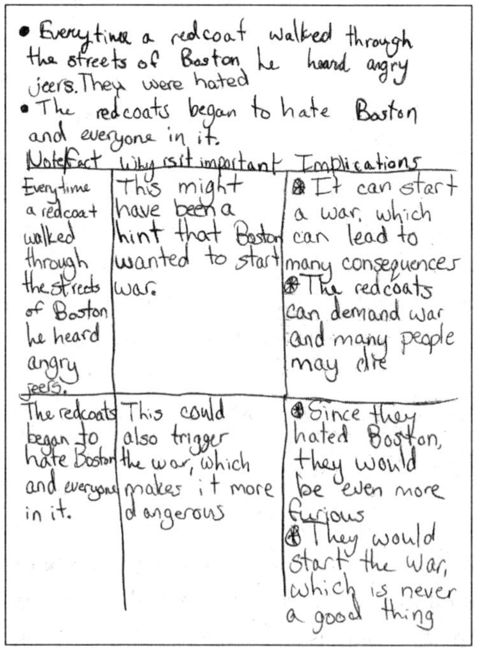

FIG. 19–1 Student notes

Session 20

Reading History for Universal Messages, for Meaning

TODAY, you draw the work of this unit to a close. In this session, you invite students to transfer all they know about interpretation to their work with the American Revolution. Interpretation is, of course, a skill that nonfiction as well as fiction readers use. It is especially important when students are reading history, because most of what they read are interpretations made by different historians. History is, by definition, interpretive. And one of the reasons that history matters is that the stories of long ago can teach us lessons that help us live our lives today.

Stories in history are told over and over again, not just because the facts matter, but because they carry themes that people believe matter. The stories of George Washington crossing the Potomac, the Boston Tea Party, the Sons of Liberty, Thomas Paine's *Common Sense* . . . those stories are told again and again in literature, in film, at the dinner table. They are told and retold, not just as reminders of what happened, but as lessons about what's possible, lessons about what's important in our lives as human beings and as Americans. In the same way that a piece of literature offers universal themes that speak to each reader in unique ways, complicated moments from the past and the stories of those times offer ideas about conflict, perseverance, leadership, and character—ideas that are meaningful to people living in any era.

The American Revolution is chock-full of these stories. It contains stories of soldiers who had nothing left—no food, no shoes—but who persevered because of a belief in the cause. It contains stories of people who had been our enemies and who put the old wounds aside to act as our friends—some of the Native Americans, the French. It contains stories of communities torn apart as neighbors became enemies when they supported different sides in the war.

This session suggests that it is worthwhile to explore the ideas behind the stories of our history. Just like some children have decided that *The Tiger Rising* was not just a story about a young boy who finds a tiger in the woods, but a story about cages—the consequences of escape as well as imprisonment—so too, some children may come to think of the American

IN THIS SESSION, you'll teach students that readers draw upon their knowledge of interpretation to ask questions about history, and to figure out the big lessons that they can learn from the past.

GETTING READY

✔ Today will be a day of celebration, the culmination of the work of this unit. Before this session, give some thought to how you would like students to share their research and learning. You may wish to celebrate a pivotal moment in the American Revolution, such as the signing of the Declaration of Independence, the creation of the first national flag, or the enactment of the U.S. Constitution. You may have other ideas about how students can share their knowledge and celebrate their achievements.

✔ Display the "How to Build an Interpretation" chart from Session 16 of Unit 1 *Interpreting Characters* (see Teaching).

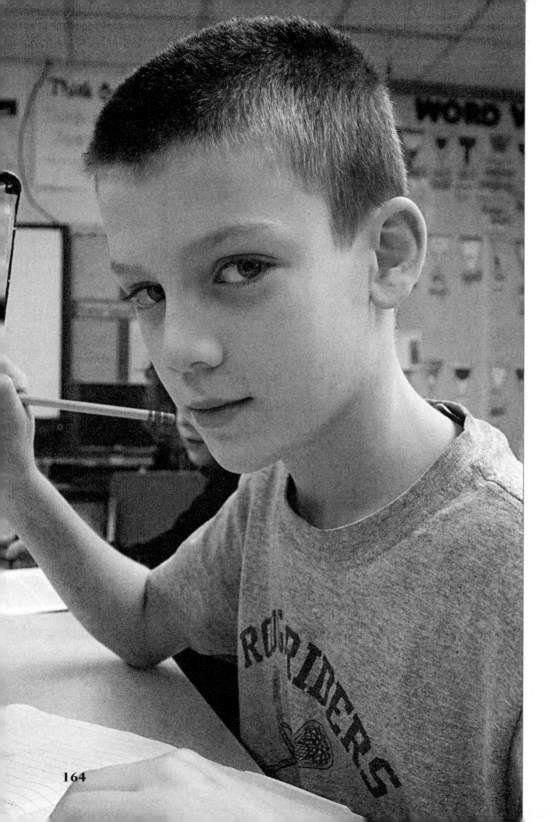

Revolution as a story about the fight for freedom, or about the "right makes might," or about the consequences of escape.

Readers of history need to learn that history is not just about memorizing dates and facts. History is about ideas. Some of these ideas are commonly taught in history courses, while others are developed by the critical and thoughtful reader. For now, this session is your way to teach your children to think like a historian, not just memorizing events, but also developing and internalizing ideas.

"Stories in history are told over and over again, not just because the facts matter, but because they carry themes that people believe matter."

Reading History for Universal Messages, for Meaning

CONNECTION

Suggest that there's a reason to study history beyond learning facts, and liken the interpretive work children did in fiction to the interpretive work they can do now.

"Readers, last night I got to worrying. I was thinking about all that I've taught you about previewing and categorizing and synthesizing information, about noticing the facts—the who, where, and when—of history. And I thought, 'Those are important skills to have, but have I spent enough time helping these kids understand *why* it's important to study history? Have I done enough to help them understand why it matters to read about the Boston Tea Party and the Boston Massacre and the Stamp Act, and the Townshend Acts?'

"Then a light bulb went off for me. I realized that you've already done this kind of interpretation work! You did it during our fiction unit. You read novels thinking not just, 'Who's in this story and what's happening?' but also, 'What's important here? What big lessons can I take away from this story?'

"Well guess what? You can do this very same work when studying history."

❖ **Name the teaching point.**

"Today I want to teach you that readers can study history for more than facts. You can study it to think, 'What's so important about this moment in time? What big lessons can I learn from it?'"

TEACHING

Reveal a familiar anchor chart from an earlier unit, and ask children to consider which interpretation skills can carry over from reading fiction to reading history.

"Readers, have you ever noticed that *history* has the word *story* inside it? History is made of countless stories, but there is a reason that the stories that we think of as history survive. There's a reason they're told again and again. There's a reason why each new class of fourth-graders reads about those stories. And one of the important things that readers

The why of teaching is as important to teaching as the what. Teaching demands that we design what our students will do on a given day. It is subtly empowering for students to know why they're doing what they're doing.

need to do is to ask, 'What's the big deal about these events? Why did these stories survive? What can we take away from them?'

"So let's think for a minute about how we might interpret these events in history that we've been studying. Let's think, 'What big lessons can we learn from this past event?'

"The good news is that you are already pros at doing this sort of thinking." I unveiled the anchor chart from Session 16 of *Interpreting Characters* and said, "Do you remember this chart?"

I gave children a few moments to glance over the chart, refreshing their memories, then said, "We used this chart to analyze fiction, but I wonder . . . might any of this help you interpret history? Turn and tell your partner which of these bullets seems applicable to reading history, if any."

History is a great vehicle to teach students about interpretation. Therefore, coach your students into becoming independent thinkers and learners and have them begin to think about transference.

As children talked, I leaned in to listen. After a minute, I voiced over, saying, "I heard many of you say that some of these bullet points, like reading intensely, and being alert to places in the text that seem extra important can be used to interpret history, too. Some thought others were about characters and they are only in fiction. But I'm wondering, if you replace the word *character* with *person*, might other strategies on this list apply, too? Keep talking."

"So let's try that now. Let's think about patterns in the way the colonists acted—say, in the Boston Tea Party, the minutemen at the Battle of Concord and Lexington, the Sons of Liberty. Think of those events as chapters in a chapter book, and think, 'What patterns do I see in the ways that the colonists acted—or in the ways stories describe those actions, anyhow?'" I gave students some time to think silently, then I said. "What do you find?"

"The colonists stood up to the British. Even though the British had their fancy uniforms and everything and seemed so strong and unbeatable, the colonists were brave," Cynthia said.

I gestured to signal that she should say more. "Why have those stories lasted all the years? What are the life lessons or the big truths those stories carry? Be brave. What else?"

Soon voices were coming from all corners of the room. "It's like, you don't need the fancy stuff to fight, if you are fighting for something you really believe in." "Yeah, it's like one of those 'little guy wins it all' stories. Even against a big power." "It's also about people like Charlotte in *Charlotte's Web* who are willing to devote their life to others." "And for freedom."

Debrief, pointing out the steps you just took in ways that are transferable to other historical events.

I nodded. "So the stories of the American Revolution carry big life lessons. And are you realizing that you can use your skills at interpretation to read history interpretively?

✳ How to Build an Interpretation ✳

- ☑ Read intensely.
- ☑ Use patterns in character's actions to form ideas.
- ☑ Why might the character act like this?
- ☑ Notice a character's desires and how they are achieved.
- ☑ Notice anything about a character that the author repeats–ask why?
- ☑ Characters are complicated–contexts, relationships, outside/inside.
- ☑ Read, thinking about many aspects of a book.
- ☑ Ask early in the story: "What is this story about?"
- ☑ Be alert to places in the text that seem extra important.
- ☑ Connect different parts of the book and think across the whole book.
- ☑ Connect ideas you've had about the book.

"Readers, do you see what we just did? We used a bullet point from our 'How to Build an Interpretation' chart to guide our thinking about a historical event—to think, 'Why does this event matter? What lesson can it teach me?'"

ACTIVE ENGAGEMENT

Set children up to try this interpretive work in partnerships, focusing on whatever topic they are currently studying.

"So, ready to give this a try yourself? Right now, with your partner, pick another question on this chart. You can probably get any of these to apply, maybe with a little tweaking, but if you find that one isn't getting you anywhere, just move on to another. Then use it to think about why the event you're studying or the story of the person or document you're researching is one that's been recorded and told and retold all these years. Why does it matter? What lessons can you take from it?"

As children talked, I circulated, listening in and offering tips as needed. I suggested that groups might look back at texts they had read to ground their ideas in the records of what people said and did. I reminded children that they should build on one another's thinking, taking an idea as far as it could go before moving to another.

After a few minutes, I reconvened the class and shared out some of their ideas.

LINK

Reiterate that just as the lessons people learn from reading literature apply not just to one character and one story, similarly, lessons from history aren't limited to the people of one time.

"Readers, just as the lessons you get from fiction are ones that apply not just to one character and one story, but also to the people who read those stories, the lessons you get from history are ones that cross time and place. It's not just colonists living in America in the 1770s who cared about what kind of society they lived in, and under whose rule. They certainly weren't the only people to fight for the freedom to govern themselves.

"As you continue reading about your subtopic today, will you take this idea with you? Keep asking, 'Why does this event matter? What's the bigger meaning? Why did this story survive? What lessons can I take from it? Are there lessons here about what it means to be a citizen? An American?' Off you go!"

The invitation to analyze history is a monumental one. You are, in essence, inviting students to study information and create an independent take on the reported facts. This is the work of real historians.

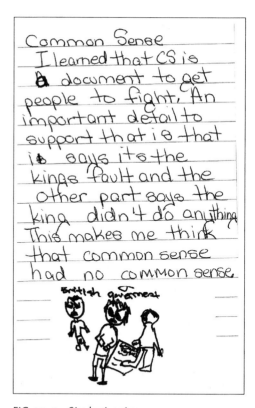

FIG. 20–1   Student notes.

Reading Different Nonfiction Genres Differently

AS YOU CONFER WITH YOUR STUDENTS, you will want to notice the genre that a given student is reading and help that student to adjust his or her reading strategies accordingly. Encourage a reader to think about the text that he or she is reading, asking, "Is this mostly a narrative? Or is it mostly expository?" If it is a narrative, for example it will be organized by time: first, then, next. There will be a main character—a person, a group of people, an animal. Students who are reading narrative should be developing theories about the people in the text—about the *he*, *she*, *it*, or *they* around which this true story (or fictionalized fact-based story) revolves. And they should be thinking about ways the characters are meeting the challenges of their lives.

If students are reading texts that are expository/informational, then they will be organized more by categories, in an all-about way, perhaps with subheadings. If there are no subheadings, readers can sort of supply their own headings. They probably need to think about gathering main ideas and supports. If students are reading texts that are mostly narrative, then they'll profit from bringing a story frame to those texts.

You might want to teach your students to tuck specific details about the American Revolution into your stories. You might coach students with questions such as who is telling the story? Whose voice is heard? How does the message we are reading go with who is telling the story? How might this story go if another person is telling it? What is the message this story or part of history is telling me? What do I learn from it?

MID-WORKSHOP TEACHING   Noticing Patterns in History

"Readers, eyes up here a minute." I waited until I had their attention. "As you've read today, have any of you found yourself thinking, 'This reminds me of something that's happened recently in the world?' Or have you compared it to something that happened during another time and place in history? Thumbs up if so."

I took note of which kids had made these connections.

"When you think about the big meanings behind historical events, you often start to notice patterns. You think, 'Hey, this group of people risked their lives to stand up for something they believe in . . . and so did this group, a continent apart and hundreds of years later.' Or 'This fight for democracy is similar to the one that's happening today, in. . . .'

"Even if you haven't done that kind of thinking, keep it at the front of your mind as you read on. Pay attention to the kinds of things that repeat. What kinds of things matter to people across time? What have people banded together to do? What battles have they fought? What things have they tried to protect?"

Readers Teach Others What They've Learned

Set readers up to plan for their teaching, and then to teach a partner what they've been learning.

"Readers, you've seen the lesson plans that I carry around. Before I teach all of you, I plan out the main ideas I'll teach and how I'll teach them. You'll need to do the same. Will you take a few minutes to get ready to teach your partner? Think again about the main ideas your texts taught, and plan for how you'll teach them. Will you use gestures? Are there visuals that will help you? And, importantly, how will you organize your teaching?"

As students talked, I moved from partnership to partnership, coaching to lift up the teaching work that each student did. "Will you get with your partner and decide who's teaching first? And if you're listening first, you've got two jobs. First, you have to listen in a way where you can learn. And second, get ready to compliment your partner on something specific they do well."

Celebrate the conclusion of the unit and the tremendous work your students have done.

After students finished teaching, I gathered them back together in the meeting area. "Researchers, we know the Patriots celebrated the ending of the American Revolution and their newfound independence from Great Britain. They celebrated their victories, the courage of their troops, their ability to make decisions on their own. Today, as we draw our American Revolution unit to a close, we also need to celebrate. You've come so far as nonfiction readers in a few short weeks.

"Right now, will you and your partner talk for a few minutes? Use our anchor charts from across the unit to help you. In what specific ways have you grow as readers of nonfiction?

"And just like the Patriots, at the conclusion of any major effort, we think about what's coming next. The Patriots asked, 'What will our new government look like? Who will lead us? How will power be distributed? What relationship, if any, will we have with Great Britain? What will we do about our family members who disagree with our efforts?' We need to ask, 'What's next for us as readers and researchers? In what areas do we still want to grow as readers of nonfiction?' Add this into your conversation with your partners. As you talk, envision the feeling these Patriots felt and the gratitude they felt as they celebrated the birth of a new nation."